LITERACY IN
THE LIBRARY

Critical Studies in Education and Culture Series

Beyond Comfort Zones in Multiculturalism: Confronting the Politics of Privilege
Sandra Jackson and José Solís, editors

Culture and Difference: Critical Perspectives on the Bicultural Experience
in the United States
Antonia Darder

Poststructuralism, Politics and Education
Michael Peters

Weaving a Tapestry of Resistance: The Places, Power, and Poetry of a Sustainable
Society
Sharon Sutton

Counselor Education for the Twenty-First Century
Susan J. Brotherton

Positioning Subjects: Psychoanalysis and Critical Educational Studies
Stephen Appel

Adult Students "At-Risk": Culture Bias in Higher Education
Timothy William Quinnan

Education and the Postmodern Condition
Michael Peters, editor

Restructuring for Integrative Education: Multiple Perspectives, Multiple Contexts
Todd E. Jennings, editor

Postmodern Philosophical Critique and the Pursuit of Knowledge in Higher Education
Roger P. Mourad, Jr.

Naming the Multiple: Poststructuralism and Education
Michael Peters, editor

LITERACY IN THE LIBRARY

Negotiating the Spaces Between Order and Desire

MARK DRESSMAN

Critical Studies in Education and Culture Series
Edited by Henry A. Giroux

BERGIN & GARVEY
Westport, Connecticut • London

Library of Congress Cataloging-in-Publication Data

Dressman, Mark.
  Literacy in the library : negotiating the spaces between order
and desire / Mark Dressman.
    p. cm.—(Critical studies in education and culture series,
  ISSN 1064–8615)
  Includes bibliographical references (p.) and index.
  ISBN 0–89789–495–2 (alk. paper)
    1. School libraries—Social aspects—Southwest, New—Case studies.
  2. Socialization—Southwest, New—Case studies.   3. Children—
  Southwest, New—Books and reading—Case studies.   4. Fiction in
  libraries—Southwest, New—Case studies.   I. Title.   II. Series.
  Z675.S3.D749   1997
  027.8′222′0979—DC21   97–18571

British Library Cataloguing in Publication Data is available.

Library of Congress Catalog Card Number: 97–18571
ISBN: 0–89789–495–2
ISSN: 1064–8615

First published in 1997

Bergin & Garvey, 88 Post Road West, Westport, CT 06881
An imprint of Greenwood Publishing Group Inc.

Printed in the United States of America

The paper used in this book complies with the
Permanent Paper Standard issued by the National
Information Standards Organization (Z39.48–1984).

10 9 8 7 6 5 4 3 2 1

Copyright Acknowledgments

The author and publisher gratefully acknowledge permission to use the following material:

Excerpts from Mark Dressman, "Congruence, Resistance, Liminality: Reading and Ideology in Three School Libraries" in *Curriculum Inquiry*. Used by permission of Blackwell Publishers.

Excerpts from "Preference as Performance: Doing Gender and Social Class in Three School Libraries" in *Journal of Literacy Research*. Used by permission of National Reading Conference.

For Megan and Dan

and for Joe Angel Flores,

who reads his world so well.

Contents

Illustrations

Series Foreword

Educational reform has fallen on hard times. The traditional assumption that schooling is fundamentally tied to the imperatives of citizenship designed to educate students to exercise civic leadership and public service has been eroded. The schools are now the key institutions for producing professional, technically trained, credentialized workers for whom the demands of citizenship are subordinated to the vicissitudes of the marketplace and the commercial public sphere. Given the current corporate and right-wing assault on public and higher education, coupled with the emergence of a moral and political climate that has shifted to a new social Darwinism, the issues that framed the democratic meaning, purpose, and use to which education might aspire have been displaced by more vocational and narrowly ideological considerations.

The war waged against the possibilities of an education wedded to the precepts of a real democracy is not merely ideological. Against the backdrop of reduced funding for public schooling, the call for privatization, vouchers, cultural uniformity, and choice, there are the often ignored larger social realities of material power and oppression. On the national level, there has been a vast resurgence of racism. This is evident in the passing of anti-immigration laws such as Proposition 197 in California, the dismantling of the welfare state, the demonization of black youth that is taking place in the popular media, and the remarkable attention provided by the media to forms of race talk that argue for the intellectual inferiority of blacks or dismiss calls for racial justice as simply a holdover from the "morally bankrupt" legacy of the 1960s.

Poverty is on the rise among children in the United States, with 20 percent of all children under the age of 18 living below the poverty line. Unemployment is growing at an alarming rate for poor youth of color, especially in the urban centers. While black youth are policed and disciplined in an out of the nation's schools, conservative and liberal educators define education through the ethically limp discourses of privatization, national standards, and global competitiveness.

Many writers in the critical education tradition have attempted to change the right-wing fundamentalism behind education and social reform in both the United

States and abroad while simultaneously providing ethical signposts for a public discourse about education and democracy that is both prophetic and transformative. Eschewing traditional categories, a diverse number of critical theorists and educators have successfully exposed the political and ethical implications of the cynicism and despair that have been endemic to the discourse of schooling and civic life. In its place, such educators strive to provide a language of hope that inextricably links the struggle over schooling to understanding and transforming our present social and cultural dangers.

At the risk of overgeneralizing, both cultural studies theorists and critical educators have emphasized the importance of understanding theory as the grounded basis for "intervening into contexts of power . . . in order to enable people to act more strategically in ways that may change their context for the better."[1] Moreover, theorists in both fields have argued for the primacy of the political by calling for and struggling to produce critical public spaces, regardless of how fleeting they may be, in which "popular cultural resistance is explored as a form of political resistance."[2] Such writers have analyzed the challenges that teachers will have to face in redefining a new mission for education, one that is linked to honoring the experiences, concerns, and diverse histories and languages that give expression to the multiple narratives that engage and challenge the legacy of democracy.

Equally significant is the insight of recent critical educational work that connects the politics of difference with concrete strategies for addressing the crucial relationships between schooling and the economy . . . between citizenship and the politics of meaning in communities of multicultural, multiracial, and multilingual schools.

Critical Studies in Education and Culture attempts to address and demonstrate how scholars working in the fields of cultural studies and critical pedagogy might join together in a radical project and practice informed by theoretically rigorous discourses that affirm the critical but refuse the cynical, that establish hope as central to a critical pedagogical and political practice but eschew a romantic utopianism. Central to such a project is the issue of how pedagogy might provide cultural studies theorists and educators with an opportunity to engage pedagogical practices that are not only transdisciplinary, transgressive, and oppositional but also connected to a wider project designed to further racial, economic, and political democracy.[3] By taking seriously the relations between culture and power, we further the possibilities of resistance, struggle, and change.

Critical Studies in Education and Culture is committed to publishing work that opens a narrative space that affirms the contextual and the specific while simultaneously recognizing the ways in which such spaces are shot through with issues of power. The series attempts to continue an important legacy of theoretical work in cultural studies in which related debates on pedagogy are understood and addressed within the larger social context of social responsibility, civic courage, and the reconstruction of democratic public life. We must keep in mind Raymond Williams's insight that the "deepest impulse [informing cultural politics] is the desire to make learning part of the process of social change itself."[4] Education as a cultural pedagogical practice takes place across multiple sites, which include not only schools and universities but also the mass media, popular culture, and other public spheres, and signals how within diverse contexts education makes us both subjects of and subject to relations of power.

This series challenges the current return to the primacy of market values and simultaneous retreat from politics so evident in the recent work of educational theorists, legislators, and policy analysts. Professional relegitimation in a troubled time seems to be the order of the day as an increasing number of academics both refuse to recognize public and higher education as critical public spheres and offer little or no resistance to the ongoing vocationalization of schooling, the continuing evisceration of the intellectual labor force, and the current assaults on the working poor, the elderly, and women and children.[5]

Emphasizing the centrality of politics, culture, and power, *Critical Studies in Education and Culture* will deal with pedagogical issues that contribute to imaginative and transformative ways to our understanding of how critical knowledge, democratic values, and social practices can provide a basis for teachers, students, and other cultural workers to redefine their roles as engaged and public intellectuals. Each volume will attempt to rethink the relationship between language and experience, pedagogy and human agency, and ethic and social responsibility as part of a larger project for engaging and deepening the prospects of democratic schooling in a multiracial and multicultural society. *Critical Studies in Education and Culture* takes on the responsibility of witnessing and addressing the most pressing problems of public schooling and civic life and engages culture as a crucial site and strategic force for productive social change.

Henry A. Giroux

NOTES

1. Lawrence Grossberg, "Toward a Genealogy of the State of Cultural Studies," in *Disciplinarity and Dissent in Cultural Studies*, ed. Cary Nelson and Dilip Parameshwar Gaonkar (New York: Routledge, 1996), 19.

2. David Bailey and Stuart Hall, "The Vertigo of Displacement," *Ten 8*, 2 (3): 19.

3. My notion of transdisciplinary comes from Mas'ud Zavarzadeh and Donald Morton, "Theory, Pedagogy, Politics: The crisis of the 'Subject' in the Humanities," in *Theory Pedagogy Politics: Texts for Change*, ed. Mas'ud Zavarzadeh and Donald Morton (Urbana: University of Illinois Press, 1992), 10. At issue here is neither ignoring the boundaries of discipline-based knowledge nor simply fusing different disciplines, but rather creating theoretical paradigms, questions, and knowledge that cannot be taken up within the policed boundaries of the existing disciplines.

4. Raymond Williams, "Adult Education and Social Change," in *What I Came to Say* (London: Hutchinson-Radus, 1989), 158.

5. The term *professional relegitimation* comes from a personal correspondence with Professor Jeff Williams of East Carolina University.

Preface

This study aims to cross an invisible but nonetheless consequential boundary that separates critical-ethnographic studies of schooling conducted mainly in secondary settings from practice-oriented ethnographic studies that are often conducted in primary and elementary grades; its ultimate goal is to contribute to conversations about curriculum and instruction on both sides of that division. On the critical-ethnographic side, researchers have tended to rely on sociological tropes of "the system" and of "resistance" in making their analyses and have argued mainly about how determining the system really is and how efficacious students' agency might be in making use of school systems on their own terms. Their focus has most often been on the politics of exchanges among students and between students and adults and on the rehearsal of power relations among stakeholders—a rehearsal that in these researchers' narratives is meant to foreshadow (i.e., to "reproduce" or to "produce," depending on one's school of thought) later adult performances of power relations between those former students and society at large. The actual academic, disciplinary knowledge whose acquisition forms the context of adult-student interactions is metaphorized as a form of currency whose procedural and declarative content is viewed as largely symbolic and cultural. Whether exchanges of such currency take place in a class that meets to study history or typing seems to make little difference to these researchers; what is foregrounded usually is the dynamics of the exchange itself. The purpose of education in these studies is viewed as the socialization of students to certain ways of being and doing.

The order of things on the practice-oriented side of qualitative, ethnographic research is in many ways quite the opposite. While the focus of most of these studies remains the nature of interactions among students and between students and teachers, the transmission of academic, disciplinary knowledge is usually perceived not as symbolic or cultural but as the purpose of each encounter that is observed and analyzed. School knowledge is not described in metaphorical terms but is conceived of as the concrete and diverse reflection of students' physical, social, and subjective realities; and its acquisition is viewed as the primary, if not total, purpose of education.

While on the one hand critical ethnographies tend to be global and highly theoretical in the ways they describe the dynamics of inequality, on the other hand practice-oriented research is often so focused on describing "best practice" that it frequently overlooks—and sometimes seems to willfully deny—the political, economic, and cultural circumstances in which acts of teaching and learning occur, or that teaching and learning are themselves political, economic, and cultural acts. As a result, critical ethnography is frequently accused of having very little impact on the dynamics of schooling, while the consequence of practice-oriented ethnographic research too often is that the more what is touted as good practice seems to change, the more differences in students' achievement and future prospects remain pegged to the politics of race, class, and gender that the discourse of best practice tries to ignore.

In conducting and presenting this study of three school libraries I hope to join a number of other recent researchers of school literacy—among them Sarah McCarthey, Tim Lensmire, Marjorie Orellana, and Margaret Finders[1]—who have undertaken to use the tools of critical theory and social constructivism to analyze the largely unacknowledged politics of difference that inform both the discourses of mainstream "experts" and the everyday practices of literacy educators in schools. Like these researchers, I have tried to maintain a stance of calculated ambivalence in this book with regard to school literacy, in order to take a position that is theoretical yet not totally abstracted from the particularities of subject matter and the demands of everyday life in schools. I have proceeded from the assumptions that reading and writing are practices that distribute knowledge in both its particular and its symbolic senses; that both views of knowledge are also forms of power; and that power itself is without conscience in the production of its effects on individuals and society. Literacy, then, is described here as a complex social phenomenon that produces knowledge and individual belief, even as it is produced by them; and it is a phenomenon with ambivalent—but not inconsequential—outcomes that are not completely within the control of the individuals whom society places "in charge" of literacy.

Readers concerned primarily with the improvement of school practices may find this approach overcritical and uninformative about how to make things better. Where are the models of best practice that may invite emulation? Where are the clear suggestions about how to work against the ways that race, class, and gender often seem to limit children's literate development? Once again, problems we already knew about have been examined in exhaustive detail, but no real solution has been proposed. Why should these readers bother with this book? Readers concerned primarily with the advancement of theoretical discussions, however, may also be disappointed with the study's approach. Why all this detail about specific children's novels and specific events in each library? Why use the work of such ardent and passé structuralists as Bourdieu and Foucault? Beyond the novelty of its setting, what real contribution to the advancement of theory does this study make?

In advance of criticism from the former, I hope readers will take the case of each library not as a critique of individual practice but as an exposition of the ways that commonsense practices grounded in long-forgotten historical, economic, and political conditions affect children's life chances for better and for worse. I also hope these readers will persevere to the final chapter, where some suggestions are forwarded about the reconstruction of the subject positions that are likely to interrupt discourses of class and gender and secondarily of race in school literacy programs. In advance of criticism from the latter, I will suggest that there is a need within theoretical discussions at present to speak both of general conditions *and* of particular situations where generalities do not seem to prevail. For it is only in the comparative, fine-grained analysis of multiple settings that issues dealing with the power of human agency to subvert, evade, or ironically accede to the hegemonic project of formal education will ever be adequately examined or explained.

Virtually all of the people in this book, myself included at the outset, believed that literacy was the key to human enlightenment, that it was always and ultimately good, and that sacrifices must be made for its acquisition. They—we—were supported by powerful cultural and historical legacies that framed literacy in this way and that made the school library seem the purest instrument of a purely good and just cause. At the outset I believed, and I am fairly certain that the participants in the study believed, that this was the sort of story I would be telling, with some theoretical complications thrown in for academic measure. Studying a social phenomenon and participating closely in such a study, however, can have the curious effect of quickly raising doubts and awareness about the unforeseen consequences of one's actions. In true panoptic effect, one begins to see oneself and the world as though one were outside looking in. Participants and observers begin to see patterns and relationships among actions and among the objects of their life world, and both may find the experience simultaneously fascinating and uncomfortable. Yet it is always the participants who must worry more, make the harder decision to go on, and give more of themselves in the end. Sometime in the second month or so of my fieldwork, I, and I believe many of the participants, began to see certain patterns that could not be ignored or denied, patterns that we both recognized as having unintended consequences for children's literacy that were not easy to acknowledge; and patterns that, when analyzed, might challenge the expressed beliefs and intentions of participants. Yet to help me and to contribute something to the study of school libraries and literacy, none of the participants in this study decided to withdraw, or was any less giving of his or her time or information as a result of that realization. For their dedication, for their generosity, for their honesty, and for their compassion, I owe the students, teachers, and librarians in this study an enormous debt of gratitude. For the extent to which their time, patience, and sacrifice might contribute to readers' knowledge of how libraries function to distribute power and knowledge within society, and so that we may see our own practices mirrored in theirs and work to do better still, they are owed a debt of thanks.

In addition to the participants who are depicted in the text I also owe a debt of thanks to scores of other caring individuals. I owe much to the Women's Club in my hometown of Erlanger, Ky, for their support of the library there and to Mrs. Taylor, the librarian now passed on, who worked there for little or no pay throughout my childhood. I thank Julie Jensen, with whom I first discussed my idea to study libraries, who helped me turn it into a manageable topic and then stuck with me through its creation as a dissertation. Thanks also to Jim

Hoffman, Diane Schallert, Doug Foley, Doug Storey, and Colleen Fairbanks for their support and advice and for bearing with me as I struggled to make sense of my project, my data, and my theoretical frames. I also thank Mike Schulte and Jason Ramay for their good humor and sympathy as I conducted the initial research and writing. Through all this time and to the present, Sarah McCarthey has put up with and given more than she had to and has helped to keep me, and this project, manageable; I owe her more than I can express.

I also owe much to Linda Brodkey, who gave me permission early on to write and read in ways I otherwise would not have dared, who worked with me in the early stages of turning the dissertation into a book, and whose example of courage and integrity as a researcher, writer, and scholar is my guide. Roger Simon's careful reading and editorial support helped me greatly in the revision of the first chapter of this book and in reconceptualizing its conclusion; I thank him for his support and encouragement to remain critical in my approach and for standing by my project during some very rough moments. I also thank Henry Giroux for giving my project a home, and Norine Mudrick and Susan Badger for their support during the editing and production stages.

During its writing and revision, other individuals read and offered important insights and suggestions about this book. Thank you to Tim Lensmire, for his Orwellian suggestions, and to Donna Alvermann for her feminist reading of Chapter 1; thanks also to Carl Herndl, Cindy Nahrwold, Thelma Kibler, Jeremy Price, Marjorie Orellana, Christine Clark, Rachel Theilheimer, and Rudolfo Chávez, for reading versions of chapters and papers and for their moral and intellectual support, and to Johanna Halbeisen, who offered her perspective as a school librarian. Laura Sujo de Montes' skill with computer graphics has made my library floor plans presentable and legible. Thanks, finally, to Rosalinda Barrera for her support and advice, and to Jeanette Martin for understanding how much time it takes to complete a book-length writing assignment. Portions of this book will have appeared first in *Curriculum Inquiry* and *Journal of Literacy Research*; I thank Blackwell Publishers and the National Reading Conference for their generosity as well.

NOTE

1. Sarah J. McCarthey, "Authors, Text, and Talk: The Internalization of Dialogue from Social Interaction during Writing." *Reading Research Quarterly*, 29: 200–231, 1994; Timothy J. Lensmire, *When Children Write*. New York: Teachers College Press, 1993; Marjorie Orellana, "Literacy as a Gendered Social Practice: Tasks, Texts, Talk, and Take-Up." *Reading Research Quarterly*, 30: 674-708, 1995; Margaret Finders, *Just Girls*. New York: Teachers College Press, 1996.

Books That Are True; Stories That Are Made Up: School Libraries and the Politics of Reading

> He was alone with seven thousand books. . . . On the top shelves near the ceiling the quarto volumes of extinct encyclopedias slumbered on their sides in piles like tiered coffins in common graves. Gordon pushed aside the blue, dust sodden curtains that served as a doorway to the next room. This, better lighted than the other, contained the lending library. It was one of those "two-penny no-deposit" libraries beloved of book-pinchers. No books in it except novels, of course. And *what* novels! But that too was a matter of course.
>
> —George Orwell, *Keep the Aspidistra Flying*

> We must be insistently aware of how space can be made to hide consequences from us, how relations of power and discipline are inscribed into the apparently innocent spatiality of social life, how human geographies become filled with politics and ideology.
>
> —Edward Soja, *Postmodern Geographies*

Beginning sometime in the eighteenth century, when penny-wise readers in the towns of Great Britain and along the Atlantic coast of North America were looking for a "good book" to read, they would most likely visit one of two different types of establishments. One of these, the "subscription" library, was patronized largely by business and professional men who were fast assuming major public roles within the new economic and political order of the Enlightenment. These men looked to classical and contemporary works on philosophy, history, religion, and the study of nature itself for their authority. The other, the "circulating" library, operated as the "lending library" described by George Orwell. It was patronized largely by women who were less capitalized and less formally educated than men. These women were fast assuming major private roles within the new economic and political order of the middle class, and for their authority they looked mostly to a new and much criticized form of "modern" writing—the popular novel, and in particular to the domestic novel of manners.

Three centuries later, it may seem very comfortable—and yet also be ironic—that the same spatialized distinctions in reader preference between those with a taste for "serious" literature arranged by subject and those whose reading tastes ran to novels—"and *what* novels!"—ordered by their authors' last names can be observed not only in a London bookshop of the early twentieth century but also in the organizational principles guiding the arrangement of texts and circulation patterns of most school and public libraries today. This distinction may seem comfortable because in the time since its inception our society has come to regard the generic distinction between "fictional" and "factual" texts as reflecting the nature of human experience in its written expression, rather than as any historically constructed sense of things; as Raymond Williams (1977) has pointed out, "The dichotomies fact/fiction and objective/ subjective are . . . the theoretical and historical keys to the basic bourgeois theory of literature, which has controlled the actual multiplicity of writing" (149). It may be ironic because in forgetting why and how this distinction was first made, middle-class culture and the institutions of the school and public library may continue to reproduce the gender politics that first motivated the divergence of subscription and circulating libraries' texts and readerships—a colonizing, hegemonic politics in which (implicitly white) middle-class females are socialized to domesticate the world, and (implicitly white) middle-class males are socialized to run it.

Where they are staffed by professional librarians and adequately stocked—and I will acknowledge at the outset that this is not the case everywhere in the United States—school libraries operate with a degree of fiscal and professional autonomy that separates them from schools and classrooms and marks them as unique cultural sites. Their underlying purpose—to preserve, as will be seen, not only a gendered division between feminine and masculine labor but, in school systems segregated by race and social class, divisions between mental, managerial labor and physical, working-class/working-poor labor, as well as determinations of who gets to read what texts and how—nicely complements the socializing function of the schools in which they are embedded. Indeed, precisely because librarians protest their political innocence so loudly and so well, and because they work through efforts to satisfy the *desire* as opposed to the *disciplining* of student readers through their texts, school and public libraries may be potentially more efficient in aligning student readers with right ways of perceiving and organizing their reality than those found in the more coercive and obviously intrusive, and so more frequently resisted, institution of the classroom.

But on the other hand, no text as historically complex and semiotically rich as a school or public library always communicates what it intends. Like all systems of human invention, libraries are fraught with contradiction and convey messages that are frequently ambiguous or that undermine themselves. As a consequence, the capacity of student readers to read the library and its texts in critical (Shor 1993), "producerly" (Fiske 1989b) ways—that is, in ways that free rather than constrain the possible uses of the library and its texts—may vary in proportion to the extent that a particular library exposes its contradictions and ambiguities to its patrons' grasp and leaves open spaces in which they can read how and what they want. This is not to suggest that school librarians are purely libertarian in their inclination to "share the wealth" of their territories; or that they do not try, some in subtle and some in not-so-subtle ways, to direct and control the distribution of text-based knowledge; or that the organization of the library itself does not reproduce a view of knowledge whose structure and authorized uses have their roots in the Enlightenment and in nineteenth century industrialism. But there is a case to be made that in its structure and mandated operations the school library is to some degree inherently more conducive to the use of information and the production of knowledge on the terms of the student reader than is the typical classroom. Moreover, it is in the relative weakness and contradictions of librarians' speech acts and in the organization of the library that students and reflexive, enterprising teachers can be observed to find some space to use the library and its contents for their own purposes.

THREE ETHNOGRAPHIC SITES

The central project of this book will be to examine, through an ethnographic study of three school libraries, the promise and problems of school libraries as cultural spaces in which student readers of varying social classes, genders, and ethnic subjectivities alternately conform to, resist, and reconstruct the hegemonic agenda of schooling in general and of school librarianship in particular. In the spring of 1992, I made a brief pilot study of six elementary school libraries within a major southwestern city in the United States. From these I selected three schools in the spring of 1993 whose student populations were representative of the cultural and socioeconomic diversity of the city and region and whose libraries were a vital part of each school's program (see Table 1.1). Roosevelt Elementary is located in a working-class neighborhood that is predominantly Mexican-American, but also has sizable numbers of European- and African-American students. Chavez Elementary is in the poorest neighborhood in the school district, and serves a predominantly Mexican-American student body, along with a minority of African-American students. Crest Hills Elementary, in one of the wealthiest parts of the city, has a predominantly European-American student body, with some Asian-American and Latina/o students also in attendance. The following spring, I returned to these three schools, and over an intensive four-month period, I interviewed the librarians there several times, sat in on story times and other activities, and observed individual students and teachers interact with each other and with the library as a system of textual organization. I also drew maps, took notes and photographs, worked as a participant observer shelving books, read with students, and generally "hung out" in each school and library for a period of six to eight hours per week.

In these three libraries, the discursive practices through which each librarian worked to socialize student readers to use text-based knowledge were multiple and interwoven in each library, but they were also found within each and so are also comparative across all three libraries. These practices can be characterized as "channels." One channel of librarian practice was the system of textual organization, which, as I describe later in this chapter, is historically constituted by the gender politics of the last three centuries. A second, closely related channel was constituted by the organizational opposition of fiction to nonfiction in each library and by the preference for fiction—i.e., children's novels and picture books—that all three librarians showed in the books that they recommended to students as "good reading" for them. I will argue that this second channel is the

Table 1.1
Chavez, Crest Hills, and Roosevelt Elementaries: Comparative Student Demographics, 1992-1993

	Chavez			Crest Hills			Roosevelt		
	No.	Pop. (%)	Diff. from Dist. (%)	No.	Pop. (%)	Diff. from Dist. (%)	No.	Pop. (%)	Diff. from Dist. (%)
Ethnicity									
Hispanic	327	85	+48	77	9	-28	493	66	+29
African-American	53	14	-5	14	2	-17	57	8	-11
White	6	2	-42	778	90	+46	201	27	-17
Total	386			869			751		
Other Designations									
Low-Income	363	94	+46	170	20	-28	563	75	+27
Bilingual	87	23	+17	41	5	-1	122	16	+10
ESL	18	5	+2	43	5	+2	12	2	-1
Gifted/Talented	10	3	-2	158	18	+13	26	3	-2

ESL = English as a second language.

central mode of school library discourse, because it is through this channel that important messages about the politics of middle-class literacy and culture are communicated. The third channel consisted of the forms that the meta- and para-discursive practices of each librarian took, that is, the nature of story-time inter-actions, how rules and procedures within each library were negotiated, and the narratives each librarian used to explain the library's system to students. To-gether, these three channels constituted each library's program.

While the discursive practices of the third channel varied widely among the three libraries, the discourses of the first two, textual organization and the gen-dered distinction between fictional and nonfictional genres, showed remarkable congruence. In the last part of this chapter and in the remainder of this book, I will address the variations in the third channel that I observed in these libraries and schools and the sense I have labored to make of them. But my primary focus at the start will be to consider the multiple historical points of origin and cul-tural implications of the first two channels that were remarkably *invariant* across all three libraries—channels of discursive practice that, as will be seen in later chapters, identify school libraries as institutional sites in the production of their patrons' subjectivities as readers, and that without historical investigation would remain largely overlooked. My plan is first to account for the surface features of these invariances—textual organization and gendered reading preferences—and then to dig deeper to trace their cultural roots.

THE SCHOOL LIBRARY AS AN INSTITUTIONAL SITE

Disciplinary Order

The first invariance across each of the three libraries was that their systems of text classification, as well as the range of texts, were remarkably similar. These principles of textual organization also held in every other library I observed within this school district, as well as in virtually every other school library I have ever visited across a wide range of geographic and demographic locales. In fact, in my experience these organizational practices have been so uniform that I feel some confidence in stating—and the historical discussion of the school li-brary below will corroborate—that the comments I make here based on data col-lected in these three school libraries are largely generalizable to the population of school libraries as a whole. Figure 1.1 diagrams the classification systems of Chavez, Crest Hills, and Roosevelt Elementary libraries. The solid lines indicate standard practice in categorizing texts; the broken lines indicate modifications in the practices of the three libraries studied. One of these modifications, the addi-tion of a third primary category for Spanish-language books, was made at Chavez and Roosevelt in response to bilingual programs there. At both schools, books in Spanish fill two bookcases: one for fiction and the other for nonfiction. There are fewer than 100 Spanish-language books at Crest Hills, they take up three short shelves in an out of the way corner of the library's nonfiction section, and they are left over from the days when busing was used to integrate the school district.

The reasons for the other modifications are symptomatic of discontinuities and contradictions inherent in the primary division of texts in the library, between

Figure 1.1
Text Classification at Three School Libraries

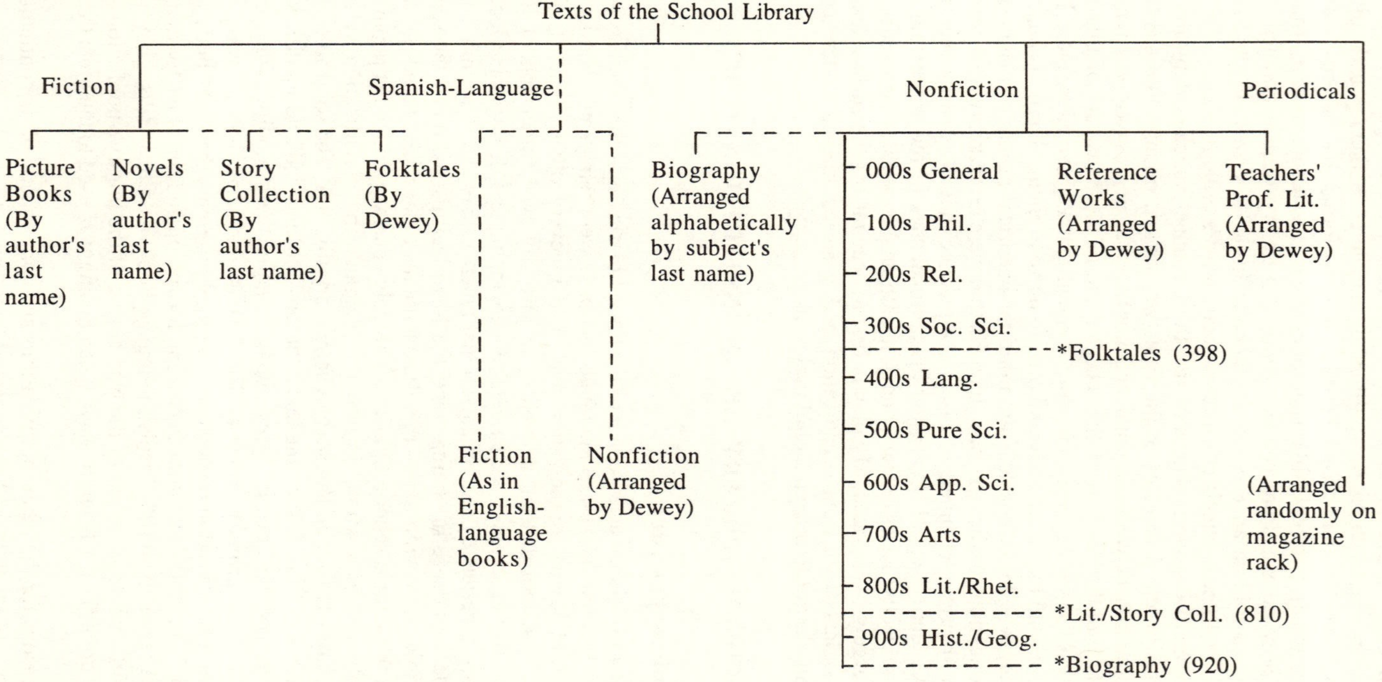

Texts of the School Library

Fiction

- Picture Books (By author's last name)
- Novels (By author's last name)
- Story Collection (By author's last name)
- Folktales (By Dewey)
- Biography (Arranged alphabetically by subject's last name)

Spanish-Language

- Fiction (As in English-language books)
- Nonfiction (Arranged by Dewey)

Nonfiction

- 000s General
- 100s Phil.
- 200s Rel.
- 300s Soc. Sci.
- 400s Lang.
- 500s Pure Sci.
- 600s App. Sci.
- 700s Arts
- 800s Lit./Rhet.
- 900s Hist./Geog.
- *Folktales (398)
- *Lit./Story Coll. (810)
- *Biography (920)

- Reference Works (Arranged by Dewey)

Periodicals

- Teachers' Prof. Lit. (Arranged by Dewey)
- (Arranged randomly on magazine rack)

*Indicates the standard Dewey classification position.

Notes: Solid lines indicate standard classification procedures. Dotted lines indicate modifications.

books designated as fiction and those books conventionally designated in the negative as nonfiction (or at Roosevelt as "fact" or, occasionally at all three libraries, as "informational"), and of librarians' attempts to deal with the problems in the overall logic of the library's system that this division creates. Fiction is divided into two main categories, children's novels (or "chapter books," because their texts are divided into chapters) and more lavishly illustrated picture books, which are alternately identified in the library as "Easy Fiction," "Easier Fiction," or "Everybody's Fiction," depending on how an individual librarian chooses to make the common point that these books are not "baby books" or inferior in their literary quality to "regular fiction." At both Chavez and Roosevelt, children's novels and picture books occupy separate bookcases in close proximity; at Crest Hills, children's novels are in a back room, separated from the picture books. Both categories are arranged in alphabetical order by the author's last name. Nonfiction books are divided into texts on a single subject or topic and reference works like encyclopedias, almanacs, and other, usually thick collections of factual information. In both sections, books are arranged according to the classification system devised by Melvil Dewey, which was based on one taken from the St. Louis Mercantile Library and modified to accommodate the application of a separate decimal numeral to each category—thus enabling the disciplining of "all of human knowledge into ten tight holes," as Dee Garrison (1979, 37) describes Dewey's inspiration.

Originally, Dewey's system did allow for the sorting of "all of human knowledge" into 10 categories—all of human knowledge that contemporary librarians deemed worthy of including in a library's collection, that is. The distinction that school and public libraries make today between books that are classified as nonfiction and fiction was not a part of any original classification scheme but came after the large-scale introduction of popular fiction to public and school library collections. Librarians' attempts to employ a commonsense logic to the library after the fact of the Dewey Decimal System in reconciling texts containing "all of human knowledge" with texts that are brazenly fictive are the cause of most of the modifications school librarians make today. This is why "folktales," whose Dewey classification is 398.2 (in the "social sciences"), are included in the fiction room at Crest Hills (but are shelved separately there). It is also why "story collections," whose Dewey number is usually 813 (for "literature"), are housed with the fiction at Crest Hills and at Roosevelt.

Even after these adjustments are made, however, problems remain. What is the explanation for why poetry and drama, which are certainly fictional, remain in the nonfiction section of all three libraries? Even more disconcerting, perhaps, is the biography section ("920"), which is usually treated like a separate literary genre and set off within the nonfiction section by special signs. The difficulty is that much of children's biography is written in a very novelistic fashion: Although people, places, and major events are historically accurate, conversations and minor incidents for which there is no historical record are often recounted with a realism that conceals their invention. Or consider the problem of classifying picture books in which just the opposite happens as with biography, where a good deal of factual information is cloaked within a story full of talking animals and other fantasy elements. Finally, consider situations like the one at Roosevelt and at Crest Hills where the children's novel *Rascal* (North 1963), about a boy who raises a raccoon cub that later turns wild, is placed in the nonfiction section in the 590s, under "zoological sciences."

When we read the classification system of school libraries this way, the easy commonsense distinction that system makes between fictional and nonfictional texts does not seem so easy to make or so commonsensical anymore; up close, the monolithic rationality of school and public libraries' organizational structure deconstructs itself in ways that require little or no tutoring to see. When we go on to look at the separate criteria by which texts deemed fiction are arranged—by the author's (father's) last name—and the criteria by which texts deemed nonfiction are arranged—by "disciplinary subject"—it becomes apparent that the school library is in fact two very separate (and different) entities joined only by its card catalog, which separately indexes each book by its title, author, and topics.

But even though all of the librarians in the study might acknowledge the contradictions and inefficiencies of their library's structure of classification when questioned, in their practices, each consistently upheld its binary order. Within each library the fiction/nonfiction dichotomy is still regarded as a natural distinction, as something self-evident that we can all believe in and agree about, and it is passed on to students by teachers and librarians in language that suggests the power of its folk quality; as I heard one teacher at Roosevelt explain to her students, "Nonfiction books are true, and fiction books are stories that are made up." Distinctions between fiction and nonfiction at Chavez became the operating principle in what texts its librarian counted as worthy sources of reading material for students, while at Crest Hills and Roosevelt, the distinction operated at spatial, architectural levels that were meant to render this difference concrete not just for the professional purposes of the librarian but for anyone who entered the library. For example, in the tour that the librarian at Roosevelt gave to visitors, she began by standing in the front and center of the library and with sweeping gestures of her right arm explained that "you can divide this library right down the middle and all the fiction is on the left, and all the fact books are on the right." To underscore this point, the words *FACT* and *FICTION* in black capital letters a foot high were taped on the walls that face each other from opposite sides of the room. At Crest Hills, fiction and "nonfiction," as it was termed there, were in separate rooms. When entering the library, nonfiction was on the right of an aisle that divided the outer, main room and that ran straight through a small hallway to a backroom where the children's novels were housed.

Gendered Reading Preferences and the Geography of Social Class Order

The three libraries' systems of textual classification and organization also seemed closely related to the second invariant finding of my study, that preference for fiction or nonfiction closely corresponded to the gender of the reader. Analysis of the books that students checked out as well as regular observation of students' locations in the library during browsing visits over the four-month period consistently indicated that students tacitly designated fiction as a feminine province, while nonfiction was territorially masculine. Over the four months that I observed browsing patterns at Roosevelt, twice as many boys as girls were regularly counted on the nonfiction side of the library, while the same was true for girls on the fiction side. Analysis of book checkouts by third graders at Roosevelt shows that across the school boys checked out more Dewey numbered "fact" books than girls by a ratio of six to one. This correlation between gender and browsing pattern acted as a general rule of thumb at Roosevelt, but at Crest Hills, it seemed to operate almost with the force of law: In four months of regular observation, I virtually never saw a boy above the first grade level (kindergarten [k]–1 students of both genders browsed almost exclusively among the picture books) fail to head straight to the nonfiction section as he entered the library to browse, while girls seldom headed anywhere but straight to the backroom for fiction.

The generalizability of this finding is supported by two major reviews of research on children's reading preferences, one by Guthrie and Greaney (1991) and the other by Monson and Sebesta (1991), which both conclude that the only consistent finding among reported studies is that girls prefer fictional texts and boys more informational, nonfictional texts. Curiously, however, neither of these reviews makes an explicit attempt to account for why this is so, although a "default" explanation may be discernible in the complete absence of any discussion by Guthrie and Greaney and in the subtext of the review by Monson and Sebesta, who note that attempts to define patterns of preference have been "elusive" (1991, 664). They also suggest that ultimately reader preferences are probably "individual and idiosyncratic" (667) and that educators would be well advised not to dwell too much on their findings, particularly as they relate to individual schools and classrooms. In the absence of any speculation or physical, material explanation—in fact, in the implication that there is no such explanation and that further investigation would be fruitless—these authors can be read as locating reader preference in the metaphysics of a Cartesian definition of subjectivity: in the immaterial, ahistorical, and asocial consciousness of a reader who "thinks therefore she is" and whose preferences must therefore originate from some mystical, unknowable, interior source rather than from external material conditions that open themselves to analysis.

An opposing explanation is suggested by Candace West and Don Zimmerman (1987), whose seminal article "Doing Gender" argues that gendered differences in the behavior of females and males have far less to do with nature than with naturalizing inequitable arrangements in the distribution of power and labor within society. According to West and Zimmerman, naturalized gender differences obscure the tacit distinction people make between *sex*, which they define as "a determination made through application of socially agreed upon biological criteria" (genitalia or chromosomal typing), and *sex category*, which, in the absence of visual confirmation, is presumed to correspond to sex because of "identificatory displays that proclaim one's membership in one or the other category" (127). *Gender*, then, refers to the social activity of managing one's conduct in such a way that the presumed correspondence between one's sex and one's sex category remains unchallenged, not only for oneself but for the maintenance of a social order predicated on the division of labor between those designated female and those designated male. Doing gender, and doing it over and over as a "recurring achievement" (126) in ways that are routinely consistent, West and Zimmerman argue, is what naturalizes socially constituted differences between what is considered appropriately male and appropriately female in any situation and culture.

It is the virtual omnipresence and virtual indisputability of genital difference—its sheer obviousness and apparent universality—that makes sex such a powerful and useful sign in the semiotics of labor distribution and identity formation, according to West and Zimmerman. They point out that more than other types of difference, sex category is "omnirelevant": That is, any social situation can become an occasion for challenging the isomorphism of one's sex with one's presumed sex category—an occasion, in other words, for the challenging of one's "meaning" and the legitimacy of one's social place—and so the activity of gendering is continually monitored and self-monitored, and its performance can be made a salient part of almost any occasion and, particularly, I will suggest, of occasions in which some challenge to the gendered division of labor is present. "Doing gender," they conclude, "consists of managing such occasions so that, whatever the particulars, the outcome is seen and seeable in context as gender appropriate or, as the case may be, gender *in*appropriate, that is, *accountable*" (135).

Feminists concerned with the relationships between gender and the uses of text and space have also applied the concept of "doing gender" to analyses of how the designation of spaces as feminine or masculine effectively also distributes knowledge and power within a society. Henrietta Moore (1986), for example, focuses on the ways that spatial arrangements are reciprocally produced by, and produce, political and economic "understandings" between (gendered) groups:

Spatial representations express in their own logic the power relations between different groups; they are therefore active instruments in the production and reproduction of the social order. The ability to provide interpretations of a spatial text . . . is political, because the power to impose the principles of representation of reality—which is no more than the construction of those principles—is a political power. (89)

Similarly, in *Gendered Spaces*, Daphne Spain (1992) argues that "a thorough analysis of gender and space would recognize that definitions of femininity and masculinity are constructed in particular places—most notably the home, workplace, and community—and the reciprocity of these spheres of influence should be acknowledged in analyzing status differences between the sexes." In her view, spatialization not only produces a division of labor along the lines of gender; it also preserves the privileged status of types of knowledge designated as masculine by effectively preventing women from accessing them. She concludes, "The power of feminist geography is its ability to reveal the spatial dimension of gender distinctions that separate spheres of production from spheres of reproduction and assign greater value to the productive sphere" (7).

The school library, with its spatialized distinctions between texts that are valorized as "true" and whose use is meant to lead to productive ends and texts that are described as "made up" and whose use is left, if not to reproduction, then to spheres where society imagines that "real work" is not done, would likely be seen by West and Zimmerman (1987) as well as by Spain (1992) and Moore (1986) as the materially realized model of spatialized relations between gender, text-based knowledge, and the division of labor, an apparatus devoted to the maintenance of gendered power relations via literacy as social practice. Just as important, the materialist perspectives of West and Zimmerman, the geographic analysis of Spain (1992), and the spatiotextual work of Moore (1986) also demonstrate how gender identity and the doing of gender serve economic impera- tives, and so their work also helps to explain how the library's disciplinary sys- tem reinforces the disciplinary order of industrial capitalism. The fiction-nonfic- tion division that school libraries instantiate can then be seen as a culturally powerful one that correlates with other organizational principles in the culture at large, not only because that distinction ostensibly separates out objective, eco- nomic, and political meanings and uses of text and invests them solely in the nonfictional category, while leaving emotional, subjective meanings to fiction, but because it routinely valorizes and reinforces the idea that the world itself is divided into two parts, which can easily be distinguished. As will be demon- strated later in this chapter, this division also channels the labor required to sus- tain and reproduce modern capitalist societies as two mutually exclusive realms, the public (masculine) workplace and the private (feminine) home. In doing so, it reserves to the home and to the idealized female who dwells there the supervi- sory labor of regulating the subjective life of the middle class through the texts of leisure, while freeing the idealized male to regulate the political and economic lives of others in a rational, well-informed, and emotionally detached way. The early children's librarian Winifred L. Taylor would likely have agreed with this statement; she made a similar observation in 1901 when she explained: "[The children's librarian] will find . . . that a distinct division in the reading of boys and girls springs from the fact that, generally speaking, the mental life of the boy is objective, that of the girl subjective" (63).

Because to sustain itself a modern industrial society like ours depends on the technologies of (multiple) cultural sites where children can learn not only to ra- tionalize the division of labor along gendered lines, but also to divide the labor of their minds from the labor of their bodies—and learn to choose which kind of labor they will perform as adults—it seems reasonable to conclude that the struc- ture of school libraries might also be used as a technology to instruct children in their roles as future members of either the working or the middle class. In fact, the librarians' practices at several of the libraries in the pilot and full studies suggest exactly this. As will be discussed in considerable detail in later chapters, both the specific texts and the ways that the librarian at middle-class Crest Hills interacted with students clearly reproduced patterns of text and information use prevalent in the professional workplace. These practices contrasted starkly with those of the librarian at working-poor Chavez, who actively discouraged students from openly using texts as informational sources and explained to me quite fre- quently that unless students there were socialized to consume fiction in mass quantities, they would never become "hooked" on reading or see the world as their peers at Crest Hills did. As an inducement to children who were depicted as having no sense of what it meant to be literate, she conducted read-for-pay pro- grams whose partial consequence was to socialize students to an economy based on piecework labor.

Moreover, even though her practices were acknowledged by both the librarian at Chavez and her peers at other schools to be extreme, that library was not an anomaly within the district but was regarded as a place where extreme problems required proportionate measures. Although no other librarian in the district went quite as far, many librarians serving children in lower-class neighborhoods bor- rowed portions of that library's practices or devised their own solutions to the less acute deficiencies that they saw in their student readers. A librarian from the pilot study, for example, expressed great concern to me about families' lack of care for school property. To dramatize this for students, she used the same prop as the one invented by the librarian at Chavez and one that she said was used by four other librarians she knew: She wrapped a book in a diaper, called it a "book baby," and regularly spent a good portion of her weekly story times lecturing students about the importance of caring for library books as though they were a baby brother or sister—keeping them away from the dog, handling them gently, and putting them up somewhere high when they weren't looking at them. As will be discussed in the next section, just as these sorts of practices are not anomalies within one school district, neither are they recent innovations in school librarianship. In fact, they may be read as part of a long tradition of service to the poor and the immigrant that can be traced to the first school and public children's libraries of little more than a century ago.

SCHOOL LIBRARIES AS HISTORICAL SITES

Within the profession of librarianship itself, there is a historical accounting for events that shaped the school library and the division of its collection into realms of objective and subjective knowledge. The U.S. federal government reported in 1876 (the same year, coincidentally, that the American Library Association [ALA] was founded) that 21 states had passed legislation providing for the creation of libraries in local school districts. Only in Massachusetts did school library collections develop in earnest, under the direction of state superintendent Horace Mann. The appropriation of funds and procedures for stocking, operating, and maintaining the collections in other states, however, was often lacking. In New York State, for example, which actually did provide funds to each school district for the purchase of library books, a loophole in the law allowed local districts to divert these funds to teacher salaries. In other cases, funds were appropriated for district or regional collections, which were then poorly administered, so that either books seldom circulated or the books purchased were considered salacious and inappropriate for students (Bowie 1986). The superintendent's report for the state of Michigan in 1869 captures the prevailing sentiments nicely:

And what kind of books were they? Some good ones, doubtless; but generally it were better to sow oats in the dust that covered them than to give them to the young to read. Every year, soon after the taxes were collected, the State swarmed with peddlers, with all the unsalable books of eastern houses—the sensational novels of all ages, tales of piracies, murders, and love intrigues—the yellow covered literature of the world. (Bowie 1986, 13)

While historians of children's libraries acknowledge these early and largely unsuccessful attempts to establish school libraries, they generally attribute the development of contemporary school libraries to two institutions of social reform promoted by the Progressive movement in the 1880s, the municipal public library and the settlement house (Garrison 1979; Jackson 1976; H. Long 1969). These two institutions constituted part of private and public efforts to ameliorate an urban, industrial environment that was ill equipped to deal with the masses of southern, central, and eastern European immigrants in the 1880s. They were motivated by concerns of civic officials and private and corporate interests (e.g., Andrew Carnegie; see Bobinski 1969) that simultaneously expressed a sincere altruism and desire to improve the lives of these "wretched masses yearning to be free" with a more political and economic desire to undercut any organized efforts to reform the social order and their own advantageous positions in it (Everhart 1983; Franklin 1976; Garrison 1979; Spring 1972).

In many cities, publicly funded libraries were built around the collections of older subscription libraries, which had been funded by user fees and run largely by the classically educated upper and middle classes, and predominantly by men. The first truly public libraries were also organized and controlled by these men, who viewed libraries as serious institutions meant to serve as "people's universities" by which the working classes could raise their standard of culture and knowledge. As nearly every urban center in the United States developed a public library system in the late nineteenth century and their services were extended into the heart of working-class neighborhoods, at first the same standards of gentility and control of the stock (open stacks were unheard of at this time) found in subscription libraries prevailed. So did criteria for the selection of "serious" works; no popular fiction, with its putatively loose moral values and transitory, emotional effects, was to be allowed.

As Garrison (1979) relates, the patriarchs of the American Library Association, Melvil Dewey among them, were adamant in their opposition to placing fiction (i.e., novels) in public library collections; the whole impulse behind the creation of municipal public libraries was, after all, to "uplift" the masses, not to pander to them. "The Fiction Problem," as Garrison labels it, raged in ALA circles for several decades, even as it became increasingly clear that public libraries that did not stock fiction went largely unused by the general public, while those that did became thriving popular institutions, albeit institutions that were largely used by women. But the disappointment of the early genteel male leadership in this turn of the library's social function away from masculine, educational interests to a marginal institution that met the recreational needs of women had nearly faded by the turn of the century, when, although still headed by men, public libraries were almost exclusively staffed and run by women from the middle and upper classes. The values of gentility that had guided them were replaced by the values of the "gentler sex" so that the "shift from 'learning' to 'taste' or 'sensibility' as a criterion defining literary quality" that Raymond Williams (1977, 48) sees originating in eighteenth century novels was finally legitimated by public libraries at the end of the nineteenth century. By this time also, not only had public libraries given up the hope of becoming "people's universities"; it seems they had also given up interest in attracting working class men; the feminization of public librarianship and of public libraries was by then a fait accompli, accepted by nearly everyone. Scott (1986), for example, quotes estimates that nearly 75 percent of the new libraries during this period were founded by women.

The first collections of children's books appeared in the settlement houses—a second institution of social reform—as a part of the wide variety of recreational and acculturating activities they provided. Later, these collections were turned over to public libraries, as children's rooms gradually extended their social outreach. Storytelling was developed among early librarians as a gentle method for inculcating proper values and standards of behavior:

Storytelling was touted as an effective method of Americanizing the foreigner, improving language, softening voices, teaching punctuality, and inculcating courtesy, honesty, neatness, industry, obedience, and gentle manners. It was also, rather incidentally, "the only means by which we can get the children to want the books 'we want them to want.'" (Garrison 1979, 209)

This is not to say, however, that early children's librarians did not share the concerns of their male counterparts about the influences of fiction or about their professional and moral obligation to direct the reading of their clients through, among other means, the careful selection of books. Harriet Long (1969) describes the efforts of one early and highly influential children's librarian, Caroline Hewins, who took over the library of the Hartford, Connecticut, Young Men's Institute in 1875: "Finding that the books by Andersen, Grimm, Hawthorne, Scott and Dickens showed little use as compared to those by Horatio Alger, Harry Castlemon, Martha Findlay and Oliver Optic, she immediately began to raise and publicize the question of better books and better reading for children" (89). Eventually, Hewins, who later became the first woman president of the ALA, threw the offending, "questionable" books out and replaced them with the higher-class "classics." "Algerism," as it was called, was viewed as a threat by children's librarians across the country because it emphasized "getting ahead" through quick strokes of luck. They feared reading Alger would leave boys "unfitted for the practical, hard realities of life" (Garrison 1979, 211).

But the Young Men's Institute, where Miss Hewins labored on behalf of children, was a private subscription library, and so she could only go so far in her proselytizing efforts with its middle-class members. Early children's librarians in public libraries were not so shy. Following practices first established by the home visitations of settlement house volunteers, public libraries set up home libraries—special collections of "the right books" (i.e., children's novels) for introduction into immigrants' homes. The Cleveland Public Library, whose children's department was directed by Effie L. Power (a prominent force in children's librarianship for years who was still writing the definitive ALA manual on children's librarianship in 1943) was a leader in this nationwide movement, beginning in 1902. By 1911, according to Harriet Long (1969), it had 53 home library collections circulating, along with a cadre of volunteers who

acted as visitors to each home library once a week to meet with the children, and by means of these visits reached the children in small groups and thereby developed a certain social influence in which the library was the motive power, but which it could not itself exert. . . . [T]he volunteer visitor prepared the way for the wider influence of books by interpreting them to the children through reading aloud and storytelling. (148)

Garrison (1979) is more direct than Long in describing the mission of the home librarian:

The home visitor . . . very often a lady volunteer, went . . . not merely to exchange books and to discuss the reading, but . . . just as importantly, to nurture children of low parentage and to spread her elevating influence over the home. The early children's librarians were repeatedly reminded that "it is a higher aim to help the boys and girls to be good than to be merely wise." . . . [The home visitor] could control, "if she will, their habits of thought, their personal cleanliness, the whole trend of character development." (209)

She also reports that in 1913 alone 3,352 such visits were made in Cleveland.

School libraries in their present form are the direct descendants of early public librarians' missionary incursions into the public schools. An enterprising librarian in Worcester, Massachusetts, Samuel Green, convinced a number of teachers in the local public school to circulate six books from the public library in their classrooms; in an alternate arrangement, books were entrusted to principals, who distributed them to children and then examined their knowledge of the book after a week or so (H. Long 1969). Garrison (1979) reports that at first, schools and teachers were reluctant to take advantage of library services, not only because they had their own curriculums to implement, but because they, too, considered recreational reading to be frivolous. Educational reform movements at the end of the nineteenth century, however, paved the way toward classroom innovations like recreational reading. For a relatively short time, school libraries were operated in close cooperation with local public libraries, and the same debates over whether, then how much, and finally what kind of fiction should be allowed in their collections that had raged earlier in the public libraries now raged between old-line male educators and more progressive, almost exclusively female, librarians and teachers: "In this first spirited discussion . . . at the ALA convention in 1879, librarians agreed that the library should issue young people no more than one work of fiction per week and that the popular 'sensational' fiction for children should be eliminated entirely from the juvenile collection" (Garrison 1979, 208). "Next it was decided appropriate to offer mediocre fiction as a bait to attract the uncultured and to serve as 'stepping stones upward' to a better class of reading" (213).

By the turn of the century, school libraries were a common fixture in elementary schools, as they had been in high schools from a much earlier period. Although they were now seldom the legal or physical adjuncts of children's rooms in public libraries, they were still run by women who had been trained in schools of library science rather than in teachers' colleges (because of the technical, largely clerical knowledge required to classify and maintain, and the training required to select, their inventory). As a result, they carried with them all the organizational markings of the public library they had developed from and became subscription libraries of "serious" academic knowledge to which a large collection of popular novels had been grafted but never quite assimilated. The same characteristics of the children's reading room in the public library were also put into place: "careful censorship, approved reading lists, separate rooms with small-scale tables and chairs, and a kindly maternal guidance designed to lead the child, unsuspecting, to a higher standard of reading" (Garrison 1979, 208).

As written in the history and revisionist histories of library science, recounting the development of school and public libraries helps to explain how school libraries came to consist of two organizationally separate and systemically different entities. The historical account indicates, as was suggested in the introduction to this chapter, that the older, nonfiction section of the school library was a throwback to earlier subscription libraries in its tone and, in its vertical, arborescent (Deleuze and Guattari 1987), "tree-like" classification system, was the product of an almost exclusively male period of library history. The introduction of popular fiction to library collections, with its more horizontal, less hierarchical arrangement of texts by their authors' (fathers') last names, similarly represents the more recent introduction of feminine interests and ways into the library, an introduction that was probably more than coincidental with the feminization of the profession of librarianship.

I will close this account by noting that librarians in general, and school and children's public librarians in particular, seem to be long-lived and tenacious people, who tend to sink deep roots into the places where they settle. Effie Power, for instance, became the director of children's library services in Cleveland in 1903; in 1943, she published her revised and authoritative manual *Work with Children in Public Libraries*, for the ALA. Of the three librarians I studied, the librarian at Roosevelt celebrated her seventieth birthday in 1993 and had completed 38 years in teaching and librarianship, with time off to raise a family. The woman who was the librarian in her town's public library when this librarian was a child was also alive at the time of my research; she had maintained their friendship for almost 60 years and visited her whenever she returned to that city. The association of the librarian at Crest Hills with that school went back 20 years; her predecessor and mentor appeared as an editor of ALA publications in the 1950s when she was at the height of her career and after many previous years of local and national influence. Time appears to move much more slowly for librarianship than it does for other fields; the influence of individuals and the traditions they stand for can be measured in scores rather than in decades. Although many of the events recounted above took place almost a century or more ago, in librarian time keeping they are removed from current practice by no more than two or three generations.

It should come as little surprise, then, that the practices of librarianship, particularly of children's librarianship, and the values and professional rights these practices instantiate—the capacity of children's librarians to determine the moral/aesthetic qualities of books, an evangelical faith in the abstract power of reading good fiction, and the moral and professional obligations of librarians, as public trustees, to guide the reading (and so the moral and intellectual development) of children and adolescents—differ surprisingly little in the publications of the *Library Journal* of 1901 and the issues of the *School Library Journal* of 1994–1995. In the published proceedings of the Waukesha Conference of the American Library Association in 1901, for example, Caroline Hewins railed against the very popular "Elsie Dinsmore" series, calling it "tearfully sentimental and priggish, where the heroine is held up as a saint and martyr for refusing to obey an entirely reasonable request of her father, and where money, fine clothes, and love-making at an early age hold too prominent a place" (61). In the February 1901 issue of *Library Journal*, W. W. Plummer blamed the "vulgarization of the child" on the lax reading habits of parents:

What if the boy's father does read the *New York Journal* and the girl's mother, when she reads anything, Laura Jean Libbey? It is our business, as librarians for children, to see that by the time the child reaches the same age he shall like something different and better. And how can this be brought about if we let him steep himself in the smart, sensational, vulgar, and up-to-date children's books that naturally lead to just such tastes in the adult? (166)

Plummer also warned librarians to "guard against false reasoning" and related the plot of one children's novel in which a girl who visits a "summer village" is at first considered by her neighbors to be beneath them socially; eventually, the neighbors decide not to snub her and finally discover that she belongs to a "fine old family" after all. Plummer concludes that this book is "full of the spirit of snobbery while professing to teach the opposite" (166), and implies that librarians have a duty to prevent such books from falling into children's hands. Throughout these issues, librarians' own good taste and moral discernment are promoted as the main, if undelineated, hedges against abusing their public trust to provide the best reading to the most people.

Ninety years later, things would seem to be different: In the monthly columns of *School Library Journal* (SLJ), for example, the profession now rails *against* censorship. But while this preoccupation with fighting censorship would seem, on the surface, to represent a change of mind over the regulation of children's and adolescents' reading, closer inspection of these columnists' arguments shows that they are less concerned with protecting the civil liberties of young readers or authors than they are with censorship's potential to hamstring their own efforts to control their young customers' (as they are now described) views on controversial social and moral issues. Indeed, if anything, the evangelical promotion of reading as an abstract virtue and remedy for whatever ails the individual and society is a stronger theme in the school library literature of the 1990s than in the 1900s. In the 1990s the reading of good books is touted as an effective response to, among other topics, homosexuality (Cockett 1995), violence (Caywood 1994), peer pressure ("Teens need to read about characters they can identify with, characters who exercise their own good judgment and model behaviors that defuse peer disapproval"; Caywood 1995b, 44), the Los Angeles riots (Mediavilla 1994), the postmodern condition (Caywood 1995c), and general struggles with the forces of good and evil ("If the hobbits and beggars and apprentices that go off to save their worlds can succeed, teens who escape into fantasy can return with the courage to confront the evils humans have created"; Caywood 1995a, 152).

"Reluctance" is the euphemism used in the 1990s to describe the "at-risk" children and adolescents who can but won't read for pleasure and so remain outside librarians' influence; the column "Practically Speaking" in 9 of the 16 issues of *SLJ* published between April 1994 and August 1995 devotes itself to strategies for "hooking" the athletic, the poor, and the generally unsupervised child reader. Now, as in 1901, it is the reading (or nonreading) habits of parents that are blamed: "Partly because fewer parents read, reading for pleasure is a way of life undreamed of by many children today" (Hodges 1994, 27). Finally, now as in the days of W. W. Plummer, librarians still take upon themselves the onus of judging, based on their own largely undelineated sense of good taste and moral discernment, the social correctness of the children's novel of manners. For example, an article on children's books dealing with mental disabilities, "Beyond the

Stereotypes" (Heim 1994) warns against the trend in which "many children's books use a character who is mentally disabled primarily as a vehicle for the growth of another character who is 'normal'" (140).

This comparison of the school library literature from 1901 and 1994–1995 also demonstrates the extent to which, then as now, the primary vehicle, or moral technology, of social action in school and public children's libraries has been and remains within the genres of fiction. Of the 74 books listed in the December 1994 issue of *SLJ*, 52, or 72 percent, were fiction; all four of the "author interviews" published in that journal from April 1994 to August 1995 featured children's authors of fiction; and of the 16 columns in the same period titled "Up for Discussion: Issues in Book Selection and Collection Development," 12 focused exclusively on the genre of children's and adolescent fiction. In 1901 as in 1994–1995, when "nonfiction" is considered, it is considered secondarily as a single unitary genre—and only after fiction is fully discussed in all its multiple subgenres.

Then, as now, novels and picture books are promoted as manuals for the straitened and as inspirations and guides to the unconverted. Yet the source of fiction's putative power and instrumentality in the lives of children, much less its hold on the imagination of those who have served for over a century as school and public children's librarians, remains both unexamined and unarticulated within the literature on the school library. The following section, then, may seem a digression from the topic of school librarianship, but it is a necessary one. For only after the textual, historical mechanics of the novel, that principal moral instrument of school librarians are examined can we begin to see not only what possessed librarians of the late Victorian age to presume to enter the homes of the immigrant underclass and the public schools with their arms full of children's novels but also what possesses school librarians today, and in particular the three librarians in the present study, to engage in their own various instructional and evangelizing projects, all of which center around the novel and its primer, the picture book.

THE IMPORT OF NOVEL READING;
OR, WHAT WORK *DOES* PLEASURE DO?

"The novel," wrote George Lukács (1920/1971), is "the representative art-form of our age. . . . [This is because] the structural categories of the novel constitutively coincide with the world as it is today" (93). So conditioned are we to the literary dominance of the form that in the population at large there are probably few educated persons outside academia who can imagine a time when to speak of literature was not to make reference first to novelistic fiction, and only second, to the epic, poetry, drama, the essay, and other, lesser, forms. Novels are, in fact, relatively new inventions, dating back only to the late seventeenth century at the earliest (Watt 1957). Along with periodicals, they were among the first works written specifically to be sold as commodities to a mass market. Novels are inextricably implicated in modern industrial society and its economic logic of mass production, mass consumption, and, consequently, mass culture (Belsey 1980; Davidson 1986; Williams 1977).

Well before the Enlightenment or the industrial age there were, of course, extended narratives, some of them in prose, that featured heroes in confrontation with the world. But these heroes—usually of noble rank or touched in some other way by a god—moved in enchanted worlds and, more like characters in a play than like conscious individuals, acted out roles prescribed by fate or divine manipulation. The hero of the novel, however, in keeping with Cartesian principles of rational action and the split of the subject from the object, is alone in his or her world—and he or she knows it. He or she is an ordinary person, no different in his or her humanity from the reader. Although the hero might be a lady or lord, or even royal, it doesn't matter; the author lets the reader know—and the novel's attraction depends in part on the reader's understanding—that he or she is "just like us" and can expect no special favors or curses. Moreover, even if the setting of the novel is some exotic locale—a desert island, a foreign land, a distant planet—we know that its enchantment has been forged and that its parts relate not allegorically to some celestial whole but analogously to some earthly reality. Again, Lukács explains, "The novel is the epic of an age in which the extensive totality of life is no longer directly given, in which the immanence of meaning in life has become a problem, yet which still thinks in terms of totality" (1920/1971, 56). In short, novels present a view of the world that has been thoroughly disenchanted and secularized, in which divine intervention in human affairs is no longer presumed or seriously expected (88). Novels, in effect, are culturally involved in the modern condition at its most problematic levels.

With the growing awareness of the individual subject's alienated condition, the objectivity of the world takes on a new fascination for him or her. Discrete objects—people, places, and things—acquire a material relevance that they did not possess in a world determined by spiritual generalities and universals, because now the possibility looms that they can be possessed and directed by conscious manipulation—a situation that in turn creates new social and ethical problems in need of an efficacious, and profitable, response. The namesake of *Robinson Crusoe* (Defoe 1719/1961), which is frequently regarded as the protonovel, is described by Ian Watt in *The Rise of the Novel* (1957) as the "illustration of *homo economicus*" (63). Shipwrecked on a desert island, for example, Defoe's lone hero becomes depressed; to cheer himself, he lists all the goods and evils that have befallen him in two columns in the novel's text, side by side: "[A]nd I stated it very impartially, like debtor and creditor, the comforts I enjoyed, against the miseries I suffered" (cited in Watt 1957, 70). The balance, it turns out, is a positive one. Crusoe is cheered and resolves to see what he can do to make his lot a more comfortable one.

But Crusoe's sense of the economic, according to Watt, is not limited to things alone; Crusoe, a good Calvinist, sees all his relations with the world, including his social relations, in economic terms. When he must choose among five women for his wife, he chooses the sturdiest but least attractive in the lot and then later congratulates himself for making a wise investment: "She proved the best wife of all the parcel" (cited in Watt 1957, 68). In a sequel to the original novel, Crusoe is befriended and on occasion saved by a Moorish boy, Xury, and several times promises to see to it that the boy's fortunes are fixed. But when another captain makes an offer that he can't refuse, Crusoe sells the boy into slavery. In Crusoe's "dealings" with people, Watt concludes that "he treats them all in terms of their commodity value" (69).

The same emphases—on individualism, on realism, and on objectified social relationships—continued as the hallmark qualities of the novels of the eighteenth, nineteenth, and twentieth centuries (Belsey 1980). These novels' major innovation, and commercial asset, was to produce a textual effect in which, according to Davidson (1986),

[t]here is a direct line of communication between the sender and the receiver. With this form, the *meaning* of the text is embedded in the experience of decoding the message and thus cannot be separated from the act of reading itself. Although a scientific treatise may be paraphrased without any significant loss of validity or substance, a novel cannot, and to summarize the argument of the plot is not to convey the essence of the fiction. In a sense, the novel *is* its reading, and that reading must finally be private and personal. (43; italics in original)

Novel Ways of Reading

It was, according to the editor of *New York Magazine* in 1797, "a novel-reading age" (cited in Davidson 1986, 39). By Watt's (1957) estimates, compiled with "the greatest possible reserve," 7 "works of fiction" per year were written between 1700 and 1740 (remember that *Robinson Crusoe*, the "first novel," was not published until 1719); but 20 per year were written from 1740 to 1770; while in the last three decades of the eighteenth century, 40 novels were written per annum (290)—for an approximate total of 2,080 works of hundreds of pages in length, each in hand-set type. Moreover, this figure does not include the even vaster numbers of novelistic texts disguised—to suggest their "educational" as opposed to amusement, value—as "travel narratives," "histories," or "lives," all of which attempted to produce the same textual effect as the novel.

It bears noting here that in the history of its narrative form as written by Watt, the novel captures and expresses the spirit of the modern age as its product rather than its engine or collaborative force. More recently than Watt, however, a new generation of feminist and poststructuralist critics, following Virginia Woolf's observation that "a change . . . of greater importance than the Crusades . . . [took place when] . . . the middle-class woman began to write" (1975, 69), has placed the novel, and particularly the domestic novel of manners, prior to, and then concurrent with, the development of the middle-class industrial state. In *Desire and Domestic Fiction,* Nancy Armstrong (1987) outlines how the sexual contract defining modern relations between men and women that novelists like Richardson and Fielding (and a host of lesser-known but well-read women writers of the same period) worked out narratively was predated by the conduct books of the seventeenth and early eighteenth centuries, in which relations between men and women were described as separating the management of the objects of the household and of the world into two separate provinces or spheres of influence, in accordance with the "natural" (i.e., God-given) properties or qualities of the male and female sex. According to Armstrong, originally these relations, as described in the Puritan conduct books of the sixteenth and early seventeenth centuries, could not be described as "contractual" at all in the modern sense that a contract is a negotiated, voluntary agreement between two consenting individuals. In these early conduct books, women were depicted as fulfilling their purpose when they served the proprietary interests of their male masters with or without their consent; under Puritan arrangements, the husband "got money and provisions" and the wife was to "not vainly spend" them; the husband was to "be skillful in talk" while the wife was to "boast of silence," and so on (Armstrong 1987, 110). But beginning with later conduct books of the seventeenth century and throughout the eighteenth, the desirable traits of a wife were gradually redefined in terms of interior, quasi spiritual qualities like "modesty," "frugality," and "discretion." In time, these qualities came to be identified as territorially, and later inherently, female; in this way the road was paved for a theory of sexuality that, in allotting certain characteristics to women and others to men as their birthright, claimed to describe the natural order of political and economic conduct as well.

As the Enlightenment and its Cartesian ideal of a conscious individual whose subjectivity originates outside political history began to empower the commercial classes of the eighteenth century to challenge the economic and political hegemony of the aristocracy, the notion of the female as a subject—as a conscious individual whose defining characteristics opposed and complemented those of the rational, male subject—also gained currency within the conduct book literature, as well as within the developing form of its narrative counterpart, the novel. Again, according to Armstrong, it was the fiction of a society composed of persons whose individuality originated outside of culture and history that necessitated the creation of the trope of the contract—now a *voluntary* agreement between two *consenting* subjects—that formed the main topic of novelists in the eighteenth and nineteenth century and the main concern of its largely but not entirely female readership.

If, as Armstrong argues, in writing the novel the social contract that became middle-class marriage was negotiated within society at large, in reading novels women were provided with critical information about how to behave in negotiating a middle-class marriage. The first "true novel," according to Watt (1957), and according to Anderson and Zinsser (1988), the most widely read of the day, was Samuel Richardson's *Pamela, or Virtue Rewarded.* In some 900 meticulously detailed pages, Pamela, a fifteen-year-old servant girl who swoons at each sexual advance of her employer, Mr. B, manages both to resist seduction and to successfully negotiate a marriage to Mr. B on her terms. Then, instead of the quick fairy-tale ceremony between Pamela and Mr. B. that signaled the happily-ever-after ending found in the less durable romances of the day, the story continues "while every detail of the marriage ceremony and the resulting new conjugal pattern is worked out according to Richardson's exemplary specifications" (Watt 1957, 149)—every detail of the marriage contract, that is. Watt acknowledges the social significance of the novel and of Pamela's behavior, noting that "the appearance of *Pamela* marks a very notable epiphany in the history of our culture: the emergence of a new, fully developed and immensely influential stereotype of the feminine role" (161). But he fails to account for the credibility to readers of Pamela's resistance in an age when aristocratic males regularly had their way with servant girls, and so he fails again to show how *Pamela* and, by extension, other novels effected social change. In Nancy Armstrong's (1987) view, however, the social contract that Pamela negotiates with Mr. B. is one that had already been written and read by women years before Richardson codified its rituals:

Pamela's "no" would have meant very little had she not been speaking with the voice of thousands who by then knew the conduct-book philosophy of reading. Nor, for that matter, would her denial have reverberated through time had it not addressed millions who came to understand themselves as basically the same kind of individual first described in these female conduct books. (115)

Armstrong goes on to point out that much of the negotiation between Mr. B. and Pamela is conducted in *writing*. At one point, Richardson presents these negotiations in the form of notes exchanged between the two; they appear in the text of the novel in two columns, side by side. What she describes as "the only genuinely erotic scene in the novel" takes place when Mr. B. finally succeeds in stealing Pamela's letters, concealed, ironically, upon her body, and by doing so "takes possession of a thoroughly self-inscribed Pamela" (120). And it is through a process of *reading* these letters, Armstrong points out, that Mr. B. is transformed, and the promise of the conduct books is realized:

Pamela's writing, Mr. B. admits at last, "has made me desirous of reading all you write; though a great deal of it is against myself" (p. 242). To her he surrenders mastery over sexual relations, which he then allows to dominate the rest of the novel: "There is such a pretty air of romance as you relate them, in your plots, and my plots, that I shall be better directed in what manner to wind up the catastrophe of the pretty novel" (p. 242). Along with the authority to write their story, he hands the regulation of the household over to her, and the novel becomes little more than the conduct book it has passed through so much peril to resemble. (120–121)

The point I am arguing, along with Armstrong, is more than an academic one, for in making it, Armstrong is also arguing for the agency of women in *writing* the terms of the new social order, one based on sexuality rather than the metaphysics of blood—and one in which women, by controlling their virtue, would eventually lay claim to control of the social order itself.

Novels were, for the young middle-class woman of the eighteenth century, "actual textbooks which furnished specific arguments to justify unusual behavior, and young ladies grew amusingly efficient in citing these works whenever the occasion arose" (Tompkins 1932, 73). One of young women's most unnerving propensities, it seems, and one of the reasons Tompkins lists for the intense opposition to novel reading that grew throughout the century, was for making new demands on potential suitors to live up to the ideals of romantic courtship described by novelists (71). "The novel, then," Tompkins concludes, "offered an outlet to the imaginative, an instrument to the didactic and a resource to the straitened" (121). Once married, women turned to periodicals and books that would provide them with information on child care and running a household, usually with at least one servant (Anderson and Zinsser 1988). But in their leisure hours, they continued to read novels, and many, according to Tompkins (1932) and J. Taylor (1943), felt enough competence with the genre to write them. As Tompkins (1932) explains (patronizingly):

Here, as they apprehended it, was a new and unexacting literary form, hedged round by no learned traditions, based on no formal technique, a go-as-you-please narrative, spun out in a series of easy, circumstantial letters, such as a young lady might write to a school-friend before domestic cares absorbed her. It did not look difficult; even the plot need not be so strictly premeditated as it is in drama, or in Fielding's elaborate comic epic in prose; one could start with a rough sketch of a group of characters, and ideas for their future relationships would surely present themselves. (119)

Both reading and *writing* novels could help people to negotiate their life world—to articulate the social terrain and realize a plan of their own, by "reading themselves into articulateness," as Tompkins (122) describes the many women novelists of the period. These new writers saw in the heavy market for the novel created by the increase in circulating libraries and in the novel's form—"a capacious vessel, into which anything could be cast, in any order" (28)—a choice opportunity for self production.

The advancement of women into the field of publishing "exploited a type of literature in which she could ably share honors with the opposite sex" (Taylor 1943, 85). But it was not penis envy that motivated women to take up their pens; as the *Critical* noted in 1776, "They seem to be animated with an emulation for vindicating the honour of women in general rather than for acquiring to themselves the invidious reputation of great accomplishments" (quoted in Tompkins 1932, 123). They also seemed to be intent on presenting a more three-dimensional portrait of women. The "mixed female character" of the female novelists, according to Tompkins, "is one which cannot be labeled good, dangerous or funny; it is kneaded out of the common virtues and follies of human nature, but none of these is heightened for the sake of dramatic effect" (136). Women authors strove to produce and reinforce, in short, the ideal of the female as a fully developed, autonomous individual. But Tompkins also goes on to note that most female novelists of the eighteenth century never quite went all the way toward placing their "mixed" female heroes in mixed plots: At the end of these novels, the female character usually subordinates herself to a man and is quickly married off. Following Armstrong's analysis, this was because, under the rules of the social contract, the fullness of female subjectivity was only achievable within a domestic scenario. Tompkins concludes: "Abortive as many of [these plots] are, however, these attempts are evidence of a resolve on the part of the women to widen the circle of female portraits" (138).

Novel ways of reading and writing received a similar reception in the early years of the United States, where, according to Davidson (1986), denunciation of the novel as a threat to the social order by ministers, the press, and many of the Founding Fathers (with Ben Franklin, whose *Autobiography* shows a great deal of the stylistic influence of Richardson and Defoe, a notable exception) was "intense," regular, and widespread. Davidson suggests that ministers, at least, saw novelistic texts as a potent threat to their previously uncontested control of textual knowledge. Most of the population of the early United States was located in rural areas supported by isolated villages; the minister in such a setting was usually the only college-educated person in the community, owned most of its books, and served usually as its only interpreter of not only religious but secular knowledge as well. The establishment of commercial circulating libraries in many small communities and a general improvement in the affordability and distribution of novels meant that ministers' monopolistic hold on the uses and meanings of the written word was about to be broken. This development was satirically portrayed in one of the most popular novels circulating in the United States at the time, *The Power of Sympathy*. In that novel, "[t]he minister delivers a lengthy diatribe that is against novel reading and seduction and in favor of sermons, satire, and didactic essays. . . . While he drones on, one of the members of his intended audience diverts herself 'with the cuts in Gay's *Fables*' while another reads a copy of Sterne's *A Sentimental Journey*" (Davidson 1986, 42).

The advent of a new view of marriage, in which women and men were, for the first time, both considered individuals whose voluntary consent was required to contract a marriage, represented a major advance in the history of sexual relations and particularly in women's rights; but that sexual contract was not without its hidden clauses. Although new ideals of subjectivity along sexual lines made it possible for middle-class women to act as their own agents in negotiating with men, their avenues of economic and political activity were concurrently narrowed within the boundaries of matrimony and limited—and remained so at least until late in the nineteenth century—to the location of the home. Whereas males' schooling of the period began to reflect both academic and vocational training for work in commercial and professional enterprise, females were often still trained at home to read and write a little but mostly to master the skills that would serve them in running a home and raising children. The business of males' education became success in business; the business of females' education, and their exclusive hope for prosperity, was marriage (Davidson 1986; Stratton 1987).

Even within the home, moreover, an ideal of female subjectivity that was described as originating outside history and politics, and whose influence depended on the purity of its spirituality, ensured that women's activities would be highly constrained and that their capacity for political and economic action would be restricted to practices that could be described and justified within the tropics of motherhood: Women, in their proper roles as wives and mothers, were supposed to nurture, to support, to guide, and to influence gently. Ironically, during the Victorian era as the nuclear family came to be defined as the nucleus of society with the mother as its defining element, women (with Victoria herself as exemplar of this phenomenon) could only act politically by appearing to act in ways that seemed to originate from, and take the form of, completely apolitical motives and actions.

The Rise of Libraries

This may be the most advantageous position from which to read and write the development of libraries as public enterprises, the legitimation of the novel as an educational tool, and finally its institutional introduction in the late nineteenth century to metropolitan, and subsequently school, libraries. As was noted in the opening of this chapter, in the same way that novels and conduct books textualized gender relations, texts themselves during the eighteenth century were similarly dichotomized and located in two separate kinds of libraries, one patronized mainly by women and the working class and the other patronized mainly by professional and commercial men. The primary vehicle for distributing novels to the public during the eighteenth century was the circulating library (Davidson 1986;

Hamlyn 1946; D. Knott 1976). These establishments were frequently adjuncts to book and printing shops and, unlike subscription libraries, which had been founded prior to circulating libraries' appearance, they were strictly commercial in form and function. The library's stock was owned by a shopkeeper, who charged a fee to readers who could then borrow usually one book at a time. A catalog of available titles was printed by the shopkeeper and distributed to members to choose from (Hamlyn 1946). Because they were such popular and frankly commercial enterprises, evidently run by persons with relatively little interest in detailed record keeping, the few catalogs that survive, along with advertisements and announcements in newspapers and their brief mention in surviving diaries and journals, form the only remaining evidence of their readership or the nature of the libraries' stock (Humphreys 1985).

Consequently, while there is some evidence of who used circulating libraries and what they stocked, there is little or no evidence of the frequency of use by patrons or of particular titles' incidence of being lent. Most scholars have relied on the record of one successful shopkeeper, printer, and would-be author, who wrote a "how-to" pamphlet on starting a circulating library; he advised that 80 percent of a business's stock be novels (Hamlyn 1946; D. Knott 1976). Other scholars, however, have questioned whether this figure should be used as a general figure (Kaufman 1967; J. Knott 1972). They point to the contents of surviving catalogs, which indicate that although novels are frequently the largest category in an inventory, they are frequently rivaled in numbers by religious texts and usually do not form the majority, much less 80 percent, of the books listed—although, again, there are few, if any, records of how often particular titles were lent (Hamlyn 1946; Humphreys 1985; Tompkins 1932).

We do know that surprising numbers of women and working-class people used these libraries—surprising numbers, considering the lack and quality of even rudimentary formal education for these groups (Humphreys 1985; J. Knott 1972). According to Tompkins (1932), by the 1770s, "Women were supposed to constitute three-quarters of the novel reading public" (120). And we know that throughout the eighteenth century the numbers of circulating libraries continued to increase at a pace at least as dramatic as the increase in the number of novels published (J. Taylor 1943) and that, in Britain at least, they were to be found almost everywhere, not only in London (Hamlyn 1946; Humphreys 1985; Joynes 1971; J. Knott 1972; Mowat 1979).

Circulating libraries filled a market niche not met by the more staid, genteel, and usually better established subscription library. The two existed side by side throughout the eighteenth century and into the nineteenth, and as Davidson (1986) relates, their distinction was often blurred; of the two, however, subscription libraries clearly were regarded as having a "higher class" of books and a more educated clientele. These "nonprofit" organizations, which charged an annual fee that was usually higher than the circulating libraries', were often created by a group of educated, middle- and upper-middle-class men (although women members were allowed) who initially pooled their resources and frequently hired someone to act as a keeper of their books. Subscription libraries were often specialized in their collections, due to certain common scholarly or professional interests shared by their members (Humphreys 1985; Joynes 1971). Their more complete records also indicate a certain reserve about what books they selected and particularly about the new form of the novel, which was regarded in those times in much the same way that the educated regard television today. In time, it was the inventories of subscription libraries, and not circulating libraries, that formed the base collections of many early public libraries in both the United States and in Britain; for example, the Philadelphia Public Library was originally a subscription library founded by Ben Franklin (Bostwick 1910).

The Novel as Moral Technology

From a distance, we now can see that the novel did not remain a completely maligned form of literature indefinitely. Authors like Samuel Richardson had long used the argument that their novels were intended for moral edification (Armstrong 1987; J. Taylor 1943), but the novel's potential as an instrument of cultural influence, or "moral education," that could be directed at the underclasses was not grasped until the 1780s by the middle- and upper-class elite (Altick 1957; Anderson and Zinsser 1988; Avery 1975; J. Taylor 1943; Tompkins 1932).

The exemplar and visionary of the movement to uplift the masses of displaced farmers that flooded the new urban industrial centers of Britain through the teaching of religious virtue was, by many accounts, Miss Hannah More. Motivated by the mix of altruism and conservative self-interest that characterizes middle-class charity work to this day, Miss More's original theater of action was the Sunday School movement, which is widely recognized as the first attempt to organize schooling for the masses in industrial Britain. In these schools, which were organized on the only day of the week when they did not work in the factories, children were taught the rudiments of reading using texts with a heavy religious and moral bent. Writing was not taught, however; Miss More believed that writing "might encourage rebelliousness" (Anderson and Zinsser 1988).

Despite her preoccupation with reform, however, Miss More was a staunch defender of established cultural values and particularly of patriarchy. In her support for the ideal of an apolitical female subjectivity, she was appalled by the French Revolution and wrote to Horace Walpole that "I have been much pestered to read the *Rights of Woman*, but am invincibly resolved not to do it" (quoted in Anderson and Zinsser 1988, 126). But it was the mass publication in Britain of Thomas Paine's *Rights of Man* in 1791 and, according to Altick (1957) and Avery (1975), the prospect of social upheaval resulting from mass literacy that drove Miss More to take up the pen and write a series of popular children's books with catchy titles (Avery 1975) and one enormously popular novel, *Coelebs in Search of a Wife* (1808), that went through 12 printings in its first year and 30 by Miss More's death in 1834 (Anderson and Zinsser 1988). In it, the dashing hero Coelebs rejects the fashionable Lady Bab Lawless in favor of the more modest, scripture-reading homemaker, Lucilla Stanley. As an exemplar, Lucilla Stanley was a hit, according to Anderson and Zinsser, but not with the working classes; rather, *Coelebs* "seems to have been so successful with the largely female novel-reading audience because of its attractive portrait of an ideal woman" (127), a woman whose "pattern" of " 'regularly devoting two evenings to making her rounds among the village poor has . . . made it a fashion and a rage'" (128).

Hannah More and her peers were the most unlikely of feminists, from a contemporary point of view, but their utter respectability and staunch defense of the status quo provided opportunities at the time that previously had not existed. By taking the high moral ground and justifying their promotion of novel reading and writing as the exertion of cultural values that upheld, rather than challenged, middle-class values and male dominance within commercial and political spheres, women's novel way of reading gained legitimacy. One eventual outcome was that in the last quarter of the nineteenth century, according to Eagleton (1983), Cambridge University admitted its first women students, and to accommodate them, it also admitted the study of literature as an academic discipline for the first time.

The Rise of "Feminine" Professions

In time, the legitimization of women's literacy practices as educational activities made it possible for women to claim for themselves a space for public action, first as teachers and volunteer charity workers, then as nurses in England during the Crimean War and in the United States during the Civil War, and finally, toward the end of the nineteenth century, as librarians and social workers. That transition, however, was one preceded by a serious and lengthy discussion within the genre of women's fiction about the nature of women's problems and how it might address them. Although in principle women's individuality and right to assent or dissent from a marriage was recognized, in practice women remained the legal and social adjuncts of their husbands and, once married, were subject to their control. "Sentimental" novels, written and read by women in the United States during the first two decades of the nineteenth century, depicted the reality of an arrangement in which women were required to act virtuously, although no such social strictures were placed on their abusive, sometimes adulterous husbands. But these reformist novelists could suggest little outside of uncomplaining submission (with the hope of a heavenly reward) or "education" in advance of marriage (to help a woman choose more perspicaciously). A middle-class woman's place, for better or worse, was always placed firmly in the home; as Davidson (1986) concludes, "The changes proposed by the reforming novelists turn out to be largely grounded in the old order, and what is advocated is a readjustment of the marriage contract rather than a second revolution led by 'the Ladies'" (130).

In the United States, according to Baym (1978) and Hart (1950), later novels written by and for women in the years 1820–1870 (and reaching a peak in the 1850s) took a different turn and achieved unprecedented popularity, becoming the most widely read and commercially successful books of the period. The women who wrote them, however, were not middle- and upper-class women of means with an interest in moral education; rather, they were middle-class, educated women who wrote because they had to make a living; as one of these authors, Ruth Hall, explained, "No happy woman writes" (M. Kelley 1984, 138). The plotlines of these novels, while containing the characteristic elements of individualism, realism, and a focus on social relations identified by Watt (1957), are something of a departure from the portraits of "virtue rewarded" that had appeared in U.S. women's fiction earlier in the century and were appearing in British women's fiction of the midcentury. According to Baym (1978):

The many novels tell, with variations, a single tale. In essence, it is the story of a young girl who is deprived of the supports she had rightly or wrongly depended on to sustain her throughout life and is faced with the necessity of winning her own way in the world. . . . The happy marriages with which most—though not all—of this fiction concludes are symbols of successful accomplishment of the required task and resolutions of the basic problems raised in the story, which is in most primitive terms the story of the formation and assertion of a feminine ego. (11–12)

Because these stories end in marriage and continue to glorify the "cult of domesticity," Baym notes that some feminist critics have tended to view these authors as traitors to their sex, women whose unenlightened views contributed to women's entrapment. Baym disagrees; she points out that hardly any of these novels, as opposed to those written in the eighteenth century, are novels of seduction, like Richardson's *Pamela*, or of abuse, like those of 20 years before; instead, men and women are viewed as capable of relating to each other in ways based on "feelings other than lust" (26)—and surely that is progress. Baym sees the feminism of these authors as "pragmatic" and concerned with managing, in that moment of time, to provide women with a view of themselves and their potential that was achievable. If we read Baym's description of these novels through the historical and theoretical accounting of women's literacy provided by Nancy Armstrong and Cathy Davidson, however, it seems that Baym has missed seeing something in them, namely, the portrait of a woman who dares to enter a public sphere controlled almost exclusively by men at the time and make her way in it with some success. In much the same way that Armstrong shows how the conduct books of more than a century before had paved the way for women's successful negotiation of a marriage contract that implied their status as individual subjects, these mid-nineteenth-century popular novels can be read as paving the way for women's tentative movement into professions outside the home. In her analysis, Baym does hint at something like that, in suggesting that these novels also helped to rewrite, or rather expand, the domestic agenda:

Their fiction is mostly about social relations, generally set in homes and other social spaces that are fully described. . . . Domesticity is set forth as a value scheme for ordering all of life, in competition with the ethos of money and exploitation that is perceived to prevail in American society. The domestic ideal meant not that woman was to be sequestered from the world in her place at home but that everybody was to be placed in the home, and hence home and the world would become one. (26–27)

Baym also notes that in the years following the Civil War the symbolic action promised to women in these plots lost much of its attraction, as professions such as nursing, social work, teaching, and librarianship—those spheres of professional activity that seemed most closely aligned with the virtues of domesticity—became respectable for women to occupy. Volunteer work during the war, and the economic boom of the postwar years in the North brought the growth of women's voluntary associations across the country (Scott 1984, 1986); the massive influx of southern, central, and eastern European immigrants to the United States in the last quarter of the century brought with it a call for the same sort of charity work, first on a volunteer basis, then, with the formation of national organizations, the rise of the new "women's" professions of social work and librarianship. The most popular women's novel of the 1850s in the United States, *The Wide, Wide, World*, had been marketed to British readers as a children's book (Altick 1957; Bratton 1981; Darton 1932) as early as 1851; in 1868, the publication of Louisa May Alcott's *Little Women*, according to Baym, marked the transition of this form of women's fiction into girls' fiction in the United States: "The story of feminine heroism now becomes a didactic instrument for little girls; as an adult genre, woman's fiction becomes the gothic romance" (Baym 1978, 296).

In the same stroke, girls' fiction, helped along by a well-publicized feud between Alcott and the leading writer of "boys' fiction," Mark Twain (Alcott remarked, "If Mr. Clemens cannot think of something better to tell our pureminded lads and lasses, he had best stop writing for them," to which Twain replied, "That will sell 25,000 copies for us sure" of *Huckleberry Finn* [Hart 1950, 150]), placed itself as a genre in opposition to boys' adventure and Alger-like novels. On this occasion, however, the genre of the girls' novel, at least within the world of school and children's public libraries, was neither subordinate nor transitory.

The actual, as opposed to the symbolic, domestication of the world had become the Victorian club woman's goal; she sought, according to Ann Douglas (1977), to achieve "Pink and White Tyranny" (i.e., control of society's mores through the assertion of the "natural rights" granted women as feminine subjects to exert a domesticating agenda). As Douglas explains, these women "made do" with the tools they had at hand:

Northeastern clergymen and middle-class literary women lacked power of any crudely tangible kind. . . . Instead they wished to exert "influence," which they eulogized as a religious force . . . [and which they exerted] chiefly through literature which was just in the process of becoming a mass medium. The press offered them the chance they were seeking to be unobtrusive and everywhere at the same time. (9)

In summary, it was in the tradition of Victorian women's fiction that women's association volunteers, charity workers, and the young women entering Melvil Dewey's and other schools of library science around the country in the waning years of the nineteenth century were raised. In time, not only women's fiction of the late nineteenth century but a large portion of both "classic" and popular children's novels, from *The Tale of Peter Rabbit* (Potter 1902/1987) to *The Wizard of Oz* (Baum 1900/1956) to the Little House series (e.g., Wilder 1935/1971) to the recent An American Girl Collection (e.g., Adler 1986), as well as a large proportion of the children's novels selected yearly by the school librarians of the American Library Association for the Newbery Award, which is given to the "best book" (on all but two occasions a novel) in children's literature published in a year—*Dicey's Song* (Voight 1983); *Island of the Blue Dolphins* (O'Dell 1960); *Witch of Blackbird Pond* (Speare 1958); *Dear Mr. Henshaw* (Cleary 1983); *Julie of the Wolves* (George 1972); *Call It Courage* (Sperry 1940); *Missing May* (Rylant 1992); *Number the Stars* (Lowry 1989); *The Slave Dancer* (Fox 1973), to name a few—tell in realistic detail of an individual who finds her/himself alone and isolated from home, struggles in an open, naturalistic world to achieve a new identity, and then is reunited, at the peak of self-recognition, with the warmth of home and the security of one or both parents. This is the same motif of women's fiction (usually sans marriage) in the United States in the years 1820–1870, and it remains today a dominant, if not the dominant, motif of the stock that school librarians recommend to their clientele as "good reading" for them.

SUMMING UP: SOME CONSEQUENCES

It also seems reasonable to acknowledge, then, not only that the "classics" of children's literature have their origins in the late Victorian and Edwardian periods but also that much of the rest of the fiction stocked by children's libraries is also directly descended from the tradition of women's fiction in the Victorian era. That fiction, in turn, derived from novel ways of reading and writing pioneered by women in the late eighteenth century, as practices opposed to the "scholarly" ways of reading dominant among formally educated, middle- and upper-class men. That opposition manifested itself in the late eighteenth and early nineteenth centuries in the separated coexistence of circulating and subscription libraries, and it manifests itself today in the fiction and nonfiction dichotomy of public and school libraries, in the designation of scholarly works in public and school libraries in terms of what they are not—as "non"-fiction—from the late Victorian era to the present, and even in the current trend in children's publishing to domesticate more and more informational material by placing it in a fictional, novelistic frame (Cullinan and Galda 1994; Huck, Hepler, and Hickman 1993; Lukens 1982).

This may also help to explain, at the close of the twentieth century, the "particular fondness for the artifacts, the literature, the *mores* of our Victorian past" that many people still feel, as Ann Douglas (1977, 3) explains in *The Feminization of American Culture*. In her research, Douglas expected to find her fathers and her mothers; but "instead I discovered my fathers and my sisters. . . . The problems of the women correspond to mine with a frightening accuracy that seems to set us outside the processes of history; the answers of even the finest of them were often mine, and sometimes largely unacceptable to me" (11). In Douglas's view, the feminization of American society was achieved in tandem by the replacement of the male-dominated and intellectually austere Calvinist theology of the Great Awakening with a more populist, sentimental type of Protestantism, marked by "its obsession with popularity and its increasing disregard of intellectual issues" (7). She argues that

literary men of the cloth and middle-class women writers of the Victorian period knew from firsthand evidence that literature was functioning more and more as a form of leisure, a complicated mass dream-life in the busiest, most wide-awake society in the world. . . . When the minister and the lady put pen to paper, they had ever in their minds their reading counterparts; the small scale, the intimate scenes, the chatty tone of many of their works complement the presumably comfortable posture and domestic backdrop of their readers. They wrote not just to win adherents to their views, but to make converts to literature, to sustain and encourage the habit of reading itself. (10)

What's wrong with that? Two things, principally. The first is that the advocacy of an escape into reading (fiction) is, as Douglas argues, "part of the self-evasion of a society both committed to laissez-faire industrial expansion and disturbed by its consequences" (12), that does not provide for any real solutions. In the feminization of librarianship, however much influence the genteel patriarchs of public and school libraries lost over the apparent form and contents of what public libraries eventually became, the hegemonic influence of middle- and upper-class gentility over the ideological content of the library's texts actually increased under the maternalism of the middle- and upper-class women who now assumed professional authority for overseeing the reading of children and of the lower classes. Whereas the acquisition of "cultural" literacy in the library had previously been signified by the cultivation of a taste for the bedrock certainty of scholarship, the acquisition of "cultural" literacy in the new order of the school and public library was signified by the acquisition of "good taste" and critical discernment in the consumption of fiction—something that the new librarians, by virtue of their social class backgrounds, professional training, and own literate standards, were in a good position, they felt, to arbitrate.

The second thing wrong is that even though Douglas is concerning herself here only with the issue of gender roles, both the historical and ethnographic evidence presented in this chapter document ways that the gendered division of labor in modern industrialized societies also helps to reinforce divisions along lines of social class and ethnicity; for not only did the feminization—or rather, the *femininization*—of white, Anglo-Saxon, middle-class society in the United States eventually provide the women of that dominant culture with public spheres of action that were separate from those of men, it provided them with the means and the logic they needed to impose that culture's texts and its practices on linguistic and ethnic minorities and other members of the working class and to make those texts and practices appear to be not merely dominant or standard but virtually universal. If issues of racial and ethnic difference have been conspicuously absent in this chapter, it is not because historically oppressed groups besides women were illiterate or because there were no texts available for them to read but because the interests of these groups have always received very marginal attention at best in school and public libraries, or sometimes none at all.

This condition of conspicuous absence or marginality persists in school and public libraries today. Most libraries may include foreign language texts, but they are few in number and are never interspersed with the English-language texts but are housed in separate bookcases that are usually not in a central area. In a city like Las Cruces, New Mexico, for example, which is 40 miles from the border with Mexico, and where one is as likely to hear Spanish spoken in shops and neighborhoods as English, a tiny portion—less than 5 percent—of the texts in the children's section of the public library are in Spanish. Although Crest Hills Elementary had significant numbers of Asian students who spoke English as a second language, there were no books in Korean or Chinese for children to read; the only foreign language books were the 30 or 40 in Spanish "left over" from the days of busing that were kept on an out-of-the-way shelf. At Chavez Elementary, whose student population was more than 90 percent Chicana/o and perhaps 50 percent bilingual (tellingly, the only statistics available describe students in terms of the amount of *English* they speak), all the Spanish-language texts of the library were kept in one (unmarked) bookcase in a corner, and none of these texts were included in the librarian's fiction-reading programs. At Roosevelt Elementary, whose "theme" was "The World We Live In," none of the knick-knacks or other decorations that stood on top of shelves or hung on walls reflected the African or Mexican background of the majority of its students; and none of its signs were in Spanish, although its Spanish-language section was larger and far more prominently marked and well maintained than at the other two. In all three school libraries only token numbers of books in English dealt with places, persons, or cultural themes relevant to the interests of linguistic and ethnic minorities. In the end, as Douglas concludes, "The cruelest aspect of the process of oppression is the logic by which it forces its objects to be oppressive in turn, to do the dirty work of their society in several senses" (1977, 11).

This may be a good place, finally, to acknowledge as ethnographer and critic my own personal involvement and interest in the topic of school libraries. I entered this study with warm personal memories of my own childhood experience with the local public library in the small town in northern Kentucky where I grew up, memories that no doubt contributed in unnoticed ways to the processes I used in selecting school libraries as sites, in framing specific questions, in what and how I gathered my data, and finally, in writing this book. That library was run almost single-handedly by an elderly librarian who was the granddaughter of the town's founder, a woman who was revered for her connection to the town's past and for her dedication to the literacy of our community. The entire town, in fact, took enormous pride in the fact that of all the many small communities in our area, only we had a library; and it was common knowledge that without Mrs. Taylor and the assistance of the Women's Club, the literacy and quality of life in our town would have suffered.

My personal interactions with Mrs. Taylor were minimal, however; she sat at her desk and quietly stamped our books and issued cards with little ceremony. I remember mostly the books I read from that library: As a child, the *Dr. Doolittle* series (e.g., Lofting 1922), a series of three books about an English woman and her husband who cared for lion cubs orphaned by native hunters in Kenya, (e.g., *Born Free*, Adamson 1960), and *The Swiss Family Robinson* (Wyss 1954). As an early adolescent, my first "adult" novel was about a teenager who is left to "find himself" on a ranch in New Mexico when his father leaves the family to fight in World War II, *Red Sky at Morning* (Bradford 1968/1986); later on in high school I became "hooked" on the social realism of John Steinbeck and *The Grapes of Wrath* (1936). In my childhood and adolescence and later as I began this study of three libraries, I never thought to consider how these books and the cultural information contained in them may have helped shape my life, much less this project. But now, thinking back on my experiences as a reader and an early library patron, I have to ask whether, in addition to contributing to my literate development and later interest in library culture, they did not also serve as the primers for the colonialist frame of mind I admit I took as a young adult to Morocco as a U.S. Peace Corps volunteer (and which Moroccans, who at the time had almost 70 years' experience of such encounters with Western adventurers, promptly and graciously disabused me of) or for the persona of self-reflexive individualist that I carry today as an academic calling card (Dressman 1996).

ACCOUNTING FOR VARIANCE
IN THREE SCHOOL LIBRARIES

Even though I have characterized them in this chapter as deeply hegemonic institutions, school libraries, unlike classrooms, must also be organized according to the imperatives of consumption more than production, and so they remain potentially more open to the demands of consumers than producers. This is because unlike classroom teachers, who have state-mandated "skills" to teach and "objectives" for which they are held accountable, the historical mandate of librarianship—to instruct *through* delight—must exercise itself through appeals to the desire, as opposed to the disciplining, of student readers—through "tasteful" discourses and presentation of the library as an attractive cultural icon, or diagram, of middle-class literacy. In the relationship between social reproduction and resistance in schools and the participation of text-based knowledge as a material medium of that process, then, the school library is a site that opens itself through its practices to conditions in which students might find the means to transform themselves by reconstructing the order of the library on their own terms.

To be sure, this is not always the case. There was wide variance among the three school libraries I studied, and it stemmed not from differences in the textual organization of the library or from librarians' focus on fiction but, ironically, from variations in how each librarian viewed the needs of her "customers" or student clientele and in the consequent ways that clientele responded to each program. It is, in fact, the conditions of institutional variation among these three libraries that forms the bulk of the following chapters. As a way of framing the discussion to follow, I will outline below (1) the conditions that appear to account for the variation in the practices of the librarians at Chavez, Crest Hills, and Roosevelt Elementaries; (2) a brief discussion of how the literature on student resistance and social reproduction might help to explain variation in student response; and (3) a very brief prospectus of how librarian practice and student response play themselves out in each of the three libraries.

The Motive Power of Class Consciousness

As I stated at the beginning of this chapter, one invariant channel of school library programs is the distinction between fiction and nonfiction that forms the first principle of their textual organization, while a second invariant channel is the use of the novel, or more broadly, "expressive realism" (Belsey 1980), as the principal technology of school libraries' social and moral mission. If we keep in mind the argument of the preceding sections of this chapter, that it was only by proposing the domesticating influence of a femininity constructed in the interests of the middle class as the solution to society's ills that women were first able to make professional spaces for themselves outside the home, then it becomes clear why the sociocultural class consciousness of school librarians is the motivational and guiding force behind the third, more variable channel of school library programs, that is, their everyday discursive practices—as well as it is the force behind the ways that these discourses differ among libraries in their local articulations.

The primacy of sociocultural class consciousness in determining librarians' discursive practices is further supported by other historical evidence also presented in this chapter, which indicates that from their inception school and public libraries were assumed to be institutions where the poor and the culturally disenfranchised might have their tastes aligned, free of charge, with the "best books" available. Although librarians might have quibbled at times over exact criteria in the name of scholarship, there has never been any doubt that "best" in practically all instances means those books that cater to the taste preferences of the sociocultural elite. When exceptions have been made to these criteria, as with the introduction of popular fiction to collections during the feminization of librarianship as a profession, even then only "the best" popular fiction was allowed, and only with the implicit hope that once readers became regular patrons of the library, they might develop a taste for a "higher class" of literature. As will be seen in the case of the library at Chavez Elementary, today when school librarians allow "series" novels (e.g., "The Hardy Boys"; "Sweet Valley Kids") or other popular magazines into their collections, they do so apologetically and only with the understanding that once hooked, "poorer" (in all that word's meanings) readers can be guided to higher classes of text or, in the case of the library at Crest Hills, to higher forms of aesthetic experience.

Just how not only librarians but nearly all members of the middle class in modern, industrialized cultures understand their positions and the positions of others in relation to the "best" is delineated in *Distinction*, Pierre Bourdieu's (1984) study of the relationship between people's expressed taste for commodities (in the present case of school librarians, children's literature) and their social class, in which individuals, by virtue of their disposition toward legitimate cultural objects, place themselves in a three-dimensional, hierarchical social space (or "field") where they can be identified, and identify themselves, by their "taste preferences." One's tastes, in Bourdieu's analysis, are informed by a materialist aesthetics in which the possession of various types of capital—social, educational, cultural, and economic—as well as one's (indirect) relation to the mode of production constructs not only one's taste preferences but one's "habitus," the "structuring structure, which organizes the perception of practices" (170). The more capitalized one is, the more one can afford to indulge in the consumption of objects "for their own sake" and to focus on an abstract, essentialist, and formalized appraisal (or "reading") of an object's "worth." The less capitalized one is, the more one is inclined to look for and value the functionality of objects and to focus on a concrete, particular, and contextualized appraisal—or reading—of an object's worth. Individuals and groups whose level of capitalization is between these two poles, according to Bourdieu, believe that either upward or downward social mobility is an imminent possibility, contingent on the increase or maintenance of their own level of capital, usually through education. They have internalized the capitalist logic of the social field they are a part of and so believe in the ultimate fairness of the capitalist system and in its implicit (and sometimes explicit) promises to them that if they "just get some" educational capital, they will be entitled to the status and rewards of others in the social space who hold the same degree of education.

With regard to school libraries, local differences among school librarians' practices can then be theorized as the material articulations of their reading through the lens of their own life experiences—which they make sense of through their professional ethos and middle-class habitus—of their student patrons' present and future needs in relation to the library and its textual capital. In practice, we might suspect that school librarians, as very well intentioned agents of educational capitalization in schools with students from lower sociocultural backgrounds, would make judgments about the distance between their own middle-class reading tastes and habits of consumption and their students' reading tastes and habits of consumption, and act in various ways in their practices either to close the gap between the two or, in the case of middle-class populations, to begin to reinforce and further develop patterns of consumption and use of texts. It would then be in the interplay between students' own taste preferences and ways of reading and the tasteful discourses of librarians in three schools serving different socioeconomic classes that one could expect to observe the processes whereby school librarians worked to forge students' subjectivities as readers and users of text.

The ways that each librarian articulated this third channel in her program discursively—that is, controlled students' access to the library's organizational system and its texts, interacted with students, and selectively presented narratives—varied dramatically by location. These locational differences can be accounted for through analysis of structuring conditions external to the history and practices of school librarianship that have been *internalized* by each librarian as part and parcel of her professional logic and inheritance—conditions that, although they stand apart from the history of school and public libraries, are the product of the same historical and economic exigencies that shaped those institutions and therefore are not alien to them but largely complementary.

As will become apparent in later chapters, one of these conditions was the individual life experience of each librarian and, in particular, her history as a student, as a child library patron, and as a reader subject as she told it (although not necessarily as she consciously understood it), as well as the lessons that each took from this story about what her student clientele needed from her. These, in turn, in combination with a second external condition described below, guided her decision-making practices. In the case of these three libraries, the influence of each librarian's personal history, as well as the force of the decisions it conditioned, was further enhanced by the considerable autonomy allowed to each librarian within her school in decisions about library circulation, book purchases, and the arrangement and use of the library facilities. Each librarian was considered by teachers and principals to be an integral part of her school's educational program, and each had enjoyed a comparatively long tenure in her position. As a consequence, the actions of these librarians were not likely to be random or accidental; instead they can be characterized as the carefully considered products of the interaction among their practical understanding of the school and its students, the lessons of their own lived experiences as middle class women, and their formal, academically acquired understanding of library practice.

A second structuring condition that guided each library program was the geopolitical discourse of social class within the school district, which itself was a product of a larger geopolitical, historical discourse within the city (and the nation). Racially, socioeconomically, and politically, the city and school district are divided by residents into three zones that are separated physically by a river and a major expressway and segregated politically by discourses of race and social class. Within the city and school district, neighborhoods that historically were overtly, publicly segregated by race and ethnicity are now more often distinguished in residents' conversations by Calvinistic references to property values and family income, which then correspond to neighborhoods that—for the predominantly white middle class, at least, and certainly by the city's print and electronic media—are *covertly* segregated by race and ethnicity. A consequence of these demographics in a district in which virtually every elementary school is a neighborhood school is that schools like Chavez are characterized throughout the district by personnel as *poor* schools (a stigma helped along by a well-publicized "priority" designation), ethnically mixed schools like Roosevelt are generally considered *working-class* schools, and those in tonier parts of town like Crest Hills are thought of as *upper-middle-class*; in fact, each school in this study was located in a different zone of the city and stood in metonymic relation to its zone's ethnic and socioeconomic composition. Interscholastic class self-consciousness was further ingrained and statistically sanctified within the city by the local newspaper, which during the study published the school-by-school results of the state achievement test at the third and fifth grade under the headline "Achievement Gap Is Income Based, Data Show." Secondary correlations among race, income, and achievement were noted in the text itself: "At almost every level, in the majority of the district's schools, there were signs of a wide achievement gap among white, Hispanic, and black students—a gap that was attributed by almost everyone to economics rather than ability." Finally, the recent and painful memory of court-ordered busing to end de facto segregation remained strong in the minds of the librarians and teachers at Chavez and Crest Hills (Roosevelt had not opened yet). Stories were told by the librarian at Chavez of parents from Crest Hills "taking over" Chavez and making indigenous parents there feel out of place "in their own neighborhood school"; students bused to Crest Hills from Chavez's neighborhood were remembered by her as "having a terrible time" and "just not understanding" what was required of them by the teachers at Crest Hills. In these tellings, the problem was always related to social class differences in families' ways of thinking about education.

The politics of social class and covertly of race within the school district was also fueled by intradistrict talk among school personnel. Teachers' and librarians' assessments of the student body at their schools were highly seasoned with both explicit and implicit references to social class: about the wealth or poverty of students' families relative to their own in the past and in the present and to other schools where they have worked. "Now, when I was at___; but here at___" was a common construction when talking to veteran teachers and librarians at all three schools. This discourse of social class, through which school personnel are constantly aligning and realigning their perceptions and expectations of students at their current school, nicely complements the social reproductive function of educational systems in general, which, according to Bourdieu and Passeron (1977), is to provide students with a sense of themselves in relation to the dominant culture of the middle class and its property—its capital—that is commensurate with the social class habitus they have inherited.

With respect to the dynamics of those processes as described by Bourdieu, because all the independent variables that combine to position subjects in social space, such as occupation, degree of educational advancement, family background, and income/economic assets (and presumably gender and ethnicity, although Bourdieu barely mentions these), are not viewed as discrete entities capable of retaining their significance when isolated (as they do in positivistic conceptions of social space), the processes whereby social positions remain fairly stable over generations are not mechanical. But they certainly are, in Bourdieu's view, deterministic and ironically inevitable (Collins 1993; Jenkins 1992). Following Bourdieu's precepts, then, one would have to conclude prior to interpretation of any evidence that the effects of the habitus were total and that any variation across librarians or among students' responses within each library would be just that—variations on central themes, or social processes, whose apparent diversity was only apparent. Or as Bourdieu himself puts it, "In fact, the singular *habitus* of members of the same class are united in a relationship of homology, that is, of diversity within homogeneity reflecting the diversity within homogeneity characteristic of their social conditions of production" (1990, 60). Ethnographic analysis and interpretation, following the precepts of Bourdieu, would therefore be likely to detail the ways in which librarian-student interactions worked to construct reader subjectivities that would ultimately prove congruent with students' social class positions.

The Conditions of Student Readership: Resistance, Congruence, Liminality

The work of Pierre Bourdieu (and of Bourdieu and Passeron [1977]) makes it clear why acquiring a taste for novels, whose expressive realism iconically diagrams the middle-class habitus, or way of life, would be seen historically and currently by librarians as the sine qua non of students' eventual entry into, or continuance within, middle-class society. By school librarian logic and by the logic of Bourdieu, unless students can be brought wholly and completely into congruence with the gendered, deep cultural structure of the children's novel or picture book, their subsequent chances of acquiring the linguistic and paralinguistic surface competencies and social graces of the white, standard English-speaking middle class, and so the rights and social privileges of that class, will be severely limited.

This also helps to explain why "reluctance"—a euphemism that in a profession whose feminine politics must remain hidden to remain acceptable cleanses both librarian practice and students' acts of resistance of their political connotations—is so often paired with the term "at risk" in the monthly issues of the *School Library Journal* and why it is such a dominant preoccupation of that journal's columnists. Reluctant readers are seen by *SLJ* to constitute an implicit social threat, not only to themselves but to the cultural, economic, and political health of the social order. In the scenario that *SLJ*'s columnists construct, students who will not come to "love reading [novels]" on their own or who cannot be hooked by librarians or their teachers are destined to live on the economic and cultural margins of society, where they may fall prey to who-knows-what influences and get into who-knows-what kinds of trouble. Similarly, as Jay MacLeod (1987) notes, there is no room in Pierre Bourdieu's writings for people who act from positions in social space that oppose or stand apart from the interests of the professional and upper classes either to advance themselves or to challenge the hierarchical logic of the social order in ways that would accord their practices more than token dignity or marginal status. In Bourdieu's scenario, seeing through the logic of one's habitus and acting apart from it constitute the ultimate act of self-delusion; whether they know it or not, the petite bourgeoisie and the poor are losers whose inevitable lot is to reproduce their position in the economic and sociocultural order, so long as their semantic and syntactic grasp of cultural capital—as signified by the semiotics of their own taste preferences—remains incongruent with that of the middle class.

But beyond mere reluctance, resistance—which presents itself in acts of open opposition as well as in subtler acts of semiotic "fooling around" with the textual currency of the social order—does exist in schools and libraries in varieties and to degrees that cannot be easily dismissed or ignored. It also produces effects that cannot be written off as merely reproducing the social class order. As Bourdieu and Passeron (1977) would predict, in the present study of three school libraries, students who identified with the habitus of the middle class did tend to conform to the discourses of the library (and the school) in anticipation of future economic and social reward; but students whose home and school cultures were less congruent seemed at times to resist schooling and the library through "moves," as Lyotard (1984) calls them, that cannot be *exclusively* characterized as "reproductive." On the contrary, there is significant evidence that many of the third graders and other students whom I interviewed in focus groups on three occasions and observed and spoke with in their classrooms and the library almost daily over four months were remarkably aware of the ways that librarians tried to construct their subjectivities as readers and were sometimes aware of the political implications of their responses as well. More specifically, some of these students did not always read the library or its texts in ways that matched the intentions of the librarian or the ideological intentions of its texts. Rather than conform to or resist the textuality of the library in outright acts of rejection, students in some instances reconstructed the meaning of the library as conveyed to them by the librarian, as well as the meanings of the texts she promoted to them, in ways that served purposes of their own making and that can also be characterized as socially *reconstructive* at micropolitical levels.

Regardless of whether students read the library in ways that bring them into conformity with, resistance against, or reconstruction of its white, gendered, middle-class ethos, however, the novel—or more specifically the interpellative project (Althusser 1971; Belsey 1980) of expressive realism—remains a central technology, not only of librarians' attempts to hook students as readers but also of students' various responses to their school library's programs. Any discussion of how students might respond to the library, therefore, must include some consideration of the novel's continuing potential, now as in the eighteenth and nineteenth centuries, to act as a technology not merely of socialization but of social reconstruction. We need, in other words, to take a closer look at novel ways of reading, and to consider the novel, psychological relationship between reader and text that it produces. Here is how Lennard Davis (1987) describes the phenomenon of novel reading:

Solitary people, often in the midst of hordes of strangers, sitting passive, silent, hunched almost fetally over a small . . . pack of papers. Most often their lips are still, their faces expressionless, their eyes fixed on some invisible moving point. In order to remain in this state, they must block outside stimuli, become virtually autistic— what is it they are doing? They are visualizing, analyzing, experiencing a fantasy not their own but which, in this autistic state, they believe in some provisional way to be true—true enough to draw conclusions, form moral opinions, and even shape their own lives to fit. (2)

Clearly, he tells us in the next paragraph, that he is being facetious. Were people so impressionable, and were the effects of any medium so well defined and one directional, human beings would be little more than programmable automatons. On the other hand, as Davis also points out, for the time that we are engaged, we have successfully shut out, or "resisted" the reality of our daily lives and temporarily replaced it with another, whose nearly whole effect turns on its capacity, through a detailed accounting of its objects, to make us believe it is real. It is a world, as has already been pointed out, in which the hero has a real fighting chance to control his or her fate, in which people are "dealt with" as though they were commodities, and where love and honor and right thinking eventually triumph.

Davis's argument is that while the novel is an important way for many people to resist life worlds that are often oppressing them by escaping into alternate realities that allow them to imagine how things could be different (and, hopefully, empowering them to move toward change), novels, as contributors to the very world that is oppressing readers, do their work by drawing the reader into a world where "the distinction between illusion and reality, between fact and fiction, between symbol and what is represented" (3) blinds the reader to the fact that this world, in fact, is one that is structurally made to order for life in a world constituted by the logic of industrial capitalism. While reading novels can be an act of resistance in itself, to read them without some reflexive awareness of their hidden cultural agenda is not to use novels against themselves or society: "I read novels and enjoy them. But does that mean I cannot recognize that the very process I love and depend on is in effect part of the social mechanism that keeps me in my place?" (19).

One-way analyses like the one facetiously proposed by Davis assume that there is a clean and uncrossable division between those who produce and those who consume. But there is considerable evidence both from the fields of cognitive science (Graesser, Golding, and Long 1991; Mandler and deForest 1979; Wittrock 1984) and from reader response criticism and research (Harste, Woodward, and Burke 1984; Iser 1980; Purves and Beach 1972) that reading is a productive, constructive act and that our habits of consumption are not passive: They are really our habits of active use. This perspective is in sympathy with the work of John Fiske (1989a, 1989b). Building on Roland Barthes's (1974) typology of texts into those that are "writerly," that is, that call attention to their form and make demands on the reader to produce their meaning, and those texts that are "readerly," that is, that are "classic" (Barthes 1974, 4) in that their intended meaning is "self-evident," Fiske (1989b) proposes a third type of text for those materials that are mass-produced to be consumed rather than used. The "producerly" text has the accessibility of a readerly one, and can theoretically be read in that easy way by those of its readers who are comfortably accommodated within the dominant ideology . . . but it also has the openness of the writerly. The difference is that it does not *require* this writerly activity, nor does it set the rules to control it. Rather, it offers itself up to popular production; it exposes, however reluctantly, the vulnerabilities, limitations, and weaknesses of its preferred meanings; it contains, while attempting to repress them, voices that contradict the ones it prefers; it has loose ends that escape its control, its meanings exceed its own power to discipline them, its gaps are wide enough for new texts to be produced in them—it is, in a very real sense, beyond its own control. (104)

In the diehard reading of Saussurean semiology upon which Fiske's theory rests (see Barthes 1973), the relationship between the signifier and the signified—that is, in the case of the novel between its images and its meaning—is "arbitrary and unmotivated," and so anything goes: readers are free to build from any imagistic materials what they will. Or as Fiske (1989a) puts it:

The active semiotic use of commodities blurs the distinction between use-value and exchange-value, and that between materially based and socially produced values, for all values are arbitrary. The values of commodities can be transformed by the practices of their users, as can those of language, for as language can have no fixed reference point in a universal reality, neither can commodities have final values fixed in their materiality. The practices of the users of a system not only can exploit its potential, but can modify the system itself. (31)

So intent is Fiske in his efforts to uphold the agency of the consumer that he neglects at times to consider the space between semiotic theory and semiotic reality, namely, that producerly, popular texts, however ingenious readers may be, are in the end only so versatile, and readers only so inventive. Nor does he consider it worthwhile to ask what proportion of the population may be reading popular texts in a producerly fashion and what proportion choose to read them in more conventional, prescribed ways. Finally, he hedges on cognitive issues. To what extent are the producerly cognizant of their activities? Or if such readings are unconscious, what cognitive processes account for the sort of subversive playfulness that he describes in his own bricolage of readings of some of the more provocative (Madonna) and pedestrian (the beach; blue jeans) texts of mass culture? These issues, in the end, are of little import to him; as he sees it, every producerly reading is an effective act of semiotic guerrilla warfare, "a constant erosive force upon the macro, weakening the system from within so that it is more amenable to change at the structural level" (1989a, 11). To appreciate Fiske fully, one must read him as a counterbalance to the Frankfurt School's more pessimistic portrayal of mass culture as the blind instrument of totalitarianism (see Horkheimer and Adorno 1944/1993), as an account of the failure of Marxist revolution, of the cultural forces that produced fascism and Stalinism, and of the stifling effects of modern industrialism in general.

So—which is it, then? Is the resistance that can be engendered by novel reading always a compromised one that pulls readers ever closer to the loins of patriarchal, white middle-class hegemony, as Davis argues, or, as Fiske insists, does it provide readers with the potential means to deliver a swift kick in the same direction—to fight back, as it were? One attempt to answer this question is Linda

Christian-Smith's (1991) study of early adolescent women who read *adolescent romance fiction* (e.g., the "Sweet Valley High" series) as part of their middle school's program for "reluctant readers." Christian-Smith found that the 29 young women she interviewed used romance novels to empower themselves by wresting some control over what and how they read away from reading teachers, by temporarily evading the drudgery of the standard school curriculum, and by reading romances in a critical way that provoked some reevaluation on their part of the way boys they knew treated them. But Christian-Smith also found that the narrative motifs of these novels were steeped in conservative values: in them an affluent, physically attractive heroine, whose ability to consume far exceeded the readers' own family resources, always falls safely into the protective arms of an equally attractive and prosperous young man. She concludes:

Through romance reading, readers transform gender relations so that men cherish and nurture women rather the other way around. This, together with readers' collective rejection of a macho masculinity, represents their partial overturning of one aspect of current traditional gender sentiments. However, readers' final acceptance of romantic love and its power structure undercuts the political potential of these insights. Romance reading in no way altered the young women's present and future circumstances, but rather was deeply implicated in reconciling them to their place in the world. (207)

In the face of such ringing ambivalence, then, perhaps the truest course at this moment is also the most pragmatic: that is, to consider the battle for the hearts and minds and labor of subordinates through their literacy a truly dialectical contest in which in the micropolitics of the moment both sides give and take something in the way of concessions from, and loyalty to, the macropolitical system.

Against the static "macro" theories of economic and sociocultural determinism of Bourdieu (1984, 1990) and Bourdieu and Passeron (1977; see also Bowles and Gintis 1976; Ogbu 1987), a number of microethnographers (e.g., Everhart 1983; Foley 1990; McLaren 1993; Willis 1981) in the past 20 years have attempted to rewrite the educational scenario of the modern industrial state in much the same way that the practice of novel reading has been described above. For example, Paul Willis (1981) details how working-class British "lads" developed an expressive culture in opposition to, and in repudiation of, the culture of the classroom—"having a laff," they called it—that mimicked the joking of shop-floor culture by disrupting classroom instruction and harassing those students—labeled "ear'oles"—who listened to, or accepted, the authority of the teacher. The lads, in Willis's analysis, created a positive working-class identity by penetrating the controlling logic of the system, but only partially; for in creating that identity, he also notes that they also effectively imposed a ceiling on their own socioeconomic futures.

Another study, *Learning Capitalist Culture* (Foley 1990), was set in a comprehensive high school in a small town in south Texas that was undergoing an upheaval in its social stratification, owing to the Mexican-American civil rights movement of the 1970s. Foley takes care to detail the "expressive practices" of the working-class Chicano and Anglo youths that, in ways similar to the youths studied by Willis, both valorized and reproduced working-class culture. But of greater interest to him are the ways that some up-and-coming students whose families had historically comprised the underclass of the town learned to perform "alienated communicative labor" in linguistic "making-out games" with teachers and each other in order to steal time in the classroom and in their dealings with each other and with authorities. In Foley's "Goffmanesque" (Goffman 1959) analysis of these making out games as performances staged in their own interest, socially ascendant Anglo and Mexicano students manage the impressions of self that are presented to others; that is, they manage a portfolio of expressive practices as they might manage any other commodity or piece of property. In this way, they become naturalized, as all middle managers in a corporate society must, to managing deceit and trading an alienated self image for the prospect of personal gain. Yet Foley (1990) found that these students also managed to retain a positive sense of their ethnic identity. By means of a fluctuation in a historically very rigid social class system, some students who came from the economic and ethnic underclass found the linguistic means to interrupt the inevitability of social reproduction and stratification.

While each of these ethnographers clearly differs in his appraisal of the long and short term efficacy of the forms of resistance observed, both characterize students as appreciating what James Collins (1993) claims Bourdieu and advocates of congruence seem to have missed: "the role of contradiction in social processes and discursive action" (117). In other words, there was some metaphorical distance between "the way the system works" in principle and the way it was enacted by authority—which provided contradictory gaps in the logic of practices that the students caught in them recognized at least tacitly, and which they were reflexively able to use to work the system even as it was working them. As Collins further explains, "This gap, lag, or lack of fit between social structure and social representation is an enabling condition, a site for struggles over that representation. By changing the representation, such struggles can change the social space, for 'representations of the real are part of the real'" (124).

It was by taking advantage of such contradictions in their everyday interactions with school authorities—that is, by driving wedges into cracks in the logic of the school and classroom through daily engagement with its practices, that students in the studies above were able to appropriate their signs as material for their own micropolitical projects of representation and so effect some change in their local social space. Such spaces, in the work of ritual theorist Victor Turner (1969), are termed "liminal" or "threshold" spaces, because in any ritual, or everyday practice of enculturation, those who occupy these physical, temporal, or symbolic spaces are neither "in the system" nor completely out of touch with its authority. As Peter McLaren notes in *Schooling as a Ritual Performance* (1993), under the right conditions—when the authority or authorities in charge possess sufficient understanding of the entire ritual process to reflexively tolerate participants' counterhegemonic acts of resistance to the social order and when resisting participants remain fundamentally in touch with the ritual's sacral nature—then a condition of liminality can exist in which, through the micropolitics of the ritual process, participants are transformed to fill new social roles, while the rituals themselves, as enactments of the social order, are reconstructed and renewed to meet changing circumstances. However, as McLaren also warns, where such conditions do not exist—as when authority moves to squelch any and all opposition to its actions or when participants have either lost or overextended their sense of the sacred—then the power of ritual to transform individuals and recon-

struct the social order falters and may lose its meaning or, worse, become an occasion for social and cultural dysfunction.

In school libraries, then, liminal conditions of student transformation and social reconstruction can be theorized as occurring when in ritual moments of librarian practice—during story times, during "skills lessons," during motivational
reading programs, during the narratives librarians use to explain the library as an
organizational system, and finally, during impromptu interactions between librarians and students—spaces are created by students and tolerated, or even incor-
porated, by librarians into their practices, in which the sense that is made of
texts is as much a product of the life world of the students as it is of the life
world constituted by the library. When this happens, the school library becomes
for students outside its culture what Mary Louise Pratt (1992) describes as a
"contact zone": a border area of transculturation and cultural renewal for both
sides of the exchange. To the extent that both sides, librarian and student, agree
to "play," both sides are changed and enriched; but to the extent that either or
both sides decide that they mean business, that they will have their way or none
at all, then the library becomes a zone of self-serving conformity or resistance—
a zone of social and cultural reproduction.

PROSPECTS

The chapters that follow are meant to provide substance and extension to this
complicated discussion. Chapters 2, 3, and 4 are case studies of each of the libraries and their programs, with the main emphasis, respectively, in the analysis
of Chavez and Crest Hills on students' practices and a more detailed analysis of
both educator and student practices in the fourth chapter on Roosevelt. In
Chapter 2 the trope of resistance is used to characterize students' reflexive responses to the librarian's attempts to get them hooked on reading fiction at
working-poor Chavez Elementary, but only partially; students there did resist in
ways that ironically socialized them to the labor of a piecework economy, but
many also resisted in ways that allowed them to read and use library texts in
ways that were of practical interest to them. In Chapter 3, third-grade students at
professional-managerial Crest Hills Elementary managed their "ways with
words" during story times and in their work on assigned reports in ways that
were discursively congruent with, and reproductive of, those of the middle-class
home and office workplace, but their success at these tasks was achieved at the
expense of great anxiety about the future and nagging doubts about whether it
was all worth it—doubts that they tried to deny by ostracizing "marginal" students who dared to express alternative dreams to college or a professional career.

But at working-class Roosevelt Elementary, which I consider in Chapter 4,
teacher and librarian practices and students' uses of library texts could not be
characterized in either the terms of resistance or the terms of discursive congruence. There the librarian and the teacher of the class I observed attended to the
surface rhetoric and ideals of the standard curriculum, but in their practices, and
particularly in the narratives of the library, of their own lives, and of the wide
range of texts they read with the children, they encouraged students to playfully
disassemble textual knowledge as it was formally structured and reassemble it in
terms that made practical sense to them. In short, activity at Roosevelt Elemen-

tary seemed to be governed by a pragmatism that took into account and dealt with the demands of both the educational bureaucracy and broader political forces without opposing, evading, or entering into a Faustian pact with them. That pragmatism, I will argue in Chapter 5, depended on a "reconstructed" view of the world—one made from bits of time and text and ways of using both that the powerful have not (yet) found a use for—in reflexive interaction with an ethos of human subjectivity constructed within a space that acknowledges immanent social realities without requiring submission to their reproductive ideologies.

Resistance: Chavez Elementary

Kids are not readers by nature.

—Mary Strauss, Librarian, Chavez Elementary

READING THE SCHOOL

Chavez Elementary is located a mile west of downtown in an aging residential area that lies sandwiched between the river and a strip of double train tracks, around which cluster many small warehouses and light industrial workshops. The West End has historically been the "ethnic" part of town, a place known in former days for its jazz clubs and ethnic cuisine, and these days, to judge from the local evening news and the daily newspaper, for its gangs and drugs and on-again/off-again efforts to organize itself as a community.

It is an old neighborhood of tree-lined, narrow streets. The West End has always been working class or, as is presently the case, working poor. There are two small and relatively old public housing developments that, from the street at least, seem well maintained, but for the most part, housing in Chavez's attendance area consists of small, singly built, and very modest bungalows and frame cottages. These homes are unevenly maintained; some appear abandoned, while others, often next door, are freshly painted and have carefully tended gardens of lush tropical and semitropical plants and flowers. Most homes have small fenced yards, and some homes have bars on the windows. It appears a quiet neighborhood: Children play ball and ride bikes in the street, and in the evening, adults drink beer and talk with neighbors on their porches or while working on old cars. But the crime rate there is high, property values are low, and the area is generally considered by outsiders to constitute the city's "inner core."

Of the 386 students enrolled at Chavez in 1992-1993, the overwhelming majority were Mexican-American (85 percent). Many of these students were Spanish-language dominant and in bilingual programs (23 percent of the student body), mostly at the pre-k and kindergarten levels, although there were several students in the fourth grade the previous year who "had just arrived" and spoke little or no English. In 1992–1993, 14 percent of students were African-American, while only 2 percent of the student body (6 students) were classified as white. Ninety-four percent of the students were from "low-income" homes—46 percentage points above the district average. When court-ordered busing was discontinued in the district in 1987, as part of the settlement 16 schools primarily in the West End and on the west side of town were designated "priority schools" and allotted extra funds to improve their instruction. As a result, per student spending at Chavez was over $1,000 more than the district average (for schools with the same grades). Most of this increase was probably spent on lowering the student-teacher ratio: There were 11.7 pupils per teacher at Chavez in 1992–1993, compared to the district-wide ratio of 18.1 pupils per teacher.

This increase in per student spending, however, was not reflected in quantitative measures of academic achievement. Of the 16 priority schools in the district, Chavez's scores were near the bottom of the list; in fact, Chavez's scores were consistently among the bottom 5 schools in a district with approximately 60 elementary facilities. Great pressure was placed on the school by both the state and the district's central administration to "do something" about this, with the result that teaching and studying for achievement tests were a constant preoccupation of Chavez's entire staff. For example, in interviews with third graders in both February and May, students complained bitterly that they were always practicing for the test. I had heard of a special writing teacher who came to work with the students several times a week and later learned that she was drilling the students on the rhetorical formulas—narrative, persuasive, expository—that would be on the state-mandated writing test. The teacher of the third-grade class with whom I worked, Kirstin Thurmon, also complained to me about the pressure that was put on teachers to be always preparing students for testing. Finally, librarian Mary Strauss expressed her appreciation to me one day in passing for a fourth-grade teacher who "didn't pass along all the pressure that teachers have on them to raise test scores" to her students and assured me that many other teachers were not managing the stress as well. She said that little, if any, science or social studies was taught in most classrooms because teachers were so preoccupied with practicing to take the next achievement test.

More informal, qualitative measures gathered from participant observation, working with students, interviews, and questionnaires provide a more contextualized picture of students' literacy and the less tangible effects of a curriculum focused on the bottom line. Four of the 13 third graders in teacher Kirstin Thurmon's class could barely decode primer-level text; because of her extraordinary patience and quiet self-control, I suspected that many of her students were "special cases" who had been placed in her charge because she could "handle them." For this reason, the rate of 33 percent illiteracy in this class—if illiteracy can be crudely equated here with fluency—is probably higher than the overall rate for the school. Still, from my contact with students as a volunteer in the library and with one other third-grade class, I estimate that one of every five children I worked with could not read any text with any fluency.

In summary, both formal and informal measures place Chavez Elementary at or near the bottom of district schools in student academic achievement, a situation that provided the rationale for its test-driven curriculum and obsession with the bottom line. The most frequent cause cited for this deficiency was poverty and, according to librarian Mary Strauss, a lack of parental and community interest in schooling. There was, however, no lack of energy in the ways that teachers approached their work at Chavez or in the resolve with which the librarian there pursued motivational reading programs designed to exercise "lazy brains" and eradicate other bad habits with a love of reading fiction.

READING THE LIBRARY

Chavez's main facility was built in 1936 and remained relatively unchanged except for additions throughout the years of an auditorium and new entrance on the north end of the building and a gymnasium off the south end; but neither of these additions was very recent. The main building was an L-shaped, two-story, yellow-brick building that stood on a narrow side street. The gymnasium and auditorium were located on either end of, and behind, the main structure, forming an enclosed playground in back of the building. Portable classrooms at Chavez outnumbered permanent ones, officially by 16 to 14. These outbuildings were located along a concrete sidewalk that extended approximately 200 feet from behind the school (Kirstin Thurmon's third-grade classroom was located in the second-last of these portables). Beyond the portables and the school was an open-air stage, the Pan-American Theater, that was painted with murals that had Latino themes and slogans. One character in the murals waved his fist and held a sign that said, "Ya Basta!" (Enough already!). Beyond the school and the theater a wide, open, grassy playing field covered an entire block.

The library was located on the second floor of the main building. It was actually two former classrooms with the wall between them partially removed and covered a little over 2,000 square feet (see Figure 2.1). South-facing windows ran along the length of the library, making it warm and bright. One room housed most of the nonfiction, fiction, and "everybody's fiction" (picture book) collections, as well as a magazine rack, a display case with a rock collection, and the librarian's work space and checkout desk. The center of the room was open and served as the spot where students sat on the floor for story time and other meetings with the librarian. The other room housed a small reference section, the Dewey 900s, and the school's audiovisual (AV) equipment. The biography, picture book, and reference sections of the library were marked but not as conspicuously as at Roosevelt or Crest Hills. The card catalog stood across from the checkout desk in a cramped space that was partially hidden by a book stand filled with volumes to be reshelved; it was the least conspicuous and farthest removed from the nonfiction section of any of the three libraries in the study.

The book collection itself was impressive. In addition to funds regularly allotted by the district, local businesses and civic groups contributed several thousand dollars per year for the acquisition of new books through a library guild formed several years before. As a result, the nonfiction and fiction collection had been well maintained, while the picture book collection was one of the largest and most extensive in the city. Although it had a student population half their size, Chavez's collection was as large and as up-to-date as Crest Hills's and nearly as extensive as Roosevelt's.

Figure 2.1
Chavez Elementary Library Floor Plan

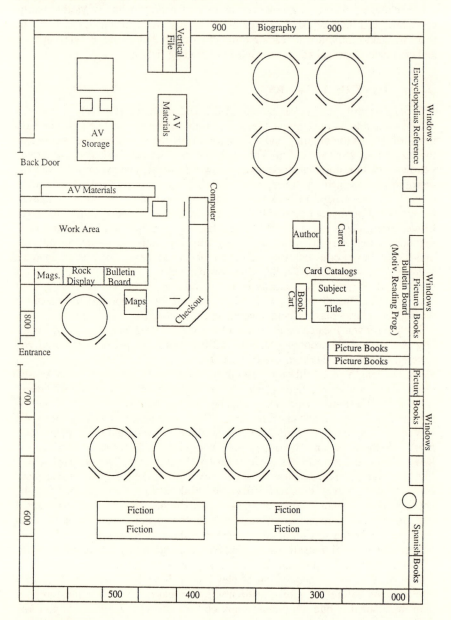

AV = Audiovisual

The Tropics of Reading

Mary Strauss scheduled formal library visits for each class in the school, from pre-k to fifth grade. The library's program of instruction followed a graded, sequential pattern and included both story times and some basic instruction in reference skills. The librarian explained that most of the practices that made up this program had evolved in response to needs or problems she had encountered over the years. For example, Mary Strauss taught nursery rhymes to pre-k and kindergarten groups, a large percentage of whom speak Spanish as their first language. She subscribed to a saying she once heard that "Mother Goose comes first." She wanted the children to have "the rhythm, the language"—that cultural/linguistic knowledge that Mother Goose provides because "they don't get it when they're one or two." Another identified problem was teaching students how to care for library books once they began to check them out in the early primary grades. She used a small book wrapped in a disposable diaper and placed in a doll crib as a prop (a "book baby") to dramatize for the students the need to take care of their books, just as they would a little brother or sister. As if to contradict this lesson, however, when the book baby was not in use, it was pushed under the table that held the card catalog.

Beyond kindergarten, one picture book was read to students in the first and second grades during the first half of scheduled library visits, and the remainder of their time in the library was devoted to browsing for new books. The programs for fourth- and fifth-grade students focused almost exclusively on their involvement in one of several motivational novel-reading programs (see below); in addition to their involvement in similar programs, third-grade students also received two or three lessons on the organizational system of the nonfiction section and the use of the card catalog. These lessons were accompanied by a series of posters telling the story of how "Mr. Dewey" found a way to organize the "piles of books" in his library and are described in more detail later in this chapter.

As at Roosevelt and Crest Hills, the stipulated policy at Chavez was that students could check out two books at any one time; but unlike the two other schools, this policy was carefully enforced at Chavez. To monitor book circulation, each classroom had its own laminated 24" x 30" poster with the teacher's name written at the top. Pocket cards, one per student, were glued to the poster in rows, with students' names written on them also. When a class entered the library, teachers usually took the book cards out of the poster pockets and returned book cards to the books students had returned. This system provided a technology superior to the standard practice of keeping students' book cards on file by a due date (as at Crest Hills) or by classroom (as at Roosevelt), for it allowed both the librarian and the teachers at Chavez to see at a glance not only how many but, more important, what kind of books a student had checked out.

The function of monitoring students' checkout so closely was, as might be suspected, to help guide students to the sorts of books that would improve their reading ability (and coincidentally raise test scores). But the guidelines imposed were described as liberal ones. Students were told that the books they checked out "have to be fun books. One of them needs to be a fun book you can read all the way through, [and] one needs to be a fun book that you just want. . . . So one that they take has to be one that they can read." Mary Strauss reported that she "[had] struggled with this." Longer, bigger books had a higher status to many children; they wanted to check them out and carry them around, but they couldn't (and didn't) read them, and so it seemed unlikely to Mary Strauss that they helped to improve students' reading. The "one they can read" was invariably also a work of fiction, because, as the librarian at Chavez argued, it was only through fiction that students were likely to develop a reading habit. When I remarked one day that many students seemed to gravitate toward the nonfiction section when they browsed (in fact, I had seen the librarian and teachers herd students away from the nonfiction section of the library and back to the picture book section), and wondered aloud if nonfiction might not be more captivating to some students, Mary Strauss agreed; but she also argued that to really engross a reader there was "just nothing like a good work of fiction."

Both "hard data" and anecdotal evidence are used to support the library program at Chavez. First, there was information supplied by standardized reading tests that showed that most students at Chavez did well on mechanical tasks of decoding and word attack but fell down on measures of comprehension. But Mary Strauss also reported witnessing rooms of students sit silently at their desks after book checkout and "read"—that is, open the book and look at the pages—but show virtually no understanding when quizzed about the book's contents. This was the most disturbing and upsetting thing to her, the thing that left her feeling the most powerless: students going through the motions of reading a book but never really engaging the text.

This problem was attributed to a lack of models at home, where parents, Mary Strauss explained, did not read for pleasure, to the easier gratification provided by television and movies, and to teachers who were not "readers" themselves (i.e., do not read for pleasure) and so saw reading as an academic skill that they had to teach and drill through worksheets:

If children don't get to read every day [they won't get hooked]. . . . It's teachers not giving kids enough time. . . . [t]here are ways to monitor if kids are reading, and that needs to be done, too, until the kids are used to doing it. Once they're hooked, then you don't have to worry about it. . . . [I become frustrated with] teachers just not understanding how crucial that time in the building is to read, because a lot of the kids are just not going to do it at home.

As this comment implies, reading was viewed by this librarian as a difficult and unnatural act. "Kids are not readers by nature," Mary Strauss once stated; and this fact, compounded by an educational, home, and general cultural environment that failed to support the act of reading as she defined it—that is, as the close attention of an isolated individual over an extended period of time to a narrative text—explained the failure of students at Chavez to become readers.

The solution, one that would get kids hooked on the reading habit, was a series of motivational reading programs that began in the second grade, as soon as most children were able to decode print with any fluency, and continued through the fifth grade. The idea for the clubs originated in a contest that was conducted several years ago to promote the reading of Buttercup Award books. Buttercups were children's novels nominated by students around the state as the best books over a year. Students who read a certain number of the nominees were then allowed to vote on which they like best. To verify whether students had actually read the books they claimed to have read, a list of 10 or so questions for each book was devised that asked about the details of settings, characters' behaviors, and plot twists—the sort of questions that might quickly determine if a student had read the book or not. According to Mary Strauss, "We realized as we were doing it that the kids liked the interviews, wanted the connection, wanted the teacher to ask them some questions about the books, and liked being held accountable."

"It had a different feel than all the other reading programs I had done before," she said. Mary Strauss decided to expand the program beyond Buttercups to "Author Fan Club," a program that would run throughout the year and provide incremental rewards—a bookmark for 5 books, a badge for 7, a pencil and one's name in the hall for 10—for reading books by a single children's author. The advantage of selecting books based on authorship was that "they tend to write all their books on the same level," and so it would be easy, once the reading level of the text was set, to match individual students with books that they could read. Civic groups, a church group, and even fourth graders across town at Crest Hills were quickly enlisted to write comprehension questions for fiction books in the library written by authors who had written multiple books, usually in a series; these questions were then filed in huge three-ring binders by the author's last name. At the time I participated in the program as a questionner, hundreds, if not thousands, of sets of questions had been compiled, enough to fill the oversized binders that just fit into the plastic milk crate that I used when I carried them out to the portables. It was the program's eventual goal to have questions on hand for every picture and chapter book in the library—perhaps 5,000 books in all.

There were two problems to be worked out to make any of these programs truly operational. First, with regard to the Author Fan Club program, there were relatively few children's authors with 10 different or even 5 different titles in the library and fewer still who wrote the sort of arty, well-crafted books that would count as legitimate cultural objects. But more critically for all these programs, these authors usually wrote in language that was above the independent reading level of most of the students. To solve this problem, mass quantities of children's pulp fiction, that is, mass-produced series with (in some cases) controlled vocabulary and stock characters and situations, were purchased for children to read. In the picture book category, these books included the "Nate the Great," "Berenstain Bears," and "Clifford" series, and in the "transitional" chapter-book category, the "Sweet Valley Kids," "American Girl," and (for the boys) "Mad Max (the Ghost)" series. Based on my observations from reshelving books and asking questions of one fourth-grade and two third-grade classes, I estimate that three fourths of the students who participated in the library's motivational reading programs read these sorts of books.

The librarian at Chavez Elementary was not unaware or unconcerned that she had to resort to using what the "experts" consider the most "tasteless" children's books—which are also the weakest sorts of academic and cultural capital available—in order to make these reading programs workable or that these texts revealed contradictions in the program's goals. Instead, she saw the development as only temporary and transitional for most students. As she put it:

Our kids watch *Star Wars*. Then we want them to read and they can read Dick and Jane. Trying to find books at their reading levels that are fun enough and exciting enough for these little appetites that have been stirred up, revved up to the degree that they want *Star Wars*, they want Eddie Murphy in their little readers, and trying to match that up is very difficult. So trying to convince children that there is a progression, that those books are there and waiting, that they're going to have to climb that little ladder to get to them; . . . that's very difficult and frustrating, because I *know* what the kids are asking for. And trying to convince them to try something else is very difficult. (her emphasis)

As these comments imply, students often selected books that were beyond what their teachers and the librarian believed they were capable of reading. In one instance that I witnessed, a second-grade boy, Tom, who was characterized as "extremely bright but hyperactive," selected a chapter book and brought it to his teacher for approval. "Oh, Tom," she said; she was sure he couldn't read it. But he persisted, and it became clear that he was determined to check out this book. His teacher was equally determined, however; she had him sit down and try to read it first. A few moments later he returned and she interrogated him with rapid-fire questions about the characters and plot of the story; he was left fumbling for a response. "You see?" she told him. She knew he couldn't read it. He needed to check out something that he could read.

Moments like these were frustrating and embarrassing, and Mary Strauss always hoped that a more diplomatic way could be found to guide students to level-appropriate reading. For example, in another instance, a group of three girls who were reading "Little House" books together (their teacher had mentioned that these were her favorites when she was a girl) were gently guided to switch to the much shorter and simpler "American Girl" series after it was decided that one of the girls in the group probably was not really reading the stories. Theoretically, as the program began to have a positive effect on students' reading proficiency, the teachers and the librarian might also be expected to suggest longer or more complex novels and picture books that students might enjoy; but every instance of guidance in book selection that I observed during four months took a downward trajectory on the ladder the program was meant to help students climb.

To help teachers to guide their students' reading, markers were placed on the spines of all the picture books for which questions had been written, along with color-coded markers that would indicate what grade level a particular book was written on. Mary Strauss wasn't "real comfortable about that—kids don't know what it means—but teachers need help." In fact, later in the year I observed a library visit by a second-grade teacher in which during the introduction of a new reading program, "Power Readers," the librarian and the teacher separated the class into groups and explained the levels to them, indicating to each group that they would only be permitted to choose books that had a specific color tab on the spine.

As is implied by efforts to justify the constraints these programs impose on students' reading, the librarian at Chavez was not unaware of the potential criticism by the "experts" both in her own profession of library science and in the field of literacy of programs where the mechanisms of control are so open. Why, then, would she go to the trouble of placing the library's motivational reading programs essentially at the center of the school's developmental reading program when, as she acknowledged, "that is not necessarily an appropriate role for librarians"? In the end, I suspect that it was social (and self-) respectability that the librarian desired for the children there, respectability that, in her eyes (and in the eyes of district administrators and the local press) was derived from the quantitative measures of literacy—from being able to *certifiably* call oneself a reader—that the questions (and for the school itself, standardized testing) provided. From where she stood, these children had so little, and such a long way to go. A sense of deprivation drove the program, deprivation that could be concluded from the students' home lives and from the community in general; but even more frustratingly, Mary Strauss drew this conclusion from her understanding of the school itself, of its teach-for-the-test curriculum and of teachers who turned reading—and learning—into "awful, awful things" that "just make me sick."

Historical Patterns

This interpretation of the library program at Chavez can be outlined from the evidence provided by incidents in the library, from the autobiographical account its librarian provided of her own education, and finally from the account of school libraries' history presented in Chapter 1. First, there is Mary Strauss's recounting of student response to answering questions for her first motivational program. In her telling, students "enjoyed being held accountable." Using questions had "a different feel . . . from [other] reading programs I had ever done before that involved kids just saying, 'Yes, I read all those books.' That didn't mean a thing to them, because anybody could say that." It "verified [it] for the other kids—see, it made it real for the other kids . . . it verifies it [for] everybody."

There was also a telling incident during one of the few "skills" lessons Mary Strauss conducted with the students to explain the Dewey Decimal System to them. When the students were not as attentive to her explanation of "Mr. Dewey's Problem" as she wanted them to be, she told the students that she was trying to help them because "other [third graders] are learning this in other parts of the city, and I would like for you to be able to do what the other kids can do. I don't want you to get into the sixth grade and go to another school, not able to do what [those kids] can do." She wanted, in other words, to spare them the embarrassment of not knowing what others took for granted.

A similar theme ran through the story this librarian told of her own literacy and upbringing in a small town in a rural part of the state—a story that complemented the ethos of the library's reading programs. Her father, the youngest child in the family, was "babied" at home and allowed not to go to college after high school, a decision he regretted all his life. Mary Strauss explained that she had much the same attitude about school as a child, but her father refused to baby her and made her get good grades in school, even though she found schooling dull and had little interest at the time in books. Reading was "not an important part of [her] childhood"; she had warm memories of a maiden aunt who read to her and her sister, and her father read, "but the books that he read weren't very exciting to me. They were Sandburg's Lincoln series, or historical kinds of things, and he loved to read, but it still didn't impress me as being anything that I, as a living, breathing teenager would care about doing." Mary Strauss also described herself as something of a social gadfly: "I was too busy running around and chasing boys." But then at the end of high school, her father issued an ultimatum: She could wait tables in a restaurant or go to the university.

She chose the university and "was stunned at what I had not read, but everybody else had." In terms that echo Bourdieu's (1984) description of lower-middle-class strategies for upward social mobility, college presented to her an attractive social world in which success depended not only on investments of social capital but on *cultural* capital as well—on acquiring a taste for, and knowledge of, the "right books." During the summer following her freshman year of college, she returned home to work in the county clerk's office. With little else to do there, she completed *The Agony and the Ecstasy* (Stone 1961), the first novel she had ever read for pleasure, and then began unsystematically to read other novels that she felt would help her to "bootstrap" her way into the world of her more cosmopolitan classmates. As Mary Strauss told the story, if her father had not made her get good grades, she would not have gone to college, she would not have seen what she was missing, and she would not love books and reading and be where she is today. Similarly, she saw herself and a few teachers at Chavez reenacting her father's role in the lives of children there, and she was willing to risk what she recognized was the anger of students and the disapproval of "experts" to frustrate students temporarily with dull texts written at their "reading level," in hope of building a habit of reading in them.

A deep and abiding strain of Calvinism informed the lesson that was taken from this story. As one of Calvinism's tenets, people are born into a "natural" state of sin and must find, or be led to, redemption. Redemption, in turn, is certified by material and cultural standing in the community—a standing that can only be gained through the hard work (in this instance) of reading. Both Mary Strauss and her father had, to use a phrase she used in the promotion of one of her programs, Power Readers, "lazy brains." Similarly, then, "[k]ids are not readers by nature": they, too, had lazy brains and little interest in exercising them without some external prodding. Once hooked, the intrinsic ("sinful") human craving for pleasure—for "fun," as she put it to students—could be turned against itself to keep students coming back for more of the innocent pleasures that derived from reading fiction, innocent pleasures that not only Mary Strauss but children's librarians since the end of the last century have been counting on to substitute for the less innocent ones of the street, pleasures that hopefully will lead to students' eventual sociocultural redemption. That is why nonfiction, which Mary Strauss told me people read selectively and not from cover to cover, wouldn't do for students to read. She explained that in her experience as a reader it did not provide the same sort of deep "pleasure"—that dreamlike, almost narcotic effect—that immersion in a "good work of fiction" did.

In summary, a desire for students' social redemption and respectability motivated the library program at working-poor Chavez and explains the sense of purpose with which the librarian there pursued her work. This analysis also helps to account for obvious similarities between the goals of the program at Chavez and the goals of early children's and public librarians discussed earlier in Chapter 1: the focus on fiction, the sense of urgency, and the missionary chutzpah with which both early librarians and Mary Strauss wielded their influence. But this analysis may also require some reconsideration of the motives of women librarians and charity workers in the late nineteenth century. Mary Strauss's rationale helps to soften their portrayal by Dee Garrison (1979) as "apostles of culture" and by Ann Douglas (1977) as crassly imperialist in their efforts to impose their own cultural values on the poor and immigrant and to see these women instead as conflicted persons who were doing their best from their own cultural perspectives and lived experience to have a positive effect on children's lives. In the time I spent at Chavez, I never saw Mary Strauss speak about students or behave toward them or anyone else with intended disrespect; rather, I saw her relate to students in ways that indicated that she saw them as she saw herself as a child in elementary school: as bored and a little recalcitrant, and in danger, lest someone like her father not be there, of failing to "make something of themselves" within a public sphere of activity—a process that began, in Mary Strauss's case and historically, in the case of middle-class women, with the habit of reading fiction.

In the end, the library program at Chavez can only be fully understood as an attempt to compensate single-handedly for the perceived deficiencies of many of its classroom teachers and the school program at large. As Mary Strauss saw it, there were all these holes in Chavez's educational program, some of them created by teachers and administrators and some of them forced on the school by unsympathetic district and state agencies. And as librarian, what could she do? A few years ago she "saw some things not being done, and some things that might help." Even though her motivational reading programs depended, ironically, on the same technologies of examination that they were meant to counteract, they also need to be interpreted as the attempt of a deeply concerned individual to patch the gaping holes and serious structural deficiencies of a curriculum that is growing, seemingly beyond anyone's capacity to stop it, ever more systematically unjust and symbolically violent (Bourdieu and Passeron 1977).

Because the read-for-pay program at Chavez did appear at times to be the product of one librarian's analysis of her school community and its students' lives, an argument can be mounted that the program was an anomaly—an exception that bears little resemblance to what happens as a rule in other schools. That was certainly the opinion of one school librarian in another district with whom I shared my findings. But in fact, while I was conducting this study, several other librarians in the district told me about a computer program they had heard of that performed essentially the same tasks electronically that were managed manually at Chavez—a program that provided comprehension questions for thousands of the novels that were a standard part of school libraries and that tested students and kept track of what they had read and how well they had done on each test—and of how interested they were in purchasing such a program, if only they could scrape together the funds. Moreover, the library program at Chavez was highly regarded by most of its faculty at Chavez, by the principal, and within the district and across the state. Two years after I completed my data collection, Mary Strauss was honored at the annual meeting of the state library association with an award for her efforts. Based on this evidence, the program at Chavez, as dramatic and idiosyncratic as it seems, can also clearly be regarded as embodying many of the assumptions that both historically and currently are made about the power of reading fiction to remediate the perceived sociocultural deficiencies of the poor.

THE MEANING OF THE LIBRARY

In addition to the cultural meanings that libraries communicate to users through their programs and through the arrangement of their texts as discussed in

Chapter 1, it is clear from the discussion at the beginning of this chapter that potent indigenous meanings are also conveyed to library patrons through the specific practices of the librarians who take charge of individual libraries. In the case of school libraries, the messages conveyed are likely to be about what exactly it means "to read" and, even more important, about the nature of the relationship between readers and texts.

One way to characterize those meanings as they were conveyed not only in the library at Chavez but later in the libraries at Crest Hills in Chapter 3 and Roosevelt in Chapter 4—on the way to discussing how they are perceived by student users—is in terms of the semiotic theory of Charles Sanders Peirce (1931/1958). In order to accomplish that, I would like to digress for a moment to explain, in terms as concise and clear as I can manage for the present purposes, Peirce's theory of semiosis, (the process of the apprehension of signs) and then, more specifically, Peirce's explication of the three modes of signification that mediate between things signified and our cognition of them.

To begin, then, it might help to draw some contrasts between the better-known semiology of Ferdinand de Saussure and "semiosis" as described by Peirce. In the nominalist foundation of Saussurean semiology, the world as human beings comprehend it is a hypothetical construct, unconnected to any absolute reality; hence, relationships between signifiers, or sensory images, and signifieds, or the meanings human beings give to them, while possessing a social and cultural connection, are ultimately arbitrary. Likewise, the rules for the arrangement of signs—their "syntagmatic" relationship—are also arbitrary and governed only by convention. Peirce, on the other hand, rejected nominalism; in his view, human beings were not alienated from the world, but an integral part of it, and beings who over the course of time had become "strongly adapted to the comprehension of the world" (cited in Ochs 1993, 54).

The world itself is a sign, in Peirce's view, whose reality makes itself known in the process of semiosis, whereby a "representamen," or signifier, is linked to its object (the thing it signifies) through the relational influence of a third element, the "interpretant," which in turn becomes a representamen, to be linked to a second object through the relational influence of a second interpretant, which in turn becomes a representamen, to be linked to a third object through the relational influence of a third interpretant, and so on, in an unending chain of signification, or semiosis. In Peircean semiotics, cognition involves the progressive semiotic interpretation of three hierarchical degrees of reality: "Firstness," or "qualitative possibility"; "Secondness," or "reactive objectivity"; and "Thirdness," or "rules, laws, mediations, and representations" (Parmentier 1987, 22). In comprehending reality, semiosis moves from the qualitative "sensibility" of Firstness to the "objectification" of Secondness (the recognition of an entity as separate from other entities), to the "intelligibility" of Thirdness, the experience of articulation or recognition.

It is the level of Thirdness, that is, the degree of human experience at which the relation between the sign vehicle (representamen) and the object is mediated by one of three types of signs, or interpretants (Parmentier 1985), that is our concern in the discussion of the relation of the sign vehicle of school library programs to their objects, reading and reader subjectivity. To put the issue more clearly, what types of signs mediate the relationship between school library programs (and in the context of the present chapter, the library at Chavez) and the socialization of students as readers? Peirce argued that sign vehicle-object relationships are mediated through three types of sign: the icon, the index, and the symbol.

Icons refer to their objects by virtue of some inherent quality that they share with that object; they establish their significance through *resemblance*. Photographs, drawings, maps and interpretive dances are all examples of icons that bear a visual resemblance to an object, but other sensory resemblances can be iconic as well, such as musical notes that imitate natural sounds. Their intention—to evoke a sense of the object—makes them the correlate of Firstness.

An *index* refers to its object by virtue of its spatial or temporal contiguity to that object: Traffic signs are indexical, as is a ringing telephone or the smell of smoke. The index differs from the icon in its dependence on context for meaning; unlike either the icon, or the third type of relational sign, the symbol, it is largely inert and meaningless unless it shares a material context with its object. Because its intention is to differentiate the object from its surroundings, the index is the correlate of Secondness.

The third type of sign is the *symbol*, which refers to its object not by any natural or physical resemblance or connection but by virtue of conventional agreement. Symbols are general signs and not dependent on context or on resemblance for their interpretation. Words, when regarded as entities, are symbols, as are laws, rules, and arguments. Because the symbol's intention is rationally understood, it correlates with Thirdness. The decontextualized, conventional nature of Thirds places them outside the physical world and makes them instead the product of human social cognition; it is signs generated as Thirds that mediate human social interaction.

And yet as a Third, every sign must embody the signs of Firstness and Secondness from which it was generated. According to Parmentier (1987):

We can observe the compositional syntax of these three kinds of semiotic entities. Every index, in order to convey information, must embody an icon. The falling grass is an index of the wind, but it is also an icon in that the direction of the grass's fall resembles the direction of the wind. (Think of this in these terms: an index directs the mind to some aspect of reality and an icon provides some information about it.) And a symbol must embody an icon and an index, the former to express the information and the latter to indicate the object. (22)

Even though all human linguistic communication is necessarily symbolic, the relations determining the chain of semiosis through which linguistic symbols—and not only words but phrases, sentences, paragraphs, and so on—are characterized by their iconic, their indexical, or their symbolic nature.

Finally, this "nested hierarchical set" of relational signs (Parmentier 1987, 22) of icon, index, and symbol can be used to characterize the cognitive relations that a user of signs intends to communicate to her audience. At Chavez, it seems clear that not only the motivational reading programs but the concrete sign vehicles of the library itself cumulatively stress the use of icons in representing literate behavior. In the chain of semiosis at Chavez, meanings are heavily dependent on the experience of Firstness. The forging of relations between student readers and texts, for instance, is considered to be dependent on getting students hooked—on getting them *addicted* to reading—by connecting the reading act with the sensation of pleasure: to inculcate in students a craving for something that does not ask for conscious understanding or recognition. While at both Crest Hills and Roosevelt the stories read during story time contained ideological lessons about how to conduct oneself in the world, the ideational content of the story-time texts for early readers at Chavez—Mother Goose rhymes—was largely nonsensical (although historically loaded with meaning) to modern young readers. It wasn't the plot or characterization or theme of rhymes like "Humpty Dumpty" that made them worth reading (and memorizing), it was their value as cultural capital and their rhythm, that is, the pleasant, physical sensation produced from the repetitive sound of the words, that made them so attractive.

Even the ideational and very *ideological* content of the pulp series recommended to students in the reading clubs was downplayed by the use of the questions. The certification that their correct answering provided was one of the few clearly indexical signs present in the library at Chavez. However, as I describe in more detail in the next section, the questions were not interested in determining whether the reader had comprehended the story but only whether the student's reading of the story matched, or at least resembled, the reading of the person who wrote the questions. In fact, I never heard anyone at Chavez have a "literary" conversation with a student about the book that student was reading; what talk there was centered on interrogating the reader to determine if the book was actually "read."

The nonlinguistic signs of the library also stressed iconicity, while discounting indexical function. In the arrangement of texts in the library (see Figure 2.1), picture books and fiction were foregrounded, while nonfictional texts were relegated to far corners of the library or to positions behind and to the side of fictional texts. Nonfiction itself was dismissed by Mary Strauss as a source of reading "pleasure," and students were discouraged from checking out nonfiction books. In an informal conversation one day, I mentioned that I liked to read nonfiction recreationally. Yes, Mary Strauss agreed, nonfiction could be interesting and useful, but there was just nothing like the experience of getting involved in a good work of fiction. The shelves of the nonfiction section did bear the numbers of their Dewey classification, but the location of the card catalog itself, the master index to the information contained in those texts, was in a spot that was far removed from those texts.

The library program's lessons about the Dewey Decimal System and the use of the card catalog also depended on icons and discounted indexical qualities. As at Roosevelt, the explanation of the Dewey Decimal System was narrativized. "Mr. Dewey" himself was the protagonist in the illustrative story Mary Strauss told, and he was a librarian with a problem: There were "piles of books" everywhere in his library, and no one could find anything. Mr. Dewey decided to put the books on shelves by their subject, and then he had his Great Idea: he'd use numbers.

In the two tellings of this story to third graders that I witnessed, Mary Strauss used a set of laminated charts on an easel. When she got to the Great Idea, she used one chart per subject category of the Dewey Decimal System, each of which had iconic representations of the topics within that category arranged on it. But there was no explanation of the logic of the numerical order, and in fact, the charts were presented out of order. As she described each subject category, she laid the charts on the floor, again out of order. Covering the call numbers on their spines, she then showed the students some books one at a time and asked them to tell her, from the pictures on the charts, to which category they belonged; the students were quick and accurate in their answers. The charts themselves were attractive depictions that used carefully chosen images to illustrate the subjects of each Dewey category clearly. When not in use for library lessons, they were placed on top of the nonfiction bookshelves along one wall of the library in numerical order but not in contiguity with the books on the shelves in each category; as a result, the indexical connection between the charts and the books on the shelves was diminished and became nonfunctional.

The use of metaphors to promote the reading programs was another indication of iconicity at work. Mary Strauss bemoaned the fact that she couldn't find texts at students' reading levels that were *as exiting as Star Wars* or Eddie Murphy; she also brought a mountain climber to school so that kids could see the resemblance between the exhilaration of reading (another feeling) and the physical exhilaration of "climbing their own mountain."

The iconization of reading in terms that rendered it a physical, as opposed to an intellectual, act became most pronounced toward the end of the school year, however, in two programs, the Power Readers program and in a day long festival that involved the entire school, Reading Rally Day. The Power Reading program was introduced late in the spring in the second grade, along with its counterpart program for the third, fourth, and fifth grades, Alpine Readers. Like Author Fan Club, these involved only the reading of fiction and used a reward system for reading in quantity; however, Power and Alpine Readers were rewarded for the number of pages they had read rather than the number of books by an author: one "line" per picture book or per 10 pages of a chapter book read.

To introduce Power Readers, Mary Strauss used a series of posters on an easel, which she flipped as she gave her pitch. The first poster read: "POWER READERS: A new reading club for kids who want to increase their BRAIN POWER by increasing their READING POWER." The next six posters stressed physical metaphors of reading and equated physical strength with "mental strength":

- Exercise builds strong muscles; Reading builds a strong BRAIN! GET TOUGH! GET BRAIN POWER!!
- ANYBODY can sit around and not learn anything and have a LAZY BRAIN. That's EASY!
- Don't let your brain be FLABBY and SOFT. GET TOUGH! GET BRAIN POWER!!
- We need HEFTY, STRONG BRAINS to run this world.
- Not WIMPY, WIMPY, WIMPY. But HEFTY, HEFTY, HEFTY!
- Here's your chance to increase your BRAIN POWER! BE A POWER READER!

The presentation that accompanied these posters attempted to cajole students into joining the program. During that presentation and in the weeks afterward Mary Strauss used the word *brain* exclusively when she talked about the act of reading and its effects. Her selection of the term clearly implied that since the brain (as opposed to the "mind") was a physical entity, like a muscle, the way to becoming a better reader was analogous to the way to get big muscles, which was to exercise—to move one's muscles (or one's brain) against some force in repetition—through essentially mindless tasks.

But the use of metaphors and parody in the promotion of the reading act was even more pronounced and public each year in mid-April, during Reading Rally Day. At the rally I observed, students entered school in the morning by ducking under a banner across the front door that read: WE'RE ROCKING AND READING WHILE EXERCISING OUR BRAINS!! The day began with an assembly in the school auditorium, in which Mary Strauss led chants of "Read to Succeed!" and "Readers Are Leaders!" One after the other, students who had read prodigious numbers of pages or books throughout the year were asked to stand and be honored; parents who "supported reading" were asked to stand; cheerleaders from the local middle school did herky-jerky mechanical cheers, while outside the auditorium doors a "reading robot" made of cardboard boxes played tapes of third graders reading fairy tales. In between awards and cheers, the librarian reminded the students that the brain was a muscle that needed exercise to get strong just like their bodies did; the best way to exercise a lazy, weak brain was to read everyday. Following the assembly, students returned to their classrooms and were visited by local civic officials and dignitaries who had been invited to come and read to the classes.

A large sign on the front lawn of the school announced READ OUT WORKOUT on the front entrance to the building. The workout was led by the PE (physical education) teacher, who "warmed the kids up" for reading with several choruses of a poem:

> The more you read,
> The more you know.
> The more you know,
> The smarter you grow.

After vocalizing, she led the students in a parody of reading as a physical act. First, the students practiced "page turning": With their arms straight out at their sides and with palms up, students and teacher raised left their arms over their heads and brought them down to meet their right arms. They repeated this motion several times, and then on the command "Now let's speed read!" they began flailing away as fast as they could, dissolving into giggles. Next, the students and teacher warmed up their eyes. Bulging her eyes out, and bobbing her head up and down, the teacher demonstrated how to read, turning at the waist from left to right as though she were moving her eyes across a page; the students followed suit, and again on the command, "Let's speed read!" they began to bob and twist wildly until out of breath. Finally, the kids were "ready to read." They sat on mats spread on the concrete walkway and opened books they had brought with them. Students who "showed they knew how to read" (by seeming particularly intent with their books) were chosen to sit in rocking chairs on the front landing. The PE teacher repeated this exercise at least 10 times over a five-hour time period that day. I wondered why this was not taking place in the gymnasium; Mary Strauss explained, "We want the community to see what's going on here."

The use of physical metaphors to describe the mental act of reading was essentially a pitch for the disciplining of the student "body" through physical parodies of the reading act that used metaphors of physical exercise to describe reading iconically as "exercise for the brain" and that turned reading into a corporately mindless activity. Like the cardboard robot whose tape had to be rewound by someone else, or like the cheerleaders whose mechanical motions acquired meaning only in unison, and then only though external direction and supervision, the erasure of the mind from the act of reading can be seen as an attempt to create a "docile" student body: "Of exercising upon it a subtle coercion, of obtaining holds upon it at the level of the mechanism itself—movements, gestures, attitudes, rapidity: an infinitesimal power over the active body" (Foucault 1979, 137).

Docility, even in a school, is not an end in itself; as Michel Foucault points out, it becomes the means of control of the "political anatomy." Reading, as a discipline,

dissociates power from the body; on the one hand, turns it into an "aptitude," a "capacity," which it seeks to increase; on the other hand, it reverses the course of the energy, the power that might result from it, and turns it into a relation of strict subjection. If economic exploitation separates the force and the product of labor [or acts of reading from their purpose], let us say that disciplinary coercion establishes in the body the constricting link between an increased aptitude and increased domination. (138)

Literacy—the capacity to make signs in space in order to defy time (Kristeva 1989)—maintains its significance as an act largely to the extent that it contributes to people's capacity to function in the world (Graff 1987; Heath 1983, 1991; Moll 1992; Scribner 1988; Scribner and Cole 1981). When that function is disregarded, as it was in the library at Chavez, literacy, and reading in particular, becomes difficult and unnatural, something requiring a solution rather than a use, a prize whose achievement demands discipline and practice.

Without a function, the literate capacity to make signs—in the Peircean sense, to manipulate signs as arguments or vehicles of symbolic exchange (Parmentier 1987; Peirce 1931/1958)—is largely ignored. Reading and writing become signs in themselves, iconic representations of literacy, where parodies of the reading act—decoding aloud, answering questions, recognizing an author's name or an illustrator's style—signify literate behavior. But even as the literate capacity to act symbolically—to function across space in defiance of time—is lost, the iconic "sense" of literacy and a sense of its connection to the procurement and order of material existence are retained. One is expected to believe in the efficacy of literate acts without their connection to material prosperity because it "makes sense."

Literate acts are justified as acts of faith, and potential literates must not just be instructed in how to read, or even in how to use what they read; they must be evangelized to a degree in proportion to their perceived lack of faith. The agency for reading and writing shifts from those who read and write to those authorities who sanctify—and sanction—reading and writing, so that the function of literacy is inverted. Literacy comes to serve as a means of control by those who would make it a difficult act of faith over those who would try to use space to communicate across it and in defiance of time.

As Foucault (1979) has demonstrated, those ideologies and their supporting technologies that control best are those that aspire to control in toto, in conditions where technologies for controlling the body are correlated, if not made isomorphic, with those for controlling the mind. Literacy, as it was characterized in the library at Chavez, lent itself well to such technologies. Of course, these technologies are present in all modern, formal schools, where ratios of roughly 30 students to 1 teacher, and 30 teachers to 1 administrator are the norm, and where the major techniques of surveillance and control—through individuation and examination—are stretched to the optimum limits of their efficiency. But their operation is the most overt and least mitigated in urban school settings like Chavez that serve the working poor, where, for the better half of two centuries, school populations have been characterized as grossly deficient materially, culturally, and intellectually (Jones 1990). As the case of the library at Chavez illustrated, it is this perceived deficiency—this apparent spiritual void—that the most sincere and dedicated educators in impoverished educational settings feel morally justifies—indeed, compels—their activities.

Reading as Ritual

Before proceeding to discuss students' responses to Chavez's library and its texts, it might be useful to consider exactly what the iconization of reading there might imply about the subjective position that readers in that setting were directed to assume vis-à-vis texts. Contrary to what might be expected in a curriculum so preoccupied with fundamentals and skills-based activities, reading in the library at Chavez was never equated with decoding, a fundamentally rational (if, at the level of fluency, automatic) activity that focuses semiotically on the relating of phonic images to visual ones, and then of morphemic images with mental concepts. This was, however, the rationalized, mental view of reading that classroom teachers at Chavez took—and the view that the reading programs of the library were meant to compensate for.

The preponderance of physical metaphors used to describe the act of reading and the quantitative goals of the reading programs—to read as many books or as many pages as possible in order to become hooked and want more—suggested an economic interpretation of marketing reading in the library as an act of consumption. Texts there were certainly viewed as commodities: Tabbing each book to indicate its reading level was an attempt, much like sizing clothes, to match the reader with something that "fit," while chapter books were recognized by both children and adults as having higher status, or exchange value, than picture books. But while this characterization has its validity, there are also serious limitations to equating reading primarily with consumption in this context, because in the end we have only metaphorized reading and not explained or defined what it means to consume. Nor does mere "consumption" explain the need for the questions, as opposed to conversations or any other monitoring device, about each text consumed. As will be discussed in the next section, there was an economic element to the library's reading programs, but it was an element generated as much by students as it was by the programs themselves.

Neither entirely conscious nor physically passive, reading in the library at Chavez might be more productively explained as a *ritual* process—one requiring submission to the questions and the authority of others who were already accounted for as readers. But what consequence is this ritual process meant to invoke? Clifford Geertz (1983) offers some insight here. Drawing on the work of

Victor Turner and other ritual theorists, Geertz characterizes rituals as the enact-ment of social dramas, moments of theater in which the performers transmute themselves into new roles and new identities. They are triggered by situations of crisis in which the old ways are perceived as having lost their meaning, and so their power to regulate the social body:

They arise out of conflict situations . . . and proceed to their denouements through publicly performed conventionalized behavior. As the conflict swells to crisis and the excited fluidity of heightened emotion, where people feel at once more enclosed in a common mood and loosened from their social moorings, ritualized forms of au-thority—litigation, feud, sacrifice, prayer—are invoked to contain it and render it or-derly. (28)

The precipitating crisis at Chavez, I suspect, was its return to the status of "neighborhood school" in 1987 after a period of court-ordered busing to achieve integration of the city's school system and, more specifically, changes in the school's program that were a negotiated condition of its return to neighborhood status. Those changes included its designation as a "priority school," one that re-ceived not only increased funds but increased attention from the media and district officials, along with promises to bring its students' academic achievement up to par with the rest of the district and the state. Concurrent with these changes on the local level were renewed demands at the state level for educational reform, re-sulting in state-mandated testing and the imposition of carrot-and-stick technolo-gies to enforce those demands. These external changes, in which neither the community nor the staff at Chavez had much of a voice, placed enormous pres-sures on the school to do something without specifying what it was or how that "something" could reasonably and practically be effected.

The year 1987 was the same year that Mary Strauss returned to active work as a librarian after a year's leave of absence and "saw some things not being done, and some things that might help." It was also the year that she decided that li-brarianship was no longer a profession for her but a vocation. And it was the time during which she began to formulate motivational reading programs whose power to transform initiates into readers derived from the performative act of questioning or, as Geertz (1983) puts it, the invocation of "ritualized forms of authority." The disciplining of the body and the brain through repetitive mo-tions, the consecration of the questions, and the emphasis on belief in place of rational argument: These were practices designed to mitigate the doubt and fear of the crisis that had befallen the school, and to set performers on the road to social regeneration.

Thinking about reading at Chavez dramaturgically helps to account for the complicity of the faculty and the administration in Reading Rally Day, as well as the meaning and the power of three other rituals besides the questioning itself that I witnessed. The first of these was the "Read Out Workout" conducted by the PE teacher in front of the school; the significance of its public ritual and its dramaturgical qualities are obvious, and I am sure do not require further explica-tion here. Two other ritual events were processions. In the first, upper elemen-tary students from both Chavez and Berger Elementaries met on the steps of Santa Cruz Catholic Church, located midway between the two schools. There they were met by an actor hired by Mary Strauss, who played a flute and was dressed in a cape, a green suit, pointed shoes, and a hat. This "Pied Piper" led the students, who carried signs with slogans on them like "Readers are Leaders," a mile down the main thoroughfare (or "liminal," threshold, space) that divided the schools' attendance areas to the local branch of the public library, where he performed a one-man morality play based on the legend of the Pied Piper of Hamlin (in this version, however, it was television, and not a flute, that hypnotized the children and stole them away).

The second procession was the culminating point of Reading Rally Day, in which the entire school marched out the front door of the school and around the block, along the edge of one of the public housing projects, around the open field behind the school, and back to the Pan-American Theater. The procession was led by a police escort and contingents from the state university marching band and cheerleaders. Following behind were students and teachers from each class in the school, each wearing costumes that iconized the reading experience in different ways: Some classes dressed in costumes from a single children's book (e.g., *The Lion, the Witch, and the Wardrobe*); others wore butcher paper ponchos with reading slogans or the titles of books on them; the last class carried brooms and mops and a sign that identified itself as "The Clean-Up Detail." Four mounted police brought up the rear; local television cameras captured the event for the evening news. On the stage of the theater, the band played, the cheerleaders cheered, the students were exhorted by the PE teacher one more time to "Read Everyday to Exercise Your Brains," and the Chicano in the mural that decorated the amphitheater clenched his fist in protest and waved a sign himself that read "Ya Basta!" (Enough already!).

C. Clifford Flanigan (1990), drawing on Victor Turner's theory of ritual, notes:

Processions were, of course, a common and important form of ritual action in late medieval Christianity. . . . They were charged with a number of symbolic meanings, representing as they did a passage from one stage of life to another. As rituals, they were not considered mere gestures or empty signs, for they were believed to function sacramentally, to effect that to which they signaled. (50)

The particular procession and play that serves as Flanigan's ethnographic instance is one that survives from Künzelsau, a small town near Würzburg, Germany. Historically, that town was "constantly involved in a quest for prominence in which the neighboring town of Ingelfinger was its greatest rival." The precipitating crisis that led to the ritual of the procession "may have been . . . when the town lost the deanery to its rival; the new practice allowed it to display its [jilted] clergy with splendor and pomp" (51).

In a similar manner, the precipitating crises of standardized testing and the institution of priority status at Chavez may have provoked the establishment of the public ritual of Reading Rally Day as a demonstration to civil authorities and the city at large that "something" was being done. It would be incorrect, however, to see Reading Rally Day and its culminating procession merely as events staged to sway local authority and public opinion. Again, with reference to Künzelsau, Flanigan notes that "[the] play sought to tie together life as it was transacted in the streets with the prevailing mythical paradigms which were thought to determine that life" (51). In the case of Chavez, the "prevailing mythical paradigm" determining "that [modern, middle-class] life" was the one articulated by Goody and Watt (1963), among a host of others, and that circulates throughout bourgeois culture in one form or another: that literacy, and in particular the effects of the phonetic alphabet, is the cornerstone of Western thought.

In the case of Künzelsau, Flanigan points out that "many of the play's constituent elements were drawn from 'secular' as well as 'religious' paradigms":

This duality of traditions points to the function of the . . . procession and plays: by enacting the paradigmatic events of the culture's prevailing myth in the places where daily life was lived and daily business was transacted, the events of biblical history were presented not as events long past, but as present realities involving German people of the fifteenth century. (51)

Here is what I think the public ritual of the processions and of Reading Rally Day as a whole was meant to effect: By iconically "enacting the paradigmatic events of the culture's prevailing myth [about the power of reading] in the places where daily life was lived and daily business was transacted," that is, in the streets, that myth was presented to the school's largely unresponsive community as its present reality. The repeated equation of laziness and weakness with people who didn't read regularly for pleasure; assertions that the students "didn't want to grow up with lazy and weak brains"; the requests for parents present during the opening assembly to "stand up" if they supported reading at home; the broad gestures of reading conducted in front of the building for most of the day; the show of police force during the procession; and finally, the parade's route that pressed to the perimeter of the public housing project made it clear that the day's activities were meant for "the community to know what [the school was] up to" and take notice. But unlike the drama at Künzelsau, where "no clear lines of demarcation between audience and players could be drawn," and where "the resulting presentation made clear the patterns of actions sanctioned as determinative for this community" (Flanigan 1990, 51–52), there were no throngs of people from the community (save the students) in the streets or in the auditorium or in front of the school to be caught up in the ritual power of the unfolding drama of the day. Because it did not originate from within the community but within the school—in this situation, an arm of centralized authority—Reading Rally Day needs also to be read as a defiant "witnessing" of its organizers' faith in reading as the icon of authority that supported the claims of moral authority and dominance by the school over the community and its families' lives.

READING STUDENT RESPONSE

Since they involve the transmutation of individuals or groups from a state of crisis to a new identity or social role, all rituals are regarded by Victor Turner (1969) as rites of passage. The central stage of this passage, and an equally central and crucial aspect of Turner's theory, is the concept of liminality. From the Latin *limen*, for "threshold," liminality occurs within a temporal/physical space in which individuals or groups undergoing change, and, in the midst of transition, are neither what they were, or yet what they will be. When liminal entities (more or less) willingly undergo such rites as part of their own cultural practice, they undergo them plainly and in anonymity and frequently in the company of others who have similarly been stripped—literally and figuratively—of their previous "status, property, insignia, secular clothing indicating rank or role, position in a kinship system—in short, [of anything] that may distinguish them from their fellow neophytes or initiands" (95). Thus, princes (and Elvis), on their way to becoming kings, join the army and serve "like anybody else" (which may explain the nation's concern with Bill Clinton's draft deferment); Jewish and Catholic adolescents must "take classes," learn to memorize arcane and ancient prayers, and do "community service" in anonymity prior to their Bar Mitzvahs or Confirmations; nominees for cabinet positions and the Supreme Court put up with answering embarrassing personal questions and having their reputations dragged through the mud by senators and the media; and patients about to have major surgery wear skimpy gowns, no makeup, get body parts shaved, and aren't allowed to eat. As Turner puts it, "It is as though they are being reduced or ground down to a uniform condition to cope with their new station in life" (95).

Here, then, is the subject position that the library program at Chavez expects of neophyte readers vis-à-vis the texts of its reading programs and the consecrating ritual interrogation of the questions. As Turner (1969) further describes the position:

The neophyte in liminality must be a *tabula rasa*, a blank slate, on which is inscribed the knowledge and wisdom of the group, in those respects that pertain to the new status. The ordeals and humiliations, often of a grossly physiological character, to which neophytes are submitted represent partly a destruction of the previous status and partly a tempering of their essence in order to prepare them to cope with their new responsibilities and restrain them in advance from abusing their new privileges. (103; italics in original)

At least, that is how I believe Mary Strauss rationalized the subjugated reader subjectivity that the library's programs and the questions imposed on student readers: as temporary and pregnant with hope for initiates' eventual transmutation into culturally capitalized readers. But the hopeful realization of that change, of course, depended again on the (more or less) willing participation and intuitive understanding of the ritual's intended effect by the initiates themselves. The initiate must surrender to the power of the ritual and thus be changed.

Were this as far as Turner carried his analysis of the social function of ritual and liminality, then, as Ronald Grimes (1990) has commented, the "stranglehold of conservatism" characterizing the study of rituals as social defense mechanisms—"as the most backward-looking, foot-dragging of cultural forms" (144)—would not have been broken. Turner's insight came from his characterization of the social subjectivity of liminal individuals or groups as not only "ground down" and "marginal" but standing in opposition to, and both defining and being defined by, the structure of the dominant social order. "It is as though there are here two major 'models' for human interrelatedness, juxtaposed and alternating" (96). One consists of a highly organized and formally structured system of relations that distribute power and resources to individuals on the basis of arbitrary rules or maxims that operate with the force of self-evident truth; the other, which Turner refers to as *communitas*, is the product of liminal situations, is relatively fluid in its social relations, and operates on communitarian principles that respond, but do not always adhere to "the general authority of the ritual elders" (1969, 96).

Citing Martin Buber as his source, Turner differentiates "the spontaneous, immediate, concrete nature of communitas, as opposed to the norm-governed, institutionalized, abstract nature of social structure": "For communitas has an existential quality; it involves the whole man in his relation to other whole men. Structure, on the other hand, has cognitive quality; as Lévi-Strauss has perceived, it is essentially a set of classifications, a model of thinking about culture and nature and ordering one's public life" (127). If authorized society is characterized by its structure, the marginal spaces of the (w)hole are antistructural, that is, characterized by their fluidity, their egalitarianism, their freedom from constraint, and most significantly, by their capacity for potent social critique. Because, within their marginal status, "[f]reedom's just another word for nothing left to lose," liminal entities can afford to hold a mirror up to society—one that is particularly revealing and potentially curative of its warts, its ulcers, and its deformations. Writing in 1969, Turner described the hippie movement as a contemporary example of communitas and also foresaw the emergence of millennarianism (e.g., the New Age movement); today he might have characterized Whole Language (or at least some of its manifestations) as the antistructural response to process-product educational research.

And yet, as Turner is quick to add, "[c]ommunitas can be grasped only in relation to some structure" (127). There is a true dialectic relationship between the two at work: Without opening themselves to critique, societies grow brittle and un- (or mal-) adaptive; without the structuring authority of society, utopian communities disintegrate or fall prey to despotism. "What is certain," Turner concedes, "is that no society can function adequately without this dialectic" (129). Which brings us, after a long but necessary side trip for theoretical supplies, to the response of students at Chavez to the library and its structured reading rituals. Recalling that Mary Strauss expected neophyte, initiate readers to surrender to the ritual of her programs and be changed by them, we have to consider alternately what happened when initiates did not surrender: when they perceived that the cultural or social experiences they were being subjected to were alien to themselves, when they didn't implicitly understand the meaning of the ritual itself, or when they had different ideas of what it meant to read and why they should have done so.

When this situation prevailed, then things, at least as they were planned, fell apart: Instead of regenerating the identity of the participants and the cultural life of the school itself, the rituality of the reading programs and the consecration of the questions, became a sterile, objectifying procedure. Explaining the difference in concrete terms, Michel Foucault compares the examination process of pre-Enlightenment *apprenticeship* with the examination process of disciplinary learning:

Whereas the examination with which an apprenticeship ended in the guild tradition validated an acquired aptitude—the "master-work" authenticated a transmission of knowledge that had already been accomplished—the examination in the school was a constant exchanger of knowledge; it guaranteed the movement of knowledge from the teacher to the pupil, but it extracted from the pupil a knowledge destined and reserved for the teacher. (1979, 186–187)

In Foucault's analysis, liminal space within society becomes increasingly constricted as technologies of individuation and surveillance (e.g., Foucault's example of the panopticon, or in the case of Chavez, the monitoring procedures of the library coupled with Mary Strauss's close cooperation with classroom teachers) become more and more sophisticated. The increasing decentralization of power and its diffusion throughout modern social systems as Foucault describes it can alternately be viewed as the extension of the cognitive-instrumental structures of society throughout the school culture, so that ultimately there is little, if any, space left for alternate modes of being, ways of thinking, points of view, or lifestyles in which to be one's own subject.

Put more simply, where one might hope for at least two agendas within a school—one official, pompous, swollen with its sense of responsibility and The Future; the other marginal, mercurial, electric with untempered possibilities— the imposition of structure and official control over every movement and every moment of the day is almost—almost but not quite—enough to shut down the capacity to play altogether. When this happens, Turner concedes, "Exaggeration of structure may well lead to pathological manifestations of communitas outside or against 'the law'" (1969, 129). Liminality under these conditions does not disappear; but liminal space does become hard to find and harder still to make.

Making Room for the Subject as Reader

As might be expected in a school where control of the body is conflated with control of the "brain," the disciplinary system at Chavez was a mirror image of the system of rewards for reading. Students received one and then two "minuses" for minor infractions, which served as warnings; three minuses and they were placed in "time-out," or temporary isolation from the group; four or more minuses got a student sent to the office and placed in time-out there. (Compare this system with the one at Crest Hills, where no explicit rules—but some powerful implicit ones—were in place, or the token system at Roosevelt, where students earned hundreds and thousands of "Rodeo Rewards"—little slips of paper with a bronco stamped on them—and they could then be "fined" for infractions of rules, rather like receiving a parking ticket.) The system at Chavez is used with such efficiency that students did not usually get beyond the three-minus level; inattentiveness—the wandering of the mind from the gaze of instruction—was the most frequent infraction that I observed. Students who consistently exceeded normalized standards of behavior were tested and pathologized as a way of explaining that behavior. But the normative standards of the state and district's central office prevented unusually high numbers of students at Chavez from being designated as "special," and so students whose behavior was merely disorderly or uncooperative tended to be described informally as having problems brought on by conditions originating outside the purview of the school. Under these conditions, open rebellion against the reading programs of Chavez's library was seldom in view. But resistance did occur: The removal of mind and functionality from discourses of reading by those programs did not result in the removal of mind or issues of functionality by the students themselves.

The broadest opportunities for antistructural response in the library were provided by inherent contradictions within the practices of the reading programs themselves. In my attempt to present the logic of the reading programs earlier in this chapter, I may also have inadvertently created the impression that in fact the programs actually functioned as they were described. On the contrary, in my experience with asking students the official questions about the books they were reading, problems were the norm rather than the exception. Although I tried to be an obedient volunteer and a good official questioner, I was constantly placed in the position of having to improvise, sometimes with authorization and sometimes without, in order to salvage a situation.

One major problem (for the program's functionality) was that there was not a set of questions for every book used in the program. In those cases, I was given license to "make up" questions of my own. On these occasions, and sometimes even when there were official questions, I took some liberty to extend my interactions with students beyond a questioning mode and make small conversation with them about their reading. I was especially able to do this during my visits with a very literate group of third graders out in the portables, where the teacher was not so concerned with whether I followed procedures to the letter.

An equally problematic situation that was less amenable to improvisation had to do with differences in the way the writers of the questions read a particular book and what they held to be significant in it—especially one in a series—and the way students at Chavez read the same book and what they held to be important in it. Students were able to explain, often in great detail, characters' histories, idiosyncrasies, relationships to each other, and other relatively static information about a story's scenario, but they had considerably less success in answering questions that dealt with plot twists; greater still were the difficulties they faced in matching their explanations of character motivation with the question writers' explanations. The first few times this happened, I questioned whether the student had really read the book; after the richness of their knowledge of the scenario convinced me that they had, in fact, read the text, I began to wonder about their "level" of comprehension; finally, I wondered if backlog and time lag were not the best explanation (it was not unusual for a week or more to go by before a student was questioned about a book she had finished). Now I wonder if students were not reading these series books in the same way that I and, according to John Fiske (1987), many people watch and enjoy television series: with great distraction punctuated by intense concern for the interrelationships among characters and the atmospheric ambiance of the setting while viewing their episodic activities as essentially inconsequential and mnemonically disposable.

A variation of this problem was posed by the questions written about picture books with extremely limited text. In one instance, a fourth-grade boy, José, had read two books by series author Crosby Bonsall and "needed questions." I hadn't seen this author's books before, and I assumed on the basis of the questions in the binder that their texts were lengthy and complex. José could not answer or even begin to answer the questions, however, and after I got the books themselves and looked at them, I saw why. Each page had 10 words at most on it; moreover, the text did not seem to relate clearly to the illustrations on the page, so that even I had some trouble in trying to construct a narrative from the text, much less relate my "reading" to the official questions.

These are problems that Mary Strauss was aware of and that she acknowledged implicitly even as she explicitly upheld the questions' value. She blamed the problem on the question-writing talents of her volunteers, however, rather than on the concept of the questions themselves. If a student could answer 2 or 3 questions (out of 10 to 15), then I could give them credit for the book, she once told me. But on one occasion, when I was still new at asking questions, she also gave credit to three girls who did not remember anything of the "Clifford" books they said they had read, after their teacher testified that she had seen them reading the books together. After this incident, I began to see how the questions were actually meant to consecrate rather than to regulate or guard the bestowal of reader status and how this contradiction enabled students to evade the consequences of examination.

If students (and questioners) were able to take advantage of glitches in the questions and so make some room for conversation and individual interpretation of the texts, however, they did so primarily through the agency of the questions themselves rather than through their own inventiveness. A far more active, clever way of playing with the program was visible in the participation of one class of very bright and very resistant third graders whom I visited in the portables on a weekly basis. These students, who had caused their teacher, Mrs. Williams, to request a transfer to another school in the course of the year (I went to this classroom my first time with the warning that I was being sent "into the lion's den"), were all fluent readers and highly active members of Author Fan Club. Each student in the class had a folder with mimeographed forms in it for recording the author's name and the titles of books by that author underneath. But instead of staying with one author, students in Mrs. Williams's classroom were constantly taking up the work of new authors. Each time they did, a new form was required for that author's name and the one or two titles the student had read; as a result, the folders were filled with half-completed forms, and keeping track of who and what a student was reading was nearly impossible. For the forfeit of their token reward—a bookmark, a badge, or a pencil—these students effectively were able to read whatever they liked (and they did like to read) and also evade the agenda of their teacher and the library program.

One student in Mrs. Williams's class, however, directly refused to participate in Author Fan Club. Mary Strauss was "out of patience," she said, with Miguel, an above-average student who refused to read anything but books about baseball; but as his command of the information in them revealed, he did read them. "He reads at the fifth-grade level," she said. "He could read [children's] novels!" She and Mrs. Williams said I "was the only hope"; maybe I could use my influence on him. The two of us did, in fact, have some great conversations about Jackie Robinson and the Brooklyn Dodgers, and eventually he did come around to read children's versions of *Dr. Jekyll and Mr. Hyde* and *Treasure Island*, and he read some other books about pirates as well. But to the end, Miguel held out against docile cooperation in the library's reading programs.

Not only Miguel but other students at Chavez, mostly boys, also evaded the program by slipping into the library at odd moments to check out nonfiction books about subjects like karate or origami (in response to an uncle's demonstration of his interest in paper folding, the student told me) or books that had funny poems or riddles in them that they enjoyed. Mary Strauss acknowledged that "we have a real run on turtle books every spring" when eggs down by the river hatched. Over the two and one half months that I recorded book checkouts for Kirstin Thurmon's class, 41 percent of the books checked out by boys and 36 percent of books checked out by girls were classified as nonfiction. But these books were largely ignored by school personnel, who were preoccupied with regulating the "legitimate" reading the students did, and by teacher Kirstin Thurmon, who had several series of "easy reading" fiction series (e.g., "The Berenstain Bears"; "Nate the Great") on long-term loan in her classroom for use with the Author Fan Club program.

Many students at Chavez also found an alternative way of making economic sense of the library's reading programs. In one case I observed, a second-grade group that had just had the details of the library's latest reading program, Power Readers, explained to them (one point per picture book; one point per 10 pages of a chapter book) understood immediately that the object was to find the longest chapter book they could with the fewest words per page. They openly went about their search for such books, pulling volumes out at random and guilelessly explaining to me what they were trying to do, until Mary Strauss and the teacher called a halt to their search and explained that they were supposed to be looking for books they would like. The students listened quietly and then resumed their search for the longest books with the fewest number of words per page.

In another case, I asked three girls who were reading the same series of books if I could interview them about their reading. When I had conducted the same sort of interview with two girls at Crest Hills a few days before, those girls, who came from professional middle-class homes, were very happy to talk to me and seemed to understand my purpose in speaking with them. But when the three girls at Chavez learned that the questions I had in mind were not the reading program questions—that I was asking them to answer my questions gratis—they balked and became very suspicious. I finally had to agree to ask the program questions after I had asked them mine to get them to cooperate at all.

These two incidents, along with the demanding, expectant behavior of the students who came into the library during lunch to redeem the slips of paper that indicated how much they'd read for a bookmark, a badge, or a pencil, suggest that most students at Chavez viewed their participation in the library's reading programs through the lens of their own working-class life world. I believe that the same tokens that the librarian and the teachers of Chavez took to be signs that their program was working and that the students were developing a habit of reading were taken by the students themselves as their *wage*: as a form of compensation, nominal as it may have been, that lent some dignity and purpose to the alienated piecework labor of exercising their brains without being expected to engage their intellects.

Liminal Theatrics

There was one other, bitterly ironic way that I observed students at Chavez make room for themselves as readers, and that was through the vehicle of my small-group interviews with Kirstin Thurmon's third-grade class. Whereas at both Roosevelt and Crest Hills students seemed to have some interest in being interviewed and in answering my protocol questions carefully and often in great detail, students at Chavez were frequently inattentive, and their responses to the same questions were short, inconsistent, and lacking in elaboration; sometimes they didn't seem to understand the question, while at other times their responses seemed to evade an issue. On several occasions when our conversation strayed from the official protocol, however, these students also seemed to take an understated pleasure in ironically speaking their minds. One of the most outspoken and best readers in the third grade, Ana, told me a "joke" her uncle had made up about RIF (Reading Is Fundamental, a national, nonprofit organization dedicated to getting poor children hooked on books): He said it stood for "Reading Is *For-the-mental* [her emphasis]." Even though she also told me she "didn't know" what that meant, and she didn't think the joke was "funny," she brought it up again at the end of our conversation, when another student picked up the phrase and began to repeat it.

In the same interview, the only boy in the group, Peter (one of the boys whose reading tastes tended toward the nonfiction section), complained that there were no books on playing pool in the library, because he'd looked and asked. Later in the interview, when I asked where the students might find books on ninjas, he challenged me with an irritated tone: "There is none. You want to go ask her [Mrs. Strauss]?" A little later still, in response to my persistent questions about locating information in the library, he mimicked how he'd seen the card catalog used:

If you don't know where a book is, you could see in [the card catalog], and if you don't know where that book is, you try and [with his hand, he imitates how to shuffle through the cards in the drawer, whisking his fingers across the top of an imaginary drawer full of cards] she pushes it back, and then you shake it like that [waves his hand], and then you find what book you're looking for, and then you go look for it somewhere else.

At other times, the students were far more direct about expressing their opinion of their education. In another interview with different students, I asked them, "What do teachers do [that is different from librarians]?"

Maria:	They read to you—
Mike:	Teachers are like, let you play outside—
Maria:	They give you work, too much work to do—
Samuel:	They give you those [standardized] tests.
Mark:	Tell me about the test. What about it?
Samuel:	It's boring.
Mark:	It's boring—you get tired of it.
Mike:	It's hard; you gotta write stories, and—
Samuel:	That's the part I hate, stories.
Mark:	You hate writing stories?
Samuel:	Yeah.
Mike:	Me, too.

Maria: I do.

Mark: How come?

Maria: We're gonna write one tomorrow and I hate it. I'm not going to do mine.

Samuel: I'm gonna stay at home.

Mike: I'm gonna miss school. I don't feel like it. [*Laughs*]

Maria: No, I'm not gonna miss school.

Another round of interviews in which I asked students to sort 35 tradebooks into "groups that [made] sense" to them went more as planned. I was trying to be as careful as possible to use the same terms with all the groups I interviewed, and I used the phrase "make sense" several times with one group. One of the girls in the group, Sonia, quickly picked up the phrase. "Does this 'make sense?'" she asked me once; another time she mockingly asked after answering a question, "Am I 'making sense' to you?"

From the text alone, and without the context of students' timing and facial expression in speaking, or the tone and gestures with which they spoke, or without knowing their personal histories, much of the reflexive irony in their remarks may be lost. Ana may have admitted that she "didn't know" what "Reading Is For-the-mental" meant; but she knew it was clever and intuitively used the phrase with much effect in the context of the interview. Peter's remarks need to be understood in the context of his continuing frustration and fascination with the card catalog (I watched him try to use it several times during the semester, usually without much success) and the Dewey Decimal System, as well as his (accurate) knowledge that the library did not traffic in subjects (ninjas; pool) that he was interested in. The stories that Samuel brought up and that the other students agreed they didn't want to write were practice paragraphs for the state's standardized writing test. Maria had only one hand and was often irritable and defensive.

Mike was a special case for me, because I had worked so closely with him. We were paired as "reading buddies" in a program I had volunteered for at Chavez the summer before my study. Early into our first book, however, I discovered that he could not read at all. Mary Strauss told me that the school was fully aware of his problem and that several teachers and special tutors had done their best with him, but no one had been successful. During the summer I recorded stories that he dictated to me, and he learned to read them back and even to recognize words from his stories out of context. The following spring we began again; two or three times a week he volunteered to meet me in the library during his lunchtime to read picture books. The more I worked with him, the more I came to appreciate his keen recall of the details of social interactions of weeks before, his ability to memorize whole texts, and his bilingual joking in Spanish and English (he got a big kick out of listening to me read in Spanish). We made it through one book, and I began to tell myself that real progress was being made. A few weeks later, in the middle of another book, Mike was having a particularly difficult struggle with the text. He stopped and said, not in anger or frustration but with great resignation, "I'm never going to learn how to read. I can't do it."

I mention these incidents here because they so clearly expose the frustration that many students, and not just Mike, experienced in their efforts to obtain a formal education at Chavez. Many children, particularly in Kirstin Thurmon's class, where they were placed, I suspect, because of her patience with them, could not read. Their problems were frequently not the product of the school, but neither were they helped by its diagnoses of their problem as motivational (i.e., moral) or due to a general lack of interest in academic knowledge (i.e., due to cultural deficiencies). On the contrary, Mike, and Peter, whose reading ability was almost as poor as Mike's, as well as many other students I talked and worked with at Chavez, were desperate to get an education. Their comments and behavior also reveal their intuitive sense that they were missing something but didn't know what it was—that there were things, both declarative and procedural, that they were supposed to know about but didn't.

It is in this context that students' evasion of, and occasional irritation with, my interview questions must be interpreted. Whereas at Roosevelt and Crest Hills students seemed to view my questions as an opportunity for them to display what they knew, at Chavez the interrogative nature of the interviews—which echoed the interrogative nature of the tests students were always practicing for (when I gave Mary Strauss the protocol questions for our first formal interview to look over in advance, she remarked that she "always liked to know what was on the test")—may very likely have been understood by students as my attempt to lure them into exposing their ignorance. It is only to their credit, then, that they were occasionally able to turn the tables and reveal the indignity of the situation in which they had been placed.

Sidelong Glimpses of Reader Subjectivity

Given the quality of their experience with text-based knowledge, it might seem unlikely that students at Chavez would continue to view texts as sources of information, or reading as an activity that had any intrinsic worth to them at all; and yet as the incidents above illustrate, many students at Chavez were acutely aware of the value of reading in their lives and of the importance of books, not only as markers of social status but as sources of knowledge. As a final glimpse into the nature of their subjective relation to texts, I present the ways that five small groups of students (of two or three persons each) from Kirstin Thurmon's class sorted 35 tradebooks into "groups that made sense" and gave names to the categories they made.

These 35 texts were selected to reproduce the range of textual genres—fiction, picture book, nonfiction (at least one from each of the Dewey categories), reference, and periodicals—that would typically be found in school libraries; also included were some texts that crossed genres and groups of texts on the same topic (e.g., "Egypt") whose individual texts were chosen from both sides of the fiction-nonfiction dichotomy. I used the same 35 books with all groups and at all schools, and I also used the same terminology and phraseology in the instructions I gave in each instance. In most cases, three students sorted the texts together, and their conversations with each other and with me as they worked were recorded on tape.

Some qualification of the results is in order here. Three of the students, Peter, Mike, and Ebony, were essentially nonreaders (Ebony was mentally handicapped), while three others, Lamont (who had severe emotional difficulties), Kelly, and Tim functioned at a very low level of literacy: They were able to decode words phonetically, but their comprehension was extremely limited. A final qualification is that the artificial, hypothetical nature of the task seemed confusing to many of the students in the class. When presented with 35 shiny new children's books, the first impulse of several students was to choose the ones they wanted, while ignoring the others; several asked me if they could keep a particular book. In these cases, the other students in the small group did sort all the books into categories, and the others eventually joined them.

Even with these qualifications in mind, the most salient characteristic of these students' sortings was how much "sense" they made. As the students sorted, I would often ask them to justify why they grouped two or more texts together. In one example, Maria and Samuel debated the classification of a large and lavishly illustrated collection of myths, legends, fairy tales, and fantasy, *The Encyclopedia of Things That Never Were*. Samuel had placed the book with *Illuminations*, an alphabet book about medieval times. But Maria, who was very assertive, insisted that "these [two books] don't go together because they weren't there. They were never there. And these [in *Illuminations*] were there." She and Samuel argued back and forth, each referring to pictures and evidence in the two texts to support her or his position. Finally, Maria cited generic differences to bolster her argument: "No. Because they were never there, and that's an encyclopedia. There are two reasons: that's an encyclopedia, and plus they were never there. And this one was there, and it's not an encyclopedia." Eventually she found other books to support her argument and convince Samuel she was right: *History Mystery*, about King Tut's tomb, and *Kingdoms of Africa*, a volume about "lost" civilizations on that continent. She argued that they should be placed with *Illuminations* because all three were about "things that were there." She also found a Halloween picture book, *hist whist*, and a story about a dragon-lady teacher, *The Teacher from the Black Lagoon*, which she said belonged with *Encyclopedia*, because all three were "scary," and all three "were never there."

Or consider, in another example, the reaction of Luis to *Anno's USA*, a picture book that tells the story of author Mitsumasa Anno's trip across the United States without any written words:

Luis: [*Opens Anno's USA*] This don't have no words. It doesn't have no words.

Mark: Uh-huh. It doesn't have any words. Where would you put it?

Mike: [*Holds up The American Firehouse Cookbook*] Luis, where does this go? Make a food one? Make a food group?

Luis: Could you write your own words?

Mark: You could make up your own story, yeah. You could sort of . . . figure it out. Pretty neat, huh?

Luis: Hold it, I saw the capitol. Yeah, here it is.

Mike: Aw, man! Look [at the illustrations].

Luis: This is from Washington, D.C., right?

Mark: Uh-huh.

Luis: This is the White House, right? No—this is the White House?

Mark: That's the White House there, yeah.

Luis: It's connected to the—?

Mark: Oh, no, no, no. That's not the White House, excuse me, that's the Capitol. The White House is not connected to it.

In short, these were not the categories or the logic or the level of interest one might expect of students who had been characterized as caring only about the status that books conveyed, rather than the substance of their contents, or of students who had been described as having no "sense" of what literacy was for or what books contained. An awareness of form and genre permeated students' discussions about the books; however, it did not constrain them in their thinking about the content of texts in ways that were idiosyncratic (and bore little resemblance to the formal categories of the library or academia) but well justified.

If there is a dominant theme to be found in the ways that these third graders related to the texts, it is probably best described as personal and utilitarian. Apart from the discussion about encyclopedias and planes of reality, the books that garnered the most discussion within one small group were in a category they named "Answers and Questions." The books that Sonia chose for herself were largely chapter books (she was one of three girls who read series books together); Tim's addition of *Michael Jordan* to that category reflected his attraction to the figure of Jordan. Luis's favorite category was "fun books," which he defined in terms of their use value: "to build things, to color." In another group, Jessica first sorted out all the books that she liked but then merged her group with Ana's and retitled it "Books for Children to Use" (versus "Grown-Up Books"). I was not willing to let such a large and amorphous category go unsubstantiated, however, and asked them to explain why those books fit together. In abbreviated form, I present their lengthy, explanatory performance below:

Ana: Children like to look at the pictures, like this is funny, and, oh, look at that! . . . And this is for children because it shows how the Indians lived and how they got here first . . . And this one's about they can be good in the bus and all that instead of dancing and saying bad words . . . And this is about a game they were playing (*The Egypt Game*) . . . and it looks pretty scary. . . . And this one's about space, going in a rocket, for them to be careful if they ever do. . . . And this one's that they can be friends and never fight if they have a brother. . . . Okay, it's your turn.

Jessica: . . . And this is like, when a kid likes to read, like and *Why Mosquitoes Buzz in People's Ears*, they want to know the answer, so they read the whole book, just to get the answer.

Ana: . . . And this is about a teacher from the Black Lon—long—

Mark: —Lagoon.

Ana: —Lagoon, and it shows you not to be afraid of, not to be mean to the teacher, 'cause they might be mean to them.

Jessica: I read it. She keeps on eating the people, and burning them up.

Ana: And, this one's about the inside of your body, and the bones. . . .

Jessica: Can I read it?

Even after I concede that this exchange was a piece of "liminal theater" that was no doubt improvised in order to put me on, it is still a striking testimony to the ways in which students were able to make sense of books. I had many "theatrical" exchanges of this sort with students at Chavez during my study, exchanges that provided a sidelong, liminal glimpse of their subjective stances as readers: a subjective position in relation to texts that enabled them to make some limited room for their own transmutation into active readers and users of text-based information.

INTERROGATING "RESISTANCE"

Here is how Samuel Bowles and Herbert Gintis (1976) describe the role of schooling in modern, industrialized societies:

Capitalist production, in our view, is not simply a technical process; it is also a social process. Workers are neither machines nor commodities but, rather, active human beings who participate in production with the aim of satisfying their personal and social needs. The central problem of the employer is to erect a set of social relationships and organizational forms, both within the enterprise and, if possible, in society at large, that will channel these aims into the production and expropriation of surplus value. (10)

They proceed to explain how, in their view, schools (and by extension, school libraries) operate as one of the principal locales where people are socialized to the "set of social relationships and organizational forms" that will "channel" their labor in such ways that realize the "production and expropriation of surplus value" by capitalists. Taking a less mechanical and more cultural (but no less overdetermined) view, Louis Althusser (1971) raises the question of why this process of alienating workers from their labor seems to proceed so silently and (usually) with such little overt violence or rebellion. Althusser characterizes schools as the *primary* "Ideological State Apparatus" (or ISA) whereby ideological dispositions necessary to "reproducing the means of production" are inculcated in students through ritual practices that enact values and align behaviors characteristic not only of the workplace but of every other location of cultural activity—a process that, through its rituals, naturalizes the unnatural condition in which people act as the instruments of the machines (or offices or businesses or institutions) they exist to operate.

If schooling exists as the one experience common to nearly everyone in industrial societies, then, what accounts for its differential outcomes—that is, how is it that the children of laborers learn to be good laborers, while the children of managers learn to be good managers? Basil Bernstein (1972) and Bourdieu and Passeron (1977) argue that children inherit from their families particular cultural tastes and linguistic and paralinguistic practices, or "cultural capital"; to the extent that these tastes and practices correspond to those favored by the middle-class culture of the school, students become capitalized; to the extent that they don't, children are socialized to settle for less. Jay MacLeod (1987) explains:

Hence, the school serves as the trading post where socially valued cultural capital is parleyed into superior academic performance. Academic performance is then turned back into economic capital by the acquisition of superior jobs. The school reproduces social inequality, but by dealing in the currency of academic credentials the school legitimates the entire process. (12)

Ethnographic studies of the same period tended to support these accounts of schooling and social reproduction but extended them to detail the ways in which social class segregation within (Oakes 1985) and among schools (Anyon 1981; Connell 1977) produced differential forms of curriculums that were ostensibly the same, in which managerial practices and values prevailed in schools serving the middle class and practices and values more reproductive of clerical and blue-collar work prevailed in schools for the working classes.

In many respects, the programs of Chavez Elementary's library readily lent themselves to characterization as proto-industrial sets of practices intended to "reproduce the conditions of production" in ways that both the theoretical and empirical studies reviewed above would predict. For example, Mary Strauss's insistence that students "are not readers by nature" presumed that reading itself was a difficult and unnatural task and one with few intrinsic benefits immediately visible to the laborer, save those for which his or her "alienated labor" could be exchanged. Industrial, working-class metaphors were reinforced by the pitches she regularly made for her program that equated reading with physical exercise. The appearance of a "reading robot," the mechanical movements of the cheerleaders, and the "Read Out Workout" sessions conducted by the PE teacher at annual Reading Rally Days all clearly mechanized the act of reading as well. That the library's programs were aimed at producing habitual consumers of textual commodities was doubly reproductive, given the demands of a late industrial economy driven less by issues of production than by the creation of consumer "needs." Finally, the use of questions as a check of whether the labor of reading had been performed can be seen as rehearsing the same sort of distrustful relationship between reader and inquisitor that governs relations between labor and management.

It should be no surprise either, then, that many students at Chavez would respond to its reading program in ways that reproduced, and so socialized them to, the work habits and lifestyle of the working class (or perhaps more accurately, the working poor); some students (often the weakest academically) did seem to accept the program's promise to "build hefty brains" and participated willingly, even enthusiastically, in the program. Others, however, responded in the same ironic practices of resistance identified by Willis (1981), Everhart (1983), and Christian-Smith (1991), which I discussed in the conclusion to Chapter 1; in these studies, students are depicted as having "partially penetrated" the program's ideology and acted to resist it. Similarly, some students at Chavez used parody and jokes that revealed the indignity of their situation; they found loopholes in the program's procedures that gave them more control over the books they read than the program was designed to allow; they found loopholes in its wage system that reduced the amount of reading labor they had to do per wage unit; and three girls refused to be interviewed about their reading (to perform the labor of answering my questions) without some form of just compensation. To the extent that each of these forms of resistance effectively rehearsed the social practices of the shop, they, too, can be characterized as reproductive.

Many students, however, also resisted in ways that cannot be theorized in terms of reproduction so easily. A few of the bravest and brightest simply refused to participate in the program altogether, insisting on reading what they chose to read. Others used their own time during lunch to come to the library and check out books on their own; many others used Mary's two-book policy to cooperate nominally with her programs, by dutifully checking out a book by "their author" every week, but reserving their second allowed book to pursue their own informational interests in topics ranging from origami to Martin Luther King, Jr. In a test-driven library and school curriculum that placed no faith in, and provided little reward or recognition for, students' capacity to find any value in the act of reading except in exchange for token wages, many students consistently strove to use text in functional ways that were of use and of value to them. In short, they seemed, at least temporarily, to be out of the loop of the reproductive cycle—to be educating themselves, against expectations, for more than a life of physical labor and mindless consumption.

The students at Chavez who were able to make their own sense of the library and its texts did so essentially by finding or making opportunities within the contradictions of the library's program. For example, it was the ideological contradiction between long-standing policies of "open access" to all readers within the profession of librarianship and Mary Strauss's need to monitor the reading of students that produced her compromise solution—one "fun" book; one fiction book "at level"—the solution that allowed students to continue their own reading agendas. In other cases, there were glitches in planning, such as in the lack of questions for some books, in teachers' reluctance or sheer inability to assert total control over their students' reading (as in the case of students who simply "started a new author" to read what they liked), or in the imprecision of the quantitative strategies used to "measure out" the reading of highly irregular quantities of texts, that provided room in the program for students to make their own moves. As John Fiske (1989b, 4) would put it, these students "made do" with the resources they had; to invert the cynicism implicit in Bourdieu's (1984, 175) observation, by making a "virtue of necessity," they reproduced what has been the principal strategy of material survival of subordinate cultural groups throughout history.

Fiske (1989b) also argues that making do not only is a strategy of survival, but is, in fact, the strategy of ultimate victory:

It is material historical conditions that produce radical reform; evasive and semiotic resistances can maintain a popular consciousness that can fertilize the growth of those conditions and can be ready to exploit them when they arise, but they cannot in themselves produce such conditions. But the resistances of popular culture are not just evasive or semiotic; they do have a social dimension at the micro level. And at this micro level they may well act as a constant erosive force upon the macro, weakening the system from within so that it is more amenable to change at the structural level. (11)

The educational counterpart to Fiske's theorizing of resistance is the work done by Henry Giroux (1983), who is as critical of the structural determinism of Althusser and Bowles and Gintis as Fiske is of Horkheimer and Adorno's (1944/1993) characterization of mass popular culture. In both authors' views, it is the overdeterminism and the resultant *inevitability* of the processes they describe that is problematic, because such a stance not only neglects but effectively *negates* the possibilities of human agency, writing them off as delusions, while it constructs a static vision of the social order in which change is more apparent than real. (This sort of discourse about the "inevitability" of the industrial machine, one might add, is also objectionable on the grounds that it, in itself, inevitably works to reproduce and perpetuate the very conditions of social inequality it claims to be exposing.) According to Giroux:

The pedagogical value of resistance rests, in part, in its situating the notions of structure and human agency, and the concepts of culture and self-formation, in a new problematic for understanding the process of schooling. . . . Educational knowledge, values, and social relations are now placed within the context of lived antagonistic relations, and need to be examined as they are played out within the dominant and subordinate cultures that characterize school life. . . . Moreover, the concept of resistance highlights the need for classroom teachers to decipher how the modes of cultural production displayed by subordinate groups can be analyzed to reveal both their limits and their possibilities for enabling critical thinking, analytical discourse, and new modes of intellectual appropriation. (1983, 111)

Thus, resistance is constructed as holding the promise of enablement, not only for resistant consumers but for resistant students (and educators) who "partially penetrate" the ideology of the school and find the means to act in counterhegemonic, counterreproductive, and ultimately regenerative, reconstructive ways, if only through the erosive "wearing down" of the system.

This view of resistance and its consequences can also be drawn from the data of Chavez Elementary. Beset by internal contradictions, by the constant drain on the resources of its librarian and teachers, and by students' continued evasion and resistance, it did seem unlikely that the library program at Chavez, or for that matter, the continuation of the school's test-driven failure to raise real academic levels of achievement, could continue indefinitely. In my time there, stress had begun to take its toll on Mary Strauss's health; she steadfastly refused to run the summer reading program that had been her pride and joy for six years and even reluctantly spoke of incorporating nonfiction into her routine—an expansion that would surely have to entail some compromise in the use of questions and reading levels, in lieu of the system's total collapse.

In the meantime, a few students at Chavez did manage to beat the system and educate—that is, liberate—themselves. But while the situation there was an instructive example of how, even under conditions of extreme coercion, people can still manage to find some space to produce their own meaning from texts, it hardly serves as a model of regenerative educational practice on the order that Henry Giroux theorizes. I strongly suspect that this is because conditions within the school and library at Chavez were just too penal (as opposed to too effective) to provide liminal spaces within the day or within the curriculum that were long or large enough in which to do more than survive. In the end, considering the many more students whose hopes for educational and social advancement were effectively crippled by the well-intentioned but terribly reproductive practices of its staff, I believe that it would be premature, if not disrespectful, to celebrate the efficacy of resistance at Chavez Elementary. Moreover, given the case of Chavez, it is difficult to see how resistance in and of itself and without the presence of other, perhaps equally critical social conditions is likely to provide the sort of space or the "cover" that is needed for the reconstruction, at the level of the individual library, classroom, school, or system, of schooling. This is a critical and central point, one that I will only mention here but that, in the examples of Crest Hills and of Roosevelt Elementary, and particularly in Chapter 5, I will return to in some detail.

While the example of Chavez Elementary provides an example of the consequences of cultural repression, the example of Crest Hills seems to be an example in the other direction, one that pushes to their limits the unacknowledged assumptions of theories of reproduction such as those of Bowles and Gintis (1976) and Bourdieu and Passeron (1977) that opened this section, in which middle-class students are implicitly characterized as the "winners" of a silent class struggle and at little or no cost to (and certainly with no consideration of the suppression of) their own humanity. It seems logical—or at least arguable—to me, then, that the case of Crest Hills and the interrogation of its suppressive, as opposed to repressive, practices of cultural congruence should follow as the next chapter of this book.

3

Congruence: Crest Hills Elementary

Mark: So you can't get in the university without good grades?

Jorge: Um-hmm.

Mark: How do you know that? That's probably true.

Jorge: Because my father's at the university—

Tiff: My mom teaches.

Jorge: You probably couldn't get through with bad grades.

Mark: Somebody'd say, "You can't go on—"

Steve: Nope. Can't go to college. You'd have to do it all over, probably.

Jorge: No, you can't do it all over.

READING THE SCHOOL

Crest Hills Elementary is situated on a hill across from a small shopping district in the center of Madison Heights, within a short drive of the city's financial and business district and in the opposite direction of Chavez Elementary. The area from which Crest Hills draws its student population is geographically among the largest in the district and includes a municipal golf course and part of a National Guard camp along its southern edge. The area is bordered on the east and north by lakes and parks and on the south by major transportation routes and "green-belts." Except for the local state university's married student housing complex within its western border, there are very few apartment buildings within Crest Hills's student attendance area.

Madison Heights is one of the wealthiest residential areas in town. It was first developed by the city's growing professional class in the middle of this century and has managed to maintain its exclusivity almost uninterrupted since then. A single main thoroughfare runs through the neighborhood, along which a branch of the local public library, smaller supermarkets, and small, locally-owned businesses—old-fashioned service stations, patisseries, dress shops, and dry cleaners—cluster in two spots. Residential side streets branch from this thoroughfare and curve around the many slopes and gentle hills that lead to the lakes. Large, individually built, single-family homes with carefully tended landscapes, lawns, and massive shade trees line these streets. The boundaries of Crest Hills's student attendance area are nearly the same as Madison Heights's cultural and socioeconomic boundaries as a neighborhood, so that the school itself can legitimately be called a "neighborhood school."

Evidence of the school's status within the city and the district can be gleaned from a comparison of its staff characteristics and student transfers. Crest Hills had 41 requests for transfer into the school by teachers within the district in 1992–1993, compared to 27 at Roosevelt, and 5 at Chavez. Its teachers had an average of 13 years' experience within the district (the district-wide average is 12 years), compared to 11 at Roosevelt and 7 at Chavez. It was also the only school of the three to have more students transfer in during 1992–1993 (5 percent of the student body) than transfer out (3 percent).

At the time of the study, only 2 percent of the student body at Crest Hills were African-American and only 9 percent were Hispanic. Ninety percent of the student body were identified as white; no Asian-origin students were reported in the official statistics of the district, although from my observations that population was also represented. Five percent of all students participated in bilingual programs (where the child's native language, again from my observations, was as likely to be Korean or Chinese as it was Spanish), a negative difference of 1 percent from the district average. Twenty percent of the student body were designated as "low income," 28 percentage points lower than the district average, but this was still a surprisingly high figure, given the neighborhood in which the school is located. One likely explanation is that many students' parents were graduate students living in married student housing, whose incomes were temporarily much lower than their educational and social class backgrounds would indicate. More surprisingly, however, 28 percent of students at Crest Hills were designated "at risk" (which was still 17 points lower than the district average), suggesting high rates of single-parent households.

There was also a high level of community and business support for the school. In 1992–1993 Crest Hills had 42 "business partners," compared to 12 partners for Roosevelt and 24 for Chavez. The Parent-Teacher Association (PTA) had raised enough money to pay the salary of a part-time clerk for the library, and in 1992–1993 they decided to increase her hours. Many parent volunteers were seen in the building throughout the day, and the audience of the one school program I observed at midmorning was packed with beaming parents in business attire.

Measures of academic performance placed Crest Hills consistently among the top 5 percent of elementary schools in the district, well apart from Chavez or Roosevelt Elementaries. Across the board, scores in both 1991–1992 and 1992–1993 placed students at Crest Hills at percentile ranks ranging from the upper 70th to the lower 90th percentile ranks, in both the state-mandated criterion-referenced tests and norm-referenced Iowa Test of Basic Skills (ITBS) achievement tests. The general trend over these two years was for a slight rise in percentile rank for students for norm-referenced testing; on criterion-referenced measures, third graders scored 1 percentage point lower in 1992–1993 (80 percent) than they had the preceding year, but grades four and five were 8 percentage points higher than in 1991–1992 (from 77 percent to 85 percent). In fact, news of this rise in achievement scores along with a financial award from the state for "academic excellence" was celebrated on the front page of the city's newspaper, furthering the school's reputation as one of the best in the city.

One final measure of Crest Hills's general orientation toward statistical achievement was its inordinately high number of students designated as "gifted and talented." In 1991–1992, 207 students, or 24 percent of the school's population, were so labeled, a positive difference of 17 points over the district average; in 1992–1993, the numbers dropped to 158, or 18 percent of the population, still 13 points higher than the district average. In contrast, only 33 students in 1991–1992 and 32 students in 1992–1993, (4 percent of the student population), were in "basic special ed" programs at Crest Hills, a negative difference in percentages from the district of 2 and 3 percent, respectively. In comparison, at Chavez Elementary, 10 students, or 3 percent of the student population, were labeled gifted and talented in 1992–1993 (2 points lower than the district average), while 31 students, or 8 percent of the student population, were in basic special ed programs, 1 percent higher than the district. At Roosevelt, 26 students (3 percent of the student population) were labeled gifted and talented in 1992–1993, while 28 students, or 4 percent of the population, were in basic special ed, 3 percentage points lower than the district average.

Based on participant observation of students in the library, on focused interviews with students in one third-grade class and examination of their written work, as well as on information gained from interviews with fellow graduate students who supervised student teachers at Crest Hills, students' literacy skills could best be characterized as uniformly meeting or exceeding grade-level heuristics for "competence." I never met a student who couldn't read or who balked at certain literacy-related tasks; students from the second grade up regularly used the card catalog, and third graders could discuss in some detail the content of books they told me they had read.

In my observation of their work habits, a consistent striving for "competence" also described the businesslike attitude most students at Crest Hills took as well as the standard of performance they strove for. While students in teacher Elaine Dawson's third-grade class seldom voiced overt resistance or resentment toward school literacy tasks as they did at Chavez, neither did they voice much overt enthusiasm as a group, as they did at Roosevelt; rather, my distinct impression was that they took a craftsmanlike pride in their ability to meet a certain standard of performance on academic assignments but never viewed them as anything more than "work."

This observation was supported by responses students in Elaine Dawson's third-grade class gave during small-group interviews with me. During one session, in which I asked students to agree, disagree, or remain neutral about a list of statements, 18 of 20 students said that they liked to read, but 35 percent agreed that they wanted a job where they "wouldn't have to read a lot," and 25 percent indicated they were ambivalent; only 40 percent of the students disagreed with the statement. What could cause this ambivalence toward work-related literacy in students from very literate, affluent professional homes with such high standards and records of achievement, particularly when the students indicated positive attitudes toward reading in general? One cause may in part have been attributable to the kinds of literacy tasks required in Elaine Dawson's classroom and, from my conversation with graduate students who supervised student teachers throughout the school, in many other classrooms at Crest Hills as well. As will be discussed in more detail later, these "projects" generally required students to research a topic using one or more informational texts, record that information in accord with preset categories of knowledge on a worksheet, and then include that information in an oral or written "report" composed within guidelines set by the teacher or other external authority.

These are the sorts of school literacy tasks that many current language arts experts in the field (e.g., Atwell 1987; Calkins 1990) have condemned in recent years as boring, meaningless, and "inauthentic." And yet this sort of formulaic reading and writing, I will also point out in defense of its pedagogy, bears a close resemblance to the routine "paperwork literacy" that characterizes the bulk of the reading and writing tasks of the managerial class—a group to which a considerable majority of these students' parents belonged. Considering, then, that over many interviews these students also revealed a knowledge of their affluent professional parents' working life that was far more detailed and comprehensive than that revealed by students at either Chavez or Roosevelt, I suspect that their less-than-enthusiastic response to the prospect of reading and writing on the job was also relatively well informed.

In summary, Crest Hills Elementary presented itself to parents, to the district, and to the city as one of the best schools in the district, one characterized in bottom-line terms by consistently high levels and standards of student achievement on standardized testing measures. While that success was due in part to the experience and competence of its staff and hard work on the part of its students, it was just as likely due, I will argue, to a number of strong demographic and cultural congruencies between the neighborhood and the student attendance area, to the cultural cohesiveness of that neighborhood, which focused much of its energy and resources on the school, and finally, to strong correspondences between ways of working at school and parents' ways of working at the office, so that the culture of the home, of the school, and of the parents' workplace all aligned with one another. If the general academic program of Crest Hills lacked the preoccupation with teaching-for-the-test and the motivational efforts of Chavez, it was because it didn't need them to compensate for any perceived deficiencies. Finally, as will be seen, if its students lacked the anger of students at Chavez or the excitement about learning of students at Roosevelt, it was because they had no use for these, either: They knew intuitively that their culture and the school's culture and society as a whole were all synchronized with each other, and that under these conditions the key to success for them was to stay cool, follow the rules, and not get too out of line by challenging assumptions or authority (too much).

READING THE LIBRARY

The physical plant at Crest Hills dated from 1951, but its growth had exceeded the 600-student capacity of its 36 permanent classrooms many years ago (in

1992–1993, 869 students were enrolled), so that 12 additional "portable" class-rooms connected to the main building by outside walkways had been added. The main building was a one-story brick edifice. A long central hallway connected several wings of classrooms, which had doors opening to the hallway and the lawn around the building outside. A combination of brick interior walls, low ceilings, and varnished woodwork and doors gave the hallways a dark but warm ambiance, and the many hallway bulletin boards and display cases were full of student artwork, posters, and papers. Classroom interiors were spacious and bright and filled with cluttered but orderly assemblages of desks, bookcases, small animal cages, chalkboards, bulletin boards, computer work areas, and the like.

Both the school program and the library at Crest Hills Elementary had a long history of association with the local state university. Crest Hills had been a lab-oratory school for that university for many years, and although that formal asso-ciation had ended some years before the study, the school had retained many close ties with the university; professors and graduate students had children in school there, and many student teachers interned in its classrooms. In the 1960s the li-brary was selected by a private foundation to become 1 of 13 model school li-braries in the nation and was headed by a nationally known children's librarian who eventually became a professor in the university's school of library science. The library's interior was remodeled, and a mezzanine, or loft, was added above its main room. Budgetary constraints and the end of the model program had taken their toll on the upkeep of both the facilities and the collection by the time of this study. Its former prestige was still evident, however, in the library's archi-tecture and in its hardwood furnishings. Barbara Henry, the current librarian, was one of two assistant librarians at Crest Hills during these years of prominence. She moved to another library in the district when grant funds ran out and then transferred back when the head librarian retired. When she took over, she "moved some furniture around," but for the most part at the time of this study the library was arranged as it had been during its years of prominence.

I estimated the total square footage of the library at Crest Hills to be about 1500 square feet, making it much smaller than six other district libraries I had been in. Architecturally, the library was composed of three distinct sections (see Figures 3.1 and 3.2). One half of the rectangular main room contained the refer-ence section, most of the nonfiction books, the card catalogs, and several round work tables with chairs. The checkout and work area took up another quarter of the main room, and an area for picture books and an open story corner area filled the remaining quarter. The library's story corner was approximately 10 feet wide and 12 feet deep; it was an open, carpeted space, with two chairs in the back for teachers and aides and a low, vinyl-covered couch in front where Barbara Henry sat when she read with students. A spiral staircase next to the checkout desk in the center of the main room led to the second section of the library, its loft, which covered half the area of the main room and contained several tables and chairs, bound editions of *National Geographic* magazine, maps and posters, and the Dewey 900s (history, geography, and biography). Downstairs, a short, tun-nellike hallway in the back of the main room led to the third section of the li-brary, another back room about half the size of the main room that housed the library's collection of novels. This back room had a low ceiling and few win-

Figure 3.1
Crest Hills Elementary Library Floor Plan: Main Floor

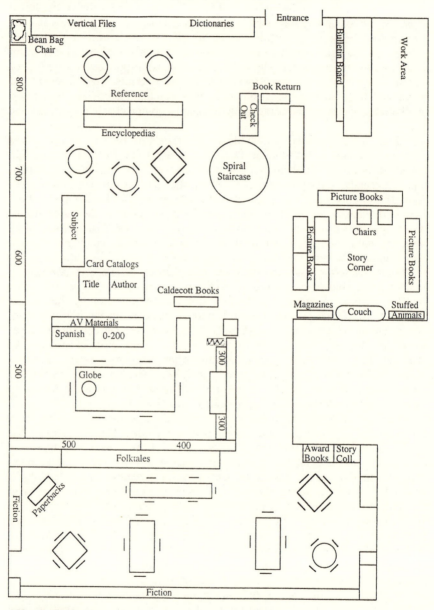

AV = Audiovisual

Figure 3.2
Crest Hills Elementary Library Floor Plan: The Loft

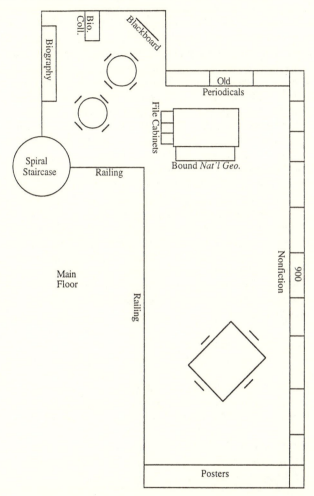

dows and was filled with tables and chairs of varying sizes and shapes and one free-standing rack for paperback books in the corner. Bookshelves lined all four walls, three of which contained children's novels, while the fourth housed the library's folklore collection.

"They Pick It Up"

Except for the inclusion of the folklore (Dewey 390) books in the fiction section, the system of text organization at Crest Hills was generally the same as that used at Chavez and Roosevelt. Large signs on the walls or hanging from the ceiling announced the location of "Easier Fiction," "Nonfiction," "Biography," and other standard sections. Across the top of each bookcase, red signs with black letters indicated the Dewey-numbered books in the that case; bookcases housing fiction were similarly lettered with "A-Br," "De-Fec," and so on.

Barbara Henry had no established formal program of instruction in library skills, and no "master narrative" that organized or moralized the library as a system of textual classification, and so there was no explicit accounting for the efficiency and purposefulness with which students of all grade levels were able to use the card catalog and find books on the shelves, more so than at Chavez or Roosevelt. Instead, as she explained, "Most of these kids pick up this stuff however and whenever," through lessons supplied by classroom teachers when students were doing research projects, from working with each other, and more speculatively, through trips to the public and university library with parents and older siblings (in interviews students told me of many such trips and in far more detail than the students at Chavez and Roosevelt).

A closer look, however, revealed an intricate network of signs, particularly in the nonfiction section. First, the nonfiction section was foregrounded in the main room of the library. Second, the card catalog, particularly the subject catalog (labeled in large red letters and housed in a much larger cabinet than the author or title catalogs), was located in close proximity (in some cases, within arm's reach) to the nonfiction books. Third, the nonfiction collection was also rather small, providing an unexpected advantage of allowing students, over many visits, to become familiar with the locations of volumes they had seen before. Fourth, there were also small laminated photographs of frequently sought topics (horses, dinosaurs, athletes) attached to the shelf above the books on that subject. Finally, when younger users had problems, the closeness of the librarian's work area made it possible for the librarian to "scaffold" (Cazden 1988) the search process for most of these children.

As for formal rules of conduct within the library, students seemed to pick them up, too. Barbara Henry explained that "by and large, because the librarian is so long-lived and the population is so stable, I just assume that students will know what the rules are." The only real policy that needed enforcement was the request that students state their business before going upstairs to the loft; because of its novelty, "Kids just like to mess around up there." In my observations, the only deviations from "good conduct" that I witnessed in the library were perpetrated by a number of boys during story times and book talks; I discuss these in more detail below.

Scheduling and the Rhythm of the Library

"I do not do half with library skills that I should," Barbara Henry explained apologetically, because "[it] would be at the expense of something else." She wondered in our interview if all grade levels needed a full year of "story time" (grades k to three) or "book talk" (grades four to six) every other week, especially in a school with more than 850 students, but then concluded that the fact that she did continue indicated what her priorities were. As well as being open throughout the day, the library was open to students before and after school and during lunch and was well patronized by students at these times. Although teachers would sometimes bring an entire class to the library to look up specific information or check out books, it was more common for groups of 2 or 4 students at a time to be sent from an individual class. Their usual mission was to browse, but some teachers, like Elaine Dawson, sent individuals or small groups of students to the library during "centers" time to work on projects or reports. When she was not occupied with a story-time or book-talk group, the librarian provided a good deal of individual assistance to students, particularly to younger students at the card catalog or to those students who expressed an interest in a specific book. From my observations, Barbara Henry seemed to know the name of nearly every student in the school (she made a sustained and serious effort to learn and use the name of each child in a group during story time), but even more remarkably, she also displayed a considerable knowledge of many individuals' reading preferences and habits, and could nearly always suggest, in a very personal, consultative manner, a book that "might be right" for a particular student.

The most sustained and regular contact that students had with the library and with its librarian, however, came in the form of whole-class reading sessions that were scheduled every other week for each class in the school. The procedures for these sessions followed a very regular and predictable sequence of events. For k-3 story time, students filed into the library in one row and moved directly to the carpeted floor of the story corner, sitting in rows on the floor, five or six students across, in the order in which they had entered the library. The librarian sat on the low couch before them, a pile of books at her side, and greeted each class by the last name of their teacher, that is, "The Dawsons," or "The Browns." Behind her and to the right were several shelves filled with stuffed animal characters from storybooks (e.g., *Winnie the Pooh*, Milne 1926/1961; and "wild things" from *Where the Wild Things Are*, Sendak 1963). Barbara Henry chose five or six students from the group to choose an animal to hold during the session, sent a student to the front door of the library with a "Shhh! Story time!" sign to hang on a hook (this was a great honor; students always clamored for the privilege), asked the teacher, "How much time have we got? . . . Good," and then proceeded to introduce the topic for the day with "Boys and girls. . . . "

There was always more than one text to be discussed during these sessions, although Barbara Henry usually read no more than one picture book. Generally, there was a "theme" to the readings, related to an approaching holiday or to a change in the seasons. Very frequently the stories she chose to read had a folktale element to them, and she was careful to bring it to the students' attention and ask for some sort of comparative structural analysis ("What other stories do you remember that have a character like this?"). The other texts either were informational and supported the reading by supplying background information about the author or setting or were stories that were thematically related to the one that was read.

Barbara Henry paused every five minutes or so during the reading to suggest, "Let's switch." On cue, students with stuffed animals passed them without hesitation and little or no fuss to the person sitting next to them, either on the right or the left; in two to three seconds, she was reading again. At the end of the story, there was a brief discussion and introduction of the other texts; then Barbara reached behind the couch and pulled out a green, home-made hand puppet called "Book Bug." This puppet was at least 10 years old, and was quite a tradition for students at Crest Hills. Book Bug would whisper in her ear, and the librarian would repeat his comments, usually about the class, to the students. Then he chose two students whose birthday fell during the month to be "bitten." The two students would sit on the couch on either side of the librarian, who reached out and shook a student's fingers or ear with the puppet. These students then recorded their names on a pad that was also kept behind the couch, and the lesson was over; students stood and filed out the door in approximately the same order they had entered the library.

Beginning in the fourth grade, students and librarian met in the fiction section of the library under slightly less ritualized circumstances. For these book-talk sessions, there were no stuffed animals or Book Bug, although the patterns of conversation between the librarian and the students followed patterns similar to story-time discourse. Again, many related texts were presented, but she read from only one. Whereas the pedagogical lesson of story times with the lower grades frequently dealt with the form of narratives, the content of the stories was more often the explicit focus of upper-grade book-talk sessions. Unlike the stories of picture books, the stories of book talk usually related directly to real or imagined, present or future problems middle class children might face. One story Barbara Henry read, *Dear Mom, Get Me Out of Here* (Conford 1992), was about a boy who is sent to live in a boarding school run by a headmaster of dubious integrity. In this story, the hero is befriended by another boy who is emotionally unstable. Together they fight the headmaster, and in the end, it is only through the detached, cool thinking of the hero that the friend, and the day, are saved.

"Tall tales" were also a featured genre of book talk. These stories characteristically use colorful language and hyperbole in their attempts to amuse; but the most salient feature of the genre is the figure of the protagonist, who is the swelled model of the Ideal Working-Class Male: physically out of proportion, always "good with his hands," intellectually raw but natively intelligent and good: a guy with a quick and permanent response to all of life's obstacles. In the tall tale that I observed Barbara Henry read, however, *Andy Jackson's Water Well* (Steele 1959), the hero, Andy Jackson, is a young lawyer trying to start a practice in Nashville. Only problem is, there's a drought and people are too thirsty and dry to worry about litigation. So Andy calls a meeting; folks have all kinds of crazy schemes, but in the end, Andy's sensible management plan prevails: He'll go to east Tennessee with his nameless Indian sidekick and bring back a well. As the story progresses, Andy and the "Chief" are confronted with one obstacle after another. These problems threaten to make Andy lose his legendary temper, but he always finds a way to manage it and the problem, too, until finally a gang of "land pirates" pushes him to use his anger to chase them away. By the end of the story, Andy Jackson emerges as the swelled model of the Ideal Professional-Managerial Male: mentally out of proportion, "good with his wits," detached and deliberate in his decision making, and possessing the management tools (including an instrumental display of temper) to overcome any obstacle: a public servant who carries a positive, can-do attitude that will take him far in life.

THE MEANING OF THE LIBRARY

The story Barbara Henry told of her own education echoed the process she described whereby students were oriented to the library and its texts in two critical ways, ways that were ultimately characteristic not only of the library but of the academic and social habitus of the third graders with whom I talked and, I suspect, of the school as well. Although she had no memory of growing up in a "print-rich environment," Barbara Henry learned to read before entering school. She knew this because early in her first-grade career, her teacher "caught her reading" a book by the window one day. She was surprised that the teacher was surprised; didn't everybody in the class read? The teacher, who had 50 other nonreading first graders to worry about, quickly promoted her to the second grade.

Barbara Henry grew up in a small town in a rural part of the state. Her family were "poor German people" from peasant backgrounds; her father farmed and later worked in a flour mill, and she said she remembered few books in her home. Her elementary school did not have a library, but there was a small room with books in her middle school. A few aunts gave books as presents, but these books, she said, made a scant impression on her. She began reading as an adolescent and read mostly fiction; Willa Cather and Charles Dickens were authors who came to mind. Like many readers—myself included—who have grown up in relative social and cultural isolation, realist fiction provided a "first look" at cultural "others." The book that (also like myself) changed her "basically as a person" during high school was *The Grapes of Wrath* (Steinbeck 1936), for, as she explained, "It was the first insight I'd ever had on how people so completely different from anything I'd ever encountered could be understood as human beings."

Barbara Henry said she was influenced more by her peers than by her parents to go to college; her classmates always assumed they would be going to college, and she assumed she'd go, too. She attended a small liberal arts college in her hometown that was sponsored by the Lutheran Church and became certified in elementary education. Her first exposure to children's literature came in a course there, and she "was floored"; she'd "had no idea all these things were available." After graduation, she moved to the city, and taught fifth grade for two years. The librarian at the school where she taught became a role model for her, and so during her second summer in the city she decided to take some library science courses. "I just adored cataloging," she recalled, although the instructor warned her and some other students that this was a serious business, not a game. But "it was just fun . . . subjects and classifications under the Dewey system. . . . There are all of these exacting little rules [about how to classify a book]."

What is intriguing about Barbara Henry's story is that while it nominally contains all the elements of bootstrapping and early "cultural deprivation" present in the stories of Mary Strauss at Chavez (no early exposure to children's literature or reading for pleasure) and Louise Currie at Roosevelt (a working-class family background; wealthier aunts) as well as a few elements of its own (no library; no parental encouragement to go to college), this librarian did not interpret her own story in this way. As her remarks about the Joads in *The Grapes of Wrath* and the complete absence of any discussion of financial difficulties in her story reveal, she clearly never identified with the poor, nor did she reveal any signs of having consciously to acquire a taste for the "right kind" of cultural objects or any sense of embarrassment or regret for having "missed" anything. Instead, she accounted for her own educational development in the same way she accounted for the ways that students at Crest Hills learn: by "picking up" knowledge as it came along.

The self-evidentness with which Barbara Henry accounted for her own learning and that of her students may indicate an acceptance of life for "what it is," but it does not suggest a point of view that lacks the capacity for self-reflexivity. Nor did I sense any evasion of questions or topics for discussion in formal interviews or any attempts at image management that exceeded normative conversational standards in our culture. Our relations throughout the study were cordial and relatively open, and I believe that her answers—or rather her attempted answers—to my protocol questions were as forthright as she could make them. But it is also clear from the data that she had far more difficulty than the other two librarians in the study in interpreting my questions about "The Meaning of the Library" and her own program goals. I suspect that to her and to the students, staff, and parents that the library at Crest Hills services, the cultural meaning of the library and its program goals were so seamlessly integrated within the "webs of significance" (Geertz 1973, 5) its users themselves had spun as to be transparent, so that these meanings therefore went largely unnoticed, or even remained invisible, to the persons within that worldview.

Under conditions such as these, the conventional would appear as the natural. A socially constituted reality, because it would be the only apparent reality, would also appear as the objective order of the world and human social relations or "human nature." Meanings would become transparent to individuals within the communities that shared their underlying assumptions. In Saussurean terms, the bond between the signifying image and that which is signified would be fused hermetically; that this bond was "arbitrary and unmotivated" in actuality might be theoretically acknowledged but practically ignored. Recalling the discussion of Peircean semiotics from Chapter 2, the consequence of a monolithic worldview such as that projected by the community that enveloped Crest Hills would be that the iconicity of the diagrammatic signs, or schema, that formed its template of human cognition and perception would disappear and seem to resist conscious apprehension. But its indices—its directive force—would be barely observable and largely implicit, which explains how individuals, through constant contact and interaction with these symbols, would tend to "pick them up." What would be foregrounded in an intact culture like that at Crest Hills, one whose primary quality was the homogeneity of its subjects and their worldview, would be its self-apparent *objectivity* and its penchant for, and fascination with, the surface rules it imposed on the world—the "natural" objectified rules by which it fully believed that not only physical reality but civilization itself operated.

Because the library had always been as it was to nearly everyone at Crest Hills, and because it seemed to work—that is, because students did pick up its system of textual organization and did seem to use the materials of the library with efficacy—it convincingly presented its system and its order to patrons as a tautology, as a closed system whose order was largely and unquestionably rational and good and culturally self-evident. While one might quibble with the application of its conventions and rules—to question, say, whether a novel based on the life of a historical figure was fiction or biography, or to challenge the placement of a picture book in the folktale and not the "Easier Fiction" section of the library—the underlying assumptions of textual classification and the boundaries of established categories would remain categorically unchallenged and would never be up for grabs at Crest Hills. In fact, one function of such quibblings would be to solidify, even celebrate, categorical boundedness by reaffirming the utility of categorical thought processes. People who thought in these terms would seldom think to make rules themselves or to challenge the idea of a universe governed by (their) rules; they would be more inclined, instead, to spend their time and energy within the parameters of any given situation studying its rules and trying to figure out how to manage a situation within the bonds of its strictures.

The second critical way that Barbara Henry's life story illuminates the meaning of the library at Crest Hills is by depicting the sort of subject-object relationship between reader and text that her program attempted to reproduce in students, one that corresponded to a rationalized view of the world. We can view this relationship in the glimpses she provided in interviews of her Self reading—that is, of herself as a reader-subject.

The first glimpse is the image of her Self reading in the first grade. The reader described is alone in this picture, apart from her 50-odd peers, and standing—not sitting in a relaxed position—by a window, reading. She is lost in the book—it's just her Self, the text, and the "poem," as Rosenblatt (1978) puts it—so that she does not even notice when her teacher approaches, observes for a moment, and then half asks/half exclaims whether she was really reading. As Elizabeth Long (1992) notes, this image of the solitary reader is the complement to Linda Brodkey's (1987) image of the solitary writer who sits alone, like Susan Sontag once did in a cold Parisian garret, and writes—and lives through her text—alone.

This image of the literate subject as detached and alienated from the world about her did not originate with Barbara Henry, however; on the contrary, it is so ubiquitous in Western civilization that it may be hard for members of the educated, modern middle class to "image in" any other literate subject position. Elizabeth Long (1992) surveys the images of the solitary reader in early Western art and observes:

These images not only oppose reading to sociability and the vita activa, but also privilege a certain kind of reading: erudite, ideational, analytic, and as morally and intellectually weighty as the tomes that inhabit these cells and are inhabited by their solitary readers. This is the visual topos of the serious reader, and, however diluted his lineage has been by secularization, mass education, democracy, and affirmative action, as academics we are all his heirs. (181–182)

Long notes that later, in the paintings of the eighteenth and nineteenth centuries, "many images of women reading alone complement those of the serious male reader/writer":

The women themselves are less contemplative than languorous, narcissistically absorbed in imaginative literature that helps them while away the hours. Although upper class or solidly bourgeois, these readers provide the iconographic ancestry for our modern conceptualizations of escapist readers of mass market genres. (182)

She concludes in a passage that echoes the divisions between "feminine" and "masculine" cultures of reading whose history I traced in Chapter 1: "Thus the solitary woman reader/writer finds her ideological place in a binary opposition that associates authoritative men with the production and dissemination of serious or high culture, and even privileged women with the consumption and 'creation' of ephemeral or questionable culture" (182). While it is significant that in both cases the idealized reader-subject is solitary, whether the feminine reader is a person who "passively consumes" popular fiction or in fact "studies" it for its informational content about social mores, is, as I also discuss in Chapter 1, a more open question than Long suggests. (Perhaps this is because in the article as a whole she is determined to make the case for the collective interpretation of literature in reading groups as a way out of the binary bondage she describes.)

In the case of Barbara Henry as reader-subject, it seems more likely that it was distanced, and not passive, contact with the world that guided her self-image as a reader. That image was further developed in the glimpse Barbara provided of her response to *The Grapes of Wrath*—a response that was as distanced and alienated (" . . . people so completely different from anything I'd ever encountered") as it strove to be sympathetic (" . . . could be understood as human beings"). Relation to others and to other worlds, in other words, came through "understanding"— through a process that was primarily cognitive and only secondarily and vicariously experiential. This relationship is underscored in a final glimpse of reader subjectivity in which Barbara Henry explained "why reading is important":

[Reading has always had] a way of giving us, if not an accurate picture of what another existence is like, at least it gives us a possible picture of what that other existence, that other being is like. . . . It gives us a possible picture in a way that no other medium can do. . . . It bridges gaps between human beings, or has that potential, and makes us more tolerant and understanding of people . . . of letting your mind see into other minds, and a way of discovering yourself as well.

One way to know the alien other, then, is not to mix with it but to place a text between it and one's Self; but the alien other is, ultimately, everything that is apart from the self, so that ironically, the more one reads and depends on reading, the more detached (and not less) one grows from the world—and the less cognizant one becomes of the distinction between the textual world as one that is possible and one that is accepted at face value as authentic. As a subject, the reader Barbara Henry depicted is a close relative to the "modernist conception of the subject" that Lester Faigley (1992) traces to Descartes, the subject who "is characterized as the final reduction of the corporeal, ethical self of classical philosophy to the state of pure consciousness detached from the world" (8). That reader-subject, Faigley goes on to point out, believes in the transparency of language as a medium of communication; or as Barbara Henry put it, that the textual world that the reader observes is "if not an accurate" then an "authentic" replication of "what another life is like," one that can be inspected at will with detachment and whose meaning, or conventions, will rationally emerge and be understood or picked up with the right tools of observation.

In summary, the meaning of the library as a collection of highly rationalized and arbitrarily collected and arranged texts is occluded by the highly rationalized worldview of the community of Crest Hills (and of Madison Heights) itself, a view that is complemented by the image of the reader-subject as a solitary figure who comes to a rational, detached understanding of the world through the seemingly transparent medium of the library's texts. Important questions still remain, however, about how students perceived and related to the library and to texts in general as reader-subjects, and it is to glimpses of their literate subjectivity that I now turn.

READING STUDENT RESPONSE

Story-Time Discourse

A detached subjectivity and preoccupation with discerning conventional meanings and patterns (or rules) of behavior similar to that described above were also characteristic of the ways that students at Crest Hills responded to stories read during story-time and book-talk sessions, of the sorts of research projects they engaged in under the direction of teacher Elaine Dawson, of the highly rationalized, conventional systems of organization they imposed on 35 books I asked them to sort into groups that "made sense" to them, and overall, of the ways I observed students treat each other.

Story-time and book-talk sessions were the principal rituals of enculturation in the library at Crest Hills. They represented the most sustained and consistent contact that the librarian had with students, and at an average of three to four sessions a day, they also represented a major portion of her time and energy, although she claimed they were less well planned and organized than they looked. Barbara Henry was, from my pedagogical point of view, a master of the form within the culture of Crest Hills, someone who had worked hard over the years to adjust and perfect her performance so that it followed as closely as it "scaffolded" (Cazden 1988) her audience's responses.

These sessions usually opened with a bid for information by the librarian. For example, Barbara Henry began a story time with one kindergarten group with the statement: "The animal I'm thinking of lived long ago. . . . " One student shouted out, "A dinosaur!" to which several others grumbled, "I knew it!" Then she offered three books they might read that day, and the students chose one. Soon after she began to read, she was interrupted by a student who made a prediction about the story; he held the floor until an exasperated girl shushed him with, "Don't tell the story!" The librarian closed the book, signaling the close of bidding. The students stopped their talking and waited for her to reopen the book.

As she continued, individual students continuously interrupted to correct the information in the text. One student noted that "the biggest animal is the blue whale [and not a brontosaurus]." The name "brontosaurus" was challenged by another student, who insisted that the "real name is 'patosaurus.' " When exchanges became heated, the librarian closed the book, and the class fell silent; she asked the students to wait until later to contribute more information. They reluctantly agreed, and from then until the end of the story, they restricted their comments to observations about character motivation and critiques of the story's plausibility, based on the raw data in the text to which the entire class was privy. At the end, the librarian returned to the subject of dinosaur names and allowed the boy with information about the "patosaurus" to report; the accuracy of his information was verified by the teacher, who led him to cite Frank, their field-trip guide, as its source.

In another session with a second-grade class, Barbara Henry gave the sign for the library door to a boy who was seated in the front row. When he returned, another boy had moved into his space; the boy complained that "it [wasn't] fair," because he had the sign, but the librarian disagreed—she said that when you take the sign, you give up your place. Three girls decided they had to move also; then two boys, Troy and Weston, decided to switch, and another insisted that one student remove his cap, because "you're supposed to take your hat off in the library." Finally, another girl in the front announced that "Shelley and I should change because Shelley's getting glasses." These bids, along with supporting arguments, reached their peak just as she began to introduce the day's book, *The Snow Party* (De Regniers 1989), when a boy, Garrison, raised his hand and stated, "I think I should get to sit on the chair because I'm so short." The librarian ignored the request and continued.

"The warning label for this book might say, 'Warning: This book could cause giggles and wiggles.' If it gets funny, are we allowed to laugh?" Barbara Henry asked the students.

"No," one student stated.

"Well, but—" she continued.

"Here's how I laugh," one student offered, and demonstrated.

"Yes, but let's try to keep it down," she said.

In the story, a farmer and his wife are stranded in their house during a snow storm and complain that they have nothing to do and nothing good to eat. The farmer has an idea and goes out to the barn. "Where do you suppose he's off to?" Barbara Henry asked. "To the bakery?" one student offered. "I think it's her birthday," another student suggested. She stopped and showed the farmer knocking at the door of the farmhouse. "Will she let them in?" she asked. "YES," the students answered in chorus. "The farmer is bringing in what?" she asked. "Chicks," all replied, to which one student added, "Three hundred."

The story continued as people who were stranded in the road knock on the farmhouse door. As each group of visitors arrived, Barbara Henry paused to show the illustration; students began to keep count. "[There are] 300 kids, if you counted the chicks," one observed. "What if you counted everybody?" another asked; she showed the picture, and students attempted to count each person.

Finally, a circus showed up at the front door. One girl observed, "I'll tell you something amazing about the parade. The horse is really little." Another student offered, "Maybe his legs are in the snow and maybe he's taller."

The comment that caught the librarian's attention, however, was one made by Weston, who noted, "It's an add-on story."

She stopped. "Did you hear what Weston said?" she asked the class. "Thank you, Weston."

Students began to make more predictions about what would happen next; the librarian acknowledged the first few but then insisted they needed to get on with the story; time was short. Finally, one boy, Joseph, who had not been recognized earlier, raised his hand and would not put it down. She called on him, "Joseph?" and then explained, half to him and half to the others, "Only because I asked you to wait before. . . . " Joseph had an involved story about the snow in

Wisconsin, where he had visited the previous winter, and began to tell about his adventures sled riding; the librarian finally interrupted with "Joseph, maybe you can tell us all about this another time. But you can really understand what these people are going through."

In one last example that is representative of story-time discourse, Barbara Henry combined several books about St. Patrick's Day with pictures from non-fiction books and an excerpt from the encyclopedia. During her reading of *Fin M'Coul* (dePaola 1981), she again entertained bids for information. She asked how to pronounce Fin's wife's name, Oonagh. One student offered that it was "more like German" and gave a likely pronunciation, which he reiterated with increasing assertiveness every time it occurred in the text. She asked what "stout" was, and one student offered, "It's disgusting." "Have you had some?" she asked. "Yes," he stated. "It's disgusting." Later in the text, she asked what a glutton was. One boy offered, "He just . . . EATS." Bids to talk were regulated through hand raising, particularly when the librarian began to ask for predictions, all of which were to the point, and quickly referenced to data in the text. At the end of the story she concluded, "And girls, isn't it good that Fin had a woman to help him out of that mess?" One boy corrected her: "Uhn-uh. It was the leprechauns," to which two more boys added in support, "Twenty-six leprechauns." Finally, as story time closed, the German expert, whose comments had been politely ignored by both the librarian and the students, conceded that "in the English language, it would be 'oona.' "

These story-time sessions suggest three important points about students' socialization to literacy as a practice and to how they responded to that socialization within the ritual process of story time. The first and most obvious is how implicitly rule governed the process was and how seriously those rules were taken—and enforced—by the students. Turn-taking was strictly observed, and the course of the conversation was extremely linear and aimed toward a clear, conventional interpretation of the story; contributing remarks had to be timely and of the appropriate sort to be considered "in play" by the class. Those that were not were called foul; those that were inappropriate were ignored.

"Appropriate" remarks—those that gained a response or even praise from Barbara Henry—were those remarks that appraised the text from a distanced, objective stance. It was, in fact, through differential recognition of those statements that indicated a distanced stance toward the text that the librarian most directly tried to shape students as distanced reader-subjects. One example of this type of statement was when Weston pointed out that *The Snow Party* was "an add-on story." More typically, however, statements receiving warm recognition were observations couched in the third person, such as the boy's comment about stout, "It's disgusting," which led Barbara Henry to verify not the boy's appraisal but the source of his information. The significance of using third person was even more apparent in other story times not recounted above. For example, in a story read during the Christmas season, a monster had trouble stealing stockings from a fireplace mantle. The students had any number of suggestions/predictions about how the monster could solve his problem; later they speculated in cold detachment about the size of a stocking and observed from the illustrations just how big the stocking did turn out to be, if they thought "a car would fit in that [stocking]" ("I think three cars would fit in that," one student noted), and "where

the reindeer were" ("I think he left them outside"). Personal, first-person statements, like those made by Joseph, were barely tolerated or were trans-
lated/salvaged by the librarian into more objective, distanced statements ("You
can really understand what these people are going through").

A second and related point is that although the floor was open to everyone, every contribution did not get the same reception or amount of attention, either
from the librarian or from the class. Any adult who has ever seen her or his idea
prevail at a staff meeting, or who has gotten a favorable response during a seminar, knows exactly how the boy with the information about the "patosaurus" felt
when he was invited to "say more" at the end of the story. That sort of recognition and control of the discourse in one's community can create a tremendous
sense of power in an individual and teach her or him that the route to that power
is through the acquisition of its capital, which necessarily includes a subtle understanding of the rules of play during that discourse (Foley 1990). As with their
skill in using the library to access information, these students had most likely
picked up and developed their oral and literate discourse practices from listening
to their parents "talk shop" with each other and with their friends, from "confer-
encing" directly with their parents, from playing "office" with older siblings and
other children from similar homes, and from having their remarks reinforced and
rewarded by teachers and during story times and book talks with Barbara Henry.

The third point, which concerns the volume and tone of voice of the students
along with their choices of words and grammatical constructions, is difficult to
convey in print form. As I listened to them speak in an impersonal, matter-of-
fact tone, couching their remarks in qualifying modals and responding to others
in civil but assertive cadences, I was struck immediately by how "professional"
these students sounded. Here was, unmistakably, the discourse of the middle-
management conference or of the graduate seminar: on one level, civil, dispas-
sionate, and to-the-point but beneath the surface, guarded, contentious, rhetori-
cally loaded, and fraught with the careful attentiveness that accompanies any ritual exchange of commodities.

At Crest Hills, then, literate practices were not only communicated as the
means to an immediate and more satisfying end; they were also communicated as
practice for the future. All text-related knowledge when used under the right conditions during story times—say, during an exchange with a more powerful adult
or in a competitive situation with one's peers—became a highly valued symbolic
commodity, which, when promulgated as an argument, could purchase certain
rewards: approval, social status, the attention of authority, and most important
perhaps, the control of discourse and the maintenance of one's position of power
within that discourse community. This was, I argue, the ultimate lesson of the
ritual of story times at Crest Hills.

RITUAL, RESISTANCE, AND REPRODUCTION

The evidence presented so far in this chapter suggests that in many ways the
rituals of the library as they were enacted at Crest Hills, in contrast to the rituals
of reader socialization in force at Chavez Elementary, were highly successful and
empowering for young readers and that they ought to be interpreted and applauded
as examples of the ritual process at its most creative and natural. Indeed, after a

morning spent at Chavez or Roosevelt Elementaries, I was often charmed by the interaction at Crest Hills between librarian Barbara Henry and students during story times and also when they were at the card catalog or just browsing—at students' earnestness in locating books, at their enthusiasm and attentiveness while the librarian read, at the scripted quality of the conversation during story time, and at the ways that everyone seemed to understand who they were, why they were there, and what to say—and could see how perhaps this was "the way it should be."

But drawing this conclusion about the efficacy of ritual processes at Crest Hills not only would require us to overlook the doing of gender that also seemed to be an integral part of nearly every story-time session I observed; it would also require us to accept the position of detached objectivity that Barbara Henry valorized —and as Pierre Bourdieu (1984) would argue, affluent professionals in general valorize—as the appropriate stance for the reader-subject to take, without further consideration of its implications. That would be a mistake because that position, the analysis above also shows, was not only some distance from being a natural position, in social situations, it may have constituted a subject "pose" that was deliberately constructed and assumed by players. This was a pose, moreover, that some students at Crest Hills like Joseph or the German expert often had difficulty in assuming or pulling off and one that others may have found difficult to sustain over long periods of time, given the demands of competing social agendas within the lives of elementary school children. It was, in other words, often a *forced* position for students to take and one that, on closer examination, many seemed to be resisting in overt and covert ways. For example, a more complex dynamic of open resistance on the part of male readers seemed to operate within the upper grades during book-talk sessions and particularly in the case of Elaine Dawson's mostly male third-grade class; but it also could be seen to operate more covertly in the reading habits of three third-grade girls in the same class who had come together informally to take their pleasure from the "An American Girl" reading series. These observed acts of resistance are significant because they extend the dynamics of resistance, which most researchers and theorists have tended to describe only with working-class students (see Everhart 1983; Foley 1990; MacLeod 1987; Willis 1981), to the analysis of middle-class students' agency as well and because they complicate the picture of these students' apparently "seamless" integration into the practices of their culture that I have presented so far in this chapter in some ironic ways.

Reading "The Dawsons"

In physical appearance, "The Dawsons," as Barbara Henry called them, were the most homogeneous of the three third-grade classes who participated in the study. There were 12 boys and 8 girls in the class, and except for one slightly overweight girl and one smaller boy, all of the girls and all of the boys were generally of the same height and build, and all projected an "All-American" image in their grooming and dress. While there was some variation among the girls in their hair length and daily costume, the boys' costume and hair were virtually uniform: hair was short on the sides, longer on top, and never out of place; all wore jeans and sweatshirts with athletic or rock-band logos in February and

March, switching to baggy athletic shorts and t-shirts also with logos as the weather warmed up in the late spring; Reeboks or other hightop, athlete-endorsed foot gear were de rigeur in all seasons. One girl, whose father was a university professor, was from an Indian family; one boy, whose father was finishing a Ph.D. at the state university, was from Nicaragua, and another boy was from Australia; the rest of the students were, to the best of my knowledge, of European-American descent.

The Dawson boys were consistently more assertive than the girls in expressing their wishes (except for the Indian girl, Emily, who was often outspoken). They also seemed more cohesive in expressing themselves, and they frequently dominated in class activities, going first to the computer work area on the mornings I observed them in the classroom and always holding most of the front-row places during story times; in their last four visits to the library, boys filled the first two rows exclusively. Barbara Henry told me she had recommended Elaine Dawson's class because it was the group of third graders most involved with the library, and I assumed that the slightly greater informality of her story-time sessions with them—more frequent negotiations of what to read and an occasional personal digression that was extremely rare with other groups—was due to more frequent contact and familiarity between the librarian and these students. In the first of six sessions I observed beginning in mid-February, Barbara Henry read an African folktale to the students about the trickster figure, Ananse, and although the students in this class seemed a little more distractible than most groups, the same pattern of story-time interaction described above also held true for them: They stayed "close to the text" in their remarks and questions, were careful in their predictions to make reference only to information available within the story itself, and remained highly task oriented and rule abiding throughout the session.

But beginning in March, the boys in this class became increasingly more aggressive in their attempts to control the agenda of the story times. When Barbara Henry introduced another Ananse story two weeks later, there was so little interest shown by the boys that she suggested other stories they might read; one, *The Seven Chinese Brothers* (Mahy 1990), drew enthusiastic roars from the first two all-male rows. This story deals with seven brothers in ancient China who all dress and look exactly the same, are named by their birth order (First Brother, Second Brother, and so on), and whose only distinguishing feature is the special power each possesses singly (e.g., tolerance of heat and cold; strength to move mountains; bones of iron). Together, these brothers work as a team to defeat an emperor who is both jealous of, and worried about, their power. The boys' involvement throughout this story was focused and energetic; they moaned or shouted at every turn and cheered at the end when the emperor was finally vanquished, while the girls sat in the back rows and tried to get a word in edgewise. By mid-March, just as the librarian began to change the nature of the story times (in anticipation of the switch to the chapter books that she would be reading to them in the fall as fourth graders, she explained to me), the boys also began to make some critical transitions in their behavior, through displays of gender that were even sharper and more direct. They made little attempt to hide their dislike of stories that had strong female characters. When they were not talking, the boys were sullen and inattentive and only engaged in discussion at the mention of some contest or game in a story, asking about what the rules were and always wanting to know who won.

Two of the last sessions of the year were particularly illustrative of these changes. The story for the day, *Three Names* (MacLachlan 1991), was introduced with a discussion of what history was and a warning that this book was a little longer than most easier fiction and that "it doesn't tell about wars or big events; it just tells about everyday life." Throughout the story, the librarian would stop to ask questions about "old-fashioned" objects, calling on girls to answer, while several boys yawned audibly. She regained the attention of the boys, however, when the subject of marbles came up. "How do you play?" she asked, asking one of the boys for advice and admitting, "I couldn't tell you all the rules and everything." After several boys eagerly explained the rules, she underscored the genderedness of her interest by telling them, "I didn't play marbles, because in my day, girls played *jacks* instead of marbles [her emphasis]." She read on, stopping a short time later to do gender one more time by asking the boys, "What's an aggie? It's *not* a person who goes to State."

The boys were more attentive to the rest of the story. They made participatory wind noises and giggled when the librarian read about a windstorm that blew an outhouse over, and she made approving comments back to them. Then, with the reading concluded, she zeroed in on the lesson she wanted the students to take from the story. "Out in the middle of the prairie, back in those days," she began, "there just was not that much that a boy or girl could find for entertainment, except for entertainment you made up on your own. . . . " Then she began to outline carefully for her listeners the sort of aesthetic experiences they might anticipate in the future from recreational reading:

Now, third graders, while you were listening to this story, I was kind of watching, because this isn't the kind of story in which the dog who's the hero saves his master from drowning, or almost gets bitten by a rattlesnake, or kidnapped by Indians; *it was more a calm, picture-making story,* wasn't it, rather than a story that tells a story, so to speak, and for the most part, I think you did a great job of paying good attention. In fact, I even saw some eyes that were up this way the whole time. I am glad you listened carefully, because some of the books that you're going to like the best in years to come, I think are going to be these books [a student yawned], *the kind of books that paint pictures for you rather than telling a real strong story.* (my italics)

This event is significant not only because it clearly demonstrates how blatant the doing of gender could be during story time in this library, but because it illustrates so clearly how the librarian tried to use gendering in order to coax these students into doing social class. For as Barbara Henry herself explained, this book, *Three Names*, was different from the books they'd shared before: Instead of "telling a story," it was "more a calm, picture-making story," the kind of story, her explanation implied, that took a "calm, picture-making" way of reading to appreciate and that she explicitly told them would be the sort of books (and the way they'd like to read) "in the years to come." This stance—one of calm, quasi-detachment and distanced appraisal of a text and of one's involvement with it—is, in fact, the same stance that, according to Pierre Bourdieu (1984), characterizes the "aesthetic disposition" of college-educated professionals. Bourdieu puts it this way:

The pure aesthetic is rooted in an ethic, or rather, an ethos of elective distance ["calm picture-making"] from the necessities of the natural and social world, which may take the form of moral agnosticism ["this isn't the kind of story in which the dog who's the hero saves his master from drowning"] or of an aestheticism which presents the aesthetic disposition as a universally valid principle and takes the bourgeois denial of the social world to its limit ["In fact, I even saw some eyes that were up this way the whole time"]. (5)

Bourdieu concludes this passage by also noting, "The detachment of the pure gaze cannot be dissociated from a general disposition towards the world which is the paradoxical product of conditioning by negative economic necessities—a life of ease—that tends to induce an active distance from necessity" (5). Consider also that both the librarian's and Bourdieu's characterizations of "tasteful" reading practices echo the "aesthetic" stance toward reading described by Louise Rosenblatt (1978) in *The Reader, the Text, the Poem*.

To produce a poem [an aesthetic experience], the reader had to pay attention to the broader gamut of what these particular words . . . were calling forth within him. . . . Sensing, feeling, imagining, thinking under the stimulus of the words, the reader who adopts the aesthetic attitude feels no compulsion other than to apprehend what goes on during this process, to concentrate on the complex structure of experience that he is shaping and that becomes for him the poem. (26)

Rosenblatt also cites John Dewey, who "says somewhere that there is nothing to prevent the man from sipping his tea from also enjoying the shape of the cup. But, one must add, his pleasure cannot be taken for granted; he must turn his attention to his response to the contours of the cup in his hand" (37). Similarly, the librarian at Crest Hills stopped frequently to pull the students back from the text and focus their attention momentarily on an object—marbles—and noted at the end that she "was watching" the students as they listened to her read—a rhetorical move that effectively interpellated or "hailed" (Althusser 1971) her listeners as observers of their own listening as well.

What is most significant about Rosenblatt's work within the present context, however, is the way the distinction she makes between the practice of aesthetic reading (which she clearly privileges) and other, "inappropriate" ways of reading closely parallels the difference Barbara Henry made between ways she and the third graders had read and enjoyed books in the past (i.e., the way they had enjoyed *The Seven Chinese Brothers*) and the ways she said they would enjoy reading "in the years to come." Rosenblatt graphically outlines this distinction by comparing her own aesthetic stance during a performance of Othello with that of "the old woman sitting next to me . . . who seemed to have wandered in mainly to rest her weary feet [and] became so involved that I thought I was going to have to physically restrain her from leaping on the stage" (1978, 80). Soap operas, she goes on to say, are also "prone to such confusion of stance." Such reading, apparently, is disdainful to Rosenblatt not only because it is "non-aesthetic" but because she associates those who read it (old women who wander in and have weary feet) and the kinds of texts that encourage it (soap operas) with the working class—that is, with *lower-class* ways of being and doing. This is why I believe the librarian at Crest Hills was so anxious to wean these students from their taste for what Rosenblatt labels "confused" and what Bourdieu (1984, 5) describes as "naive" and "quasi-ludic" ways of enjoying texts: because if, as Bourdieu also argues and Rosenblatt implies, "[t]aste classifies, and it classifies the classifier" (1984, 6), then their future professional-managerial status and privilege would hinge on acquiring an aesthetic detachment and disposition toward (textual) objects.

The disastrous implications of failing to acquire this aesthetic disposition were boldly underscored in the book that Barbara Henry selected for her last story time with this third-grade group, *The Wretched Stone* (Van Allsburg 1991). She introduced the book as a fable, a story that "people have been making up for hundreds of years, so they can kind of make people learn some lessons that they want them to learn." Then she made a bid for the students' "careful attention" by warning them that the lesson was hidden and requested that "in case anybody catches on before the end of the story to the lesson, please keep it secret . . . just sit on it." The "fable," in fact, was a heavy-handed parable about the seductive pleasures of television. The tale is told as a series of log entries by a nineteenth-century sailor who for some mysterious reason is immune to the glowing stone his fellow sailors found on an island and that, offstage, has turned his comrades in the book's illustrations into apes. Reduced to whimpering, passive beasts by their addiction to the "glowing stone," they no longer "sing or tell stories or dance" as they used to; all they do is watch the stone. When the ship is struck by lightning and the stone's glow fades, they are completely lost, and it is up to the narrator, as the surviving literate, to begin to read to his comrades and tell them stories, thus bringing them back to the light of human consciousness.

The librarian had barely gotten past the title page when a boy raised his hand to announce that another boy had "stuck [a stuffed animal] in his pants." Some of the boys giggled; she shushed them with "No visiting time. No visiting time." Another boy raised his hand; she told him to put it down, but the boy repeated the first remark aloud, "Tom stuck his animal inside his pants." The librarian stopped and scolded the boys for their interruptions, threatening to send them off to another table in the library. The boys fell silent, although one child continued to hiccup softly. She resumed reading with little student participation.

Half way through the reading, Barbara Henry stopped to ask if anyone had an idea yet of what the stone was; many hands went up. As an observer, I was not surprised by this, because the story was so laden both with clichés about the evils of television and with outright clues about the object's identity that I was certain any child of five could have guessed what "the glowing stone" was. At the end of the story, she asked, "Let's hear some of your ideas." The students' ideas were: "Never go to strange places." "Never pay attention to things that are weird." "Don't take things from places if you don't know what they are."

She tried again: "Listen again to the description. And what comes from the strange surface? A glowing light? And what happens to the men . . . ? It's kind of hypnotizing . . . and after a while they start forgetting their singing, their stories. . . . Ladies and gentlemen, what do each of you have in your home that has a smooth, glasslike surface . . . ?" The students suggested a window, a table, and a marble. She said, "And sometimes, if I were to come visit your house, I might see some people sitting around it." The students repeated windows, stained glass,

and a table. "Not talking to each other, but just looking at the strange light coming from this . . . "

"Whatever," one boy said. Finally, she asked, "What does your mother sometimes tell you that you are spending too much time—" And several students
shouted, "TV!" But then another student stated flatly, "That couldn't be a TV."
She took a vote, and there were several other students who could not (or, I wonder in retrospect, *would* not) see the analogy or take "Mr. Van Allsburg's message" for what the librarian said it was.

I was careful not to comment throughout these events, but my sympathies
were with Barbara Henry as I watched, and I wondered, as no doubt she did, what
had made these children, the boys especially, who had formerly always been so
cooperative during story times, now resist her attempts to guide their reading at
almost every turn. I wondered if their rude remarks and behavior had been staged
for my tape recorder, but actually the students paid very little attention to the
machine or to me. I never saw them look at it or at me as if to gauge any reaction, and although some stunts, like the stuffed-animals-in-the-shorts caper, and
the coughing and muttered sounds, seemed designed to provoke some notice deliberately, most seemed to be spontaneous reflections of a true attitude change on
their part, and one that I believe had nothing to do with their personal affection
for Barbara Henry as an individual.

Perhaps the simplest explanation would be that at the end of the year the boys
had outgrown the story-time format—that is, that they began to see sitting on
the floor, listening to a story book, as a challenge to their developing "male"
identities—and were expressing this by acting the role of "bad boys." In support
of this thesis, Mary Alice Wheeler (1984) also noticed changes in the attitudes of
her son and two other boys toward reading once they had entered the fourth grade.
She and the mothers of the other boys were very concerned about this at first,
but then Wheeler noted that other changes in these boys' lives were also taking
place and that, in fact, they were reading all the time—for example, cereal boxes,
the sports page—although they were no longer reading as many library books.
Physically, they had developed to a point where they were strong and agile
enough to play sports with some skill and were quite taken with their new-found
capacities. Intellectually and emotionally they were increasingly able to sit and
concentrate for extended periods of time on televised sporting events with their
fathers, and they were "more interested in the rules of games and learning their
jargon" (613). She observed that socially

being a fourth grade boy is tough in a number of ways. You cannot be just a little kid
anymore and you have got to be recognizably a boy. You have to dress like other
boys, wearing sneakers, sweatshirts, and jeans . . . .You have to move and gesture
like a boy . . . .You have to talk tough. You have to at least appear to like things that
boys like (such as sports) and dislike things that boys are supposed to dislike (such
as reading). (609–610)

At the same time, the mothers also began to notice that "the boys' fathers are in
technical, business, and educational occupations that demand reading. All of
these men read at home, but the forms of reading are almost exclusively work-related or for information. These reading materials are chosen and may be pleasur-
able to the men, but are essentially instrumental and in the domain of work.

This pattern is striking" (613). Wheeler concluded that "the variety of types as well as the meaning of the boys' reading is beginning to strikingly resemble the patterns of their fathers," and that the mothers saw "their sons being socialized to a male's view of literacy, a notion of literacy different from their own" (614).

Mary Alice Wheeler's explanation of the changes in her subjects' literacy practices, then, provides a parsimonious, developmental way to account for the third-grade boys' resistance—if not outright rejection—toward the literary experience their school librarian held out to them, as the painful and inevitable adoption of "a male's view of literacy." But this explanation contradicts the argument about "doing gender" (West and Zimmerman 1987) that was made in Chapter 1, because to accept it, we must do gender ourselves and accept Wheeler's naturalized dichotomization of "male" and "female" literacy. Moreover, exclusively focusing on gender identity as the issue here obfuscates another point made in the discussion of Bourdieu (1984) above and in Chapter 1, that what was at stake for the librarian in these lessons was not the students' future comfort with their status as women and men but their acquisition of professional-managerial tastes and aesthetic dispositions toward reading.

Instead, I wonder whether this well-intentioned concern on the librarian's part was not misguided and whether the boys' doing of gender in this case might not be interpreted as a justifiable (albeit rude) reaction to her prescriptive demonstrations of what the class's future preferences should be in the way of recreational reading. For it seems to me that the kind of isolated, subjective gaze ("the kind of books that paint pictures for you rather than telling a real strong story") and "calm," aesthetic appraisal of texts that she was advocating as *entertainment* must have looked an awful lot like *work* to boys who were already beginning to anticipate, through the projects their teacher was assigning as well as their own observation of their parents' professional literacy, the kind of intellectually detached reading and writing they would do in their future careers.

I am suggesting, then, that the type of "gaze" or detached aestheticism the librarian privileged is also the hallmark of the professional's vision—of "male literacy," as Wheeler calls it. This argument, as any student of Louise Rosenblatt is aware, directly contradicts the difference Rosenblatt insists on making between aesthetic (i.e., artistic) and efferent (i.e., informational) reading; but at the same time, Rosenblatt also concedes that the two exist on a continuum, acknowledging that the two must have not only points of contrast but also points of similarity. What they share—and in this case, I believe it is far more important than how they differ—is what Bourdieu calls the social habitus of the middle class: a detached, objectivized way of separating oneself as a subject from the objects of the world (including one's own objectivized feelings), with the end goal of better managing them.

What these boys were resisting was not an aesthetic stance toward reading per se but the librarian's suggestion to them that from now on not only library story times but ultimately all of their leisure reading experiences must take place from the same detached, objectivizing perspectives that they and their professional-managerial parents applied to their work. This way of reading, again, is not a natural, relaxed way of seeing at all but a constrained and highly rationalized intellectual pose that takes hard work to achieve and a good deal of energy (at least in my experience) to sustain; moreover, it is very isolating socially. In reality and in opposition to this suggestion, the sorts of recreational activities these boys anticipated enjoying were probably similar to those enjoyed by their professional fathers who used their minds to earn a living—activities characterized by an alert and intense emotional participation within, and not apart from, a sphere of physical action, such as following and watching spectator sports live or on television among a circle of friends. These are the kinds of ludic, communal activities of identification and human reattachment that release the tensions and constraints built up in an otherwise extremely competitive, isolating, and frequently dehumanizing social order like the modern "office." And these were also the kinds of communal reading activities the boys had reveled in before the librarian tried to guide the class in a new direction.

This account of middle-class boys doing gender as a way of interrupting their librarian's hegemonic vision of their future reading preferences begs the question, What about the girls in this class? Did they also find ways to resist, but in less overt and observable ways, or was their seeming noninvolvement in the episodes described above an indication of their tacit willingness to go along with the librarian, or is there another explanation that completely escapes my analysis? I admit that perhaps because of my own doing of gender I have very little data from this study that suggests a clear explanation. In my observations of and interviews with Elaine Dawson's class, I never saw a girl join the boys in their pranks or argue or behave in any way to express resistance or discontent with the school or library program. I did, however, interview two girls in the class who were reading books from the same "An American Girl" series that three girls at Chavez had been reading.

"An American Girl" is designed around the adventures of four nine-year-old white girls who each live in different periods of American history: 1774, 1854, 1904, and 1944 (a fifth, featuring an African American protagonist during the Civil War, was added after the study); there are five books per protagonist. Each book at the time cost $5.95 in paperback and consists of the following: an introductory portrait gallery, in which all the characters of the story are introduced; a short, six-chapter story of abandonment by their fathers, trial, and reunion with home and loved ones, which virtually diagrams the plotline of mid-Victorian "woman's fiction," as Nina Baym (1978) describes it; and a concluding appendix that gives a historical overview of life in the United States during that period of time. These books are part of a larger marketing scheme by their publishers, which includes a magazine and a collection of (at the time) four period dolls, each modeled after the protagonist in one historical period. An ad at the back of each book shows the dolls and invites readers to write for a catalog of "An American Girls Collection" and to nominate a friend ("And send a catalog to my friend") as well.

Considering the gendered nature of these students' experience in coming to these texts, the clearly mid-Victorian ethos of the books themselves, and the considerable amount of research and theory about the sociological and historical impact of popular fiction to date (Armstrong 1987; Baym 1978; Christian-Smith 1991; Davis 1987; Douglas 1977; Lukács 1920/1971; Tompkins 1932; Williams 1977), we might expect to see these girls completely enamored with the series' project and caught up in the plots and the dilemmas of the hero(ine)s. But rather than fully instantiate the historical image of the "languorous" middle-class female reader who is "narcissistically absorbed in imaginative literature" (E. Long 1992, 182), and so, presumably, who is unconscious of its ideological control, these girls' accounts of their reading complicate that image in several ways.

First, these girls originally found the dolls to be an enticing part of the series' overall project, although one girl, whose grandmother had purchased one of the dolls for her, complained that because they were so expensive, "You really aren't allowed to play with the dolls, just look at them." Second, they clearly grasped and were able to articulate the overall scheme of publication and plot construction. They explained to me that there were four different protagonists, each of whom lived in a different historical period (and they knew the dates of each period); they understood the significance of the three-part family portrait/story/historical overview design of each book; and they saw how parallel the plots of each book were ("This one has a fire, and this one has a tornado"), indicating that they were also aware of the mass-produced, as opposed to "artistic," "authentic," nature of the stories themselves.

But most significantly, what stands out about the ways these two girls described their reading of this series is the conscious attention they paid to the historical details about life in each period that the books' stories described and especially to the historical overview contained in their appendices. Instead of naming the trials and tribulations of the stories' protagonists as what drew them to the books, both girls said the appendices of the books were their most interesting part. They said they had never read history before, and found it very interesting, and they were able to tell me a great deal about what they had learned about life in different historical periods.

These two girls' accounts of their reading the books of "An American Girl" may provide at least a tentative explanation, then, of why the girls in Elaine Dawson's class did not join the boys in resisting Barbara Henry's attempts to socialize them to enjoying fiction with a detached aestheticism, because in some critical ways this more restrained reading stance was one that they were already enjoying and were familiar with. However, these two girls' practices and the way of reading Barbara Henry promoted also differed in one apparent way: While Barbara Henry (along with Louise Rosenblatt [1978] and Pierre Bourdieu [1984]) might describe the pleasure of leisure reading as deriving from an aesthetic appreciation of the form, as opposed to the substance, of the (textual) object under appraisal, the pleasure of these girls was taken not only from their comprehension of the series' overall form; it was also largely derived from their interest in the information in the text—information not about the life problems of the stories' protagonists and how they solved them but information about the historical contexts—"facts"—in which the stories were embedded.

It is arguable, then, although I concede that it is also arguable that insufficient evidence exists to do more than speculate here, that in the case of these two girls the primary strategy for resisting ideological interpellation by the "An American Girl" series was to assume the same "detached" stance with regard to fictional texts that the boys in their class had found so objectionable. Ironically, it seems that one gender's means of resistance may have been viewed by the other gender as the instrument of its control, apparently because what the girls in this class viewed as a present and future leisurely pursuit—the detached comprehension and appraisal of information—the boys regarded as more characteristic of their present and future labor. How can this be? In the late twentieth century and in a school that served the children of the professional-managerial class, surely all the students, boys and girls alike, were hearing the same messages about the need to work hard in school so they could get "a good job" later on; surely the girls as well as the boys expected to build their lives around careers as doctors, lawyers, college professors, or senior managers, and therefore surely both girls and boys should have rejected detachment as an emotionally satisfying leisure-time activity. I thought so; and as a result, I was surprised when in our closing interview Elaine Dawson volunteered that many girls in the class really were not all that interested in going to college and that many believed they would "marry up or even "—that is, marry someone whose family already "had money" or whose prospects of making money were excellent—and so enter or remain in the upper middle class that way.

In summary, I have tried to show in this section that students at Crest Hills were not merely passive participants in a regime of literacy that, due to the congruence of the practices of home, school, and library, presented them with no opportunity to resist or negotiate the terms of their socialization to professional-managerial ways of reading and using texts. On the contrary, the boys in Elaine Dawson's class could be very vocal and effective in interrupting the agenda of the librarian, while at least two girls in the same class concentrated on the informational side of the books they were reading. But it should also be clear by now that by repudiating detachment as a suitable leisure-time activity the boys in Elaine Dawson's class were also reaffirming important separations between the objectivity required for work and the subjectivity demanded by play within professional-managerial contexts. Moreover, while the two girls' quiet use of fictional texts as a source of factual information may demonstrate their capacity to follow their own agendas when they read, such an activity never really challenged the gendered nature of their reading practices, because although these girls were reading fiction "efferently" (Rosenblatt 1978), they were still reading fiction and doing so within the confines of a series of books that could have been subtitled "A Primer of Victorian Feminine Subjectivity."

Finally, it should be noted how comparatively rare it was to observe students at Crest Hills challenge the system there, either openly or covertly, and how much more often students did read and write and speak and act in ways that conformed to the wishes and expectations of peers and adults. The two examples cited above, of boys' resistance during story time and of two girls' ways of reading a fictional series for its historical content, were in fact the only two examples of anything approaching resistance or contradiction that I observed in my four months of near daily observation. In the end, then, what kept these bright, resourceful children so steadfastly in line with the agendas of home, school, and library? In the final section of this chapter, I provide examples of the interpersonal and cognitive consequences of cultural congruence as it is practiced in Madison Heights and at Crest Hills, followed by an analysis of its enforcement by means of an extraordinary, and yet ubiquitous, ritual process: "talk," whose lesson is reinforced through cautionary examples of what happens to people who fail to get ahead because they have failed to go along.

INTERROGATING "CONGRUENCE": GOING ALONG TO GET AHEAD

Going Along

To reiterate a point made earlier in this chapter, the principal mode of signification at Crest Hills is, in Peircean terms, the "symbol," a sign created entirely by human convention that is characterized by its rationality and rule-governed, or principled, nature. The cognitive lesson that guides teaching and learning at Crest Hills is one about how to abstract principles from a body of data (to reify the data, in other words) and then reapply those principles at a later date in one's own work or to one's own behavior.

Concrete evidence of these processes and applications of reified knowledge was in sight everywhere at Crest Hills. Barbara Henry regularly peppered her talk about the folktales she read during story times with references to character "types," plot "elements," and her own "commonsense" explanation of their origin and cultural function. She was usually careful to identify the "type" of folktale—myth, fable, or tall tale—being read that day and was lavish in her praise and in the attention she paid to students who made similar observations or comparative references to other folktales they'd read. Like the formalist tradition from which her analyses, however indirectly, were derived, the types and categories she made reference to were presented not as hypothetical constructs but as factual realities—as though these genres and character types were the mere reflections or shadows of a more certain world of forms.

That students had to some extent internalized the principle of formal categorization was evident not only in the frequency (about once per session) with which primary grade students were able to comment with or without solicitation about issues of type and genre but in the formal strategies and ease with which Elaine Dawson's students managed the texts I asked them to sort during small-group interviews. As with students at Chavez and Roosevelt Elementaries, I conducted each book sort with groups of two or three students chosen by the teacher, at a table in the classroom rather than in the library. My instructions were the same for all groups and schools. Spreading the books across the table in random order, I told each group that they were to "sort the books into groups that make sense to you" and that when finished, I would ask them "to give each group a name."

These students' sortings were strikingly different from those at Chavez. Knowing students at Crest Hills to be bright and academically successful, and having by this point observed many involved discussions about the meaning of stories during story times in the library, my strong expectation was that the students would either create imaginative categories of their own or would categorize the books by academic subject, for example, "history," "poetry," "folktales," "reference books," or by some combination of the two with some library categories (e.g., "easier fiction") thrown in for good measure. I was very surprised, then, when the first small group decided to sort the books alphabetically by title, then by author, and then by size. I was surprised by the seemingly superficial criteria these students used to sort the books and decided that the results were a fluke. But the third group also sorted the books initially by size, then by alphabetical order, and only when pressed ("How *else* might they make sense?"), by library/subject categories. Students in another group created a "thick book" category and also "talked" alphabetization, and one high-status male student in yet another group (I am defining status here as a function of grooming, size, and verbal assertiveness as I observed it in other interviews and during students' time in the library—observations that were corroborated in discussions with the class teacher), where the students chose to group certain books apart from each other, also insisted on initially ordering his books by size.

Looking at these seven groups' sorting strategies in isolation, it might seem that there was no common pattern or thread of logic running through each. But when the strategies that students at Crest Hills used are placed against the background of the groupings made by students at the other two schools, one very distinctive difference stands out. Whereas at the other schools students' sorting patterns were situated in contexts of personal interest or classroom instruction, the strategies students at Crest Hills used were largely abstract and noncontextual—that is, with the possible exception of a single group, they were preexisting strategies independent of the specific texts I asked the students to sort, not strategies created in response to the task and those particular texts. In other words, students at Crest Hills used rule-driven criteria to make sense of the texts before them, rather than take a more contextualized, pragmatic approach to the task, one that would have required them to derive maxims and justifications for their decisions, as was the case with students at Roosevelt and Chavez. Using a rule rather than deriving a maxim implies that the strategy was selected prior to the organizational action of placing the books in groups. So it can be said that students at Crest Hills did not "make sense" of the texts; they "imposed sense" on them, by selecting an organizational strategy and applying it—and frequently with a rigor and consistency that far surpassed the homegrown maxims used at Chavez and Roosevelt. In short, the highly formalized and abstract quality of the strategies students at Crest Hills used supports Bourdieu's (1984) work on the relationship between class and cognition.

At Crest Hills also, however, transcripts of each sorting session suggest that the doing of social class was more complicated than it first appears and that it might not have been accomplished so regularly were it not for the doing of gender and, on occasion, for the doing of hierarchy as well among students in the class. In contrast to the other two schools, and in keeping with sound management practices, groups at Crest Hills *planned* their strategies as they began to sort the books, discussing whether size or alphabetical order or genre should be the determining rule. During these sessions, as in the one reported above, the boy in the group with the highest status always took the lead, while other students either deferred or tried to negotiate with him; moreover, the dominant boy's preferred strategy usually had to do with form (genre, size, alphabetical order) as opposed to content, that is, subject matter. For example, in one group composed of a high-status boy, a boy who was younger and smaller, and a girl, the high-status boy took the lead and began to sort the books by size, but the other boy argued that subject order made more sense. The girl in the group followed the high-status boy's lead at first, but when the smaller boy complained and refused to cooperate, they compromised and decided to sort the books by title. Within other groups, although the strategy proposed by the highest-status boy in each

group did not always prevail, it was clearly the one with which others were required to negotiate. As a result, the variety of ways that students in this class
might otherwise have sorted the books was restricted by the attention they paid
to gender and within-class status.

There is other less tangible but equally revealing evidence that students' out-
looks and behavior were governed by a strong consideration for the rules of social and intellectual convention. Although I originally had considerably more and
freer personal access to students at Crest Hills than at Roosevelt, our relations
remained very distant and businesslike throughout my study, in contrast to relations with the students at both Chavez and Roosevelt, where both boys and girls
regularly hugged me in greeting or after some personal exchange. A favorite
piece of schtick for me as I walked to the library with an interview group was to
tell students to "walk this way," then hunch my back like Quasimodo and drag
one leg down the hall. Students at Roosevelt got the joke immediately, and we
giggled and hunched down the hall together. But when I tried the same gag at
Crest Hills, the students were not amused; they seemed embarrassed and increased
the distance between me and them. In the end, I never really broke through the
barrier of "civility" that separated myself as an outsider from these students or
felt that I had established a personal relationship with any student at Crest Hills,
as I had with many students at Chavez and Roosevelt. I came to feel that I, too,
had been objectified: that I had been placed in a category, that of "researcher" or,
as the tag I was given to wear read, "University Graduate Student," and was being treated accordingly.

The attitudes and work habits of students at Crest Hills as I observed them
complete two library projects, a comparative study of two animals and a biography report, also revealed much about their capacity and regard for regularity and
convention. In the animal study, which was largely completed by the time I began to gather data, students chose two wild animals that were different but also
closely related (e.g., the Arctic fox and Siberian husky; bees and wasps) and then
recorded information about them on a semantic map worksheet; then they wrote
a two-page report that included an introductory paragraph, paragraphs on their
similarities and differences, and a summative concluding sentence. Obvious similarities in wording and organization indicated clearly that Elaine Dawson had
scaffolded a great deal of the exercise for the students. Although there didn't seem
to me to be much personal investment in the writing, in interviews with the
students they were quite proud of their accomplishment. The process had been
long and involved for them, and it was the most writing many had done to date;
many spoke of how hard they had worked on this report.

For their second project, students were to make a poster or other audiovisual
aid to present in an oral report about a famous person whose biography they had
read. As with the first project, Elaine Dawson gave the students worksheets with
topics about the person to be investigated, and the students completed these
sheets during "library centers" time. In the groups that I observed, usually half
the students (mostly the girls) chose a book from the biography section of the
library, which was housed in the loft, and completed the questions as best they
could. The other half (usually boys) took books off the shelf (of sports figures,
mostly) but did not pay much attention to the texts, filling in blanks on the
worksheets from their own knowledge of the famous person (in interviews they

admitted that they picked people they already knew a lot about for this project). I missed the actual oral reports, but in interviews, the students laughed about each other's presentations; their teacher had told them that they could give "pay backs" to anyone who heckled them during their presentations, and they indicated they had had a good time trying not to get caught in the act of screwing up someone's report and of trying to ignore students who teased them during their time on stage.

In short, and as I noted at the beginning of this chapter, these projects typify many of the attributes of traditional classroom literacy tasks that the experts (e.g., Atwell 1987; Calkins 1990) regularly vilify as lacking personal relevance or "voice," encouraging formulaic writing, damaging students' self-images, and generally trouncing on children's capacities for creative self-expression. Such criticisms, however, overlook the future world of work in which students will read and write instrumentally (see Odell and Goswami 1985, for example), a world that, while it pays some lip service to creativity and innovation, more frequently prizes the worker who is able to crank out informational reports with efficiency, who writes freely in a predictable, conventional organizational style, whose rhetorical register is distanced and "objective" (that is, personally uninvolved) and whose work remains well within the mainstream; work that will distinguish itself by making few substantive ripples—and had better not make any waves—within the corporate culture; and writing for reading by important people that conveys that its author's interests are the interests of the persons who read it.

Getting Ahead

Early sociolinguistic studies of children's literacy development theorized that the achievement problems of "nonmainstream" school children could be traced to incongruence between the discourses of home and school and not to any deficiencies in the expressive quality of children's home discourse (Cazden, John, and Hymes 1972; Labov 1972). Fine-grained comparative analyses of home and school patterns of discourse repeatedly demonstrated that middle-class teachers consistently misinterpreted nonmainstream children's ways with words and consequently responded in ways that confused and alienated their students (Boggs 1985; Heath 1983; Philips 1983). The general solution sociolinguists proposed was to reconstruct the discursive patterns (the "participation structures") of classrooms to make them more congruent with students' cultures, on the premise that the more transparent the medium of language could be made to seem, the less of a barrier it would be to students' cognitive understanding and subsequent academic achievement (Cazden 1988; Jordan 1985).

Crest Hills, therefore, makes an intriguing test of that premise, because as a "best-case" scenario of discursive/cultural congruence, it is the virtual opposite of the "worst-case" scenarios in which most of the seminal sociolinguistic research in schools has been conducted to date. It serves as a test case, in other words, of (professional middle-class) researchers' unexamined assumptions about the desirability of discursive and cultural congruence—that is, about the necessity of a unified worldview as the prerequisite of educational achievement. This is because the apparent success of Crest Hills's educational program is attributable to the shared expectations of teachers and parents and of shared ways of using language to delineate and construct an objectified view of the world. The discourse practices of the library can be seen not only consistently to guide students to abstract information from text and use it in decontextualized ways that are congruent with the measures of standardized testing (see Heath's [1983] study of "mainstream" literacy) but also to rehearse the "educated," professional-managerial discourse their parents need and use to "get ahead" at work and that presumably—because middle-class parents know the value of "educated" language—is modeled and encouraged at home. The careful overlap, or layering, of these discursive patterns can be seen as effectively constructing a transparent psycholinguistic (and ideological) template from which individual subjects are stamped.

After spending only a few days at Crest Hills observing how seamlessly these discourses were integrated, then, one could come to believe that the productivity and general harmony of life at Crest Hills were unconflicted and were largely the natural result of a good match between the cultures/discourses of the school and the students' homes; that way one could also believe that the same principle of cultural/discursive congruence, if applied, for example, to the situation at working-poor Chavez, would produce a similar result. But this solution neglects to consider that the condition by which the effect of harmony is achieved is also the same condition by which the remarkable homogeneity in students' position within the text of the school and library is constructed and enforced. At Crest Hills, discursive congruence is the principal apparatus by which "the role of language in the construction of the subject" (Belsey 1980, 67) escapes notice—and by which readers, believing all the while that they are "free" to "be themselves" are guided to become interchangeably normal, that is, just like everybody else. For not only are there appropriate (i.e., normal) ways to speak and read and write at Crest Hills; there are clearly also appropriate ways to think and appropriate ways to act. In my interviews with Elaine Dawson's class, I was regularly surprised at the degree to which students there had not only the same ways with words but the same ways with dress, the same tastes in recreation, and remarkably similar game plans for their futures.

It also seemed that the congruent texts of home, school, and library that constructed the attitudes and beliefs of students at Crest Hills also taught them that there was only one path to a prosperous future. But this observation may overestimate middle-class parents' confidence in their ability to control these texts and to direct their children to a prosperous future, for as Barbara Ehrenreich (1989) has also observed, "It is one thing to have children, and another thing . . . to have children who will be disciplined enough to devote the first twenty or thirty years of their lives to scaling the educational obstacles to a middle-class career" (83). As members of the *middle* class, one whose really very tenuous social position, according to Pierre Bourdieu (1984), depends almost entirely on the acquisition of educational, as opposed to inherited, cultural capital, affluent-professional parents sense not only that everything is to be gained by their children through education but that without the right kinds of educational experiences—the kind they believe worked for them—all will most certainly be lost.

How to convey this notion to one's children is the problem, according to Ehrenreich, that every affluent-professional parent and educator faces. Their first

impulse, perhaps, is to make things "tough" for kids, to make them study demanding and largely irrelevant subjects for the "mental discipline" they build;
but in a materially affluent culture, where kids know that rebellion and dropping
out (at least temporarily) are survivable options, adults know that kind of lever-
age isn't available to them, at least directly. The alternative strategy parents and
educators resort to, claims Ehrenreich, is "talk," or a "permissive relationship"
between adult and child that becomes a "ceaseless, intense dialogue" of unending
discursive rationalizations in the course of which "the child . . . has little inner
space to retreat to" (90).

In an interview with Elaine Dawson about how students see their future, she
reported that while there was a good deal of talk by the children about which colleges they would be attending as extensions of their family's traditional loyalties
(usually large state institutions), there was more talk of the sorts of lifestyles
students expected to lead. Many girls, she said, "still have it in their head" to
marry someone rich (marrying either up or even) so they wouldn't have to go to
college; boys' talk was about making money, working in the family business,
driving a sports car, and owning a boat. She described her students as "very con-
fident and self-assured" about the future. However, she also expressed great concern and anxiety on the part of parents (and herself) that a "potential exists for
dropouts." Two families, she reported, had serious problems with older sons who
"had to be boarded" once they reached adolescence; she felt that a younger son in
her classroom from this family also "might be headed in that way."

For the students' part, their talk during interview sessions revealed a clearer and
consistently more detailed knowledge of the instrumentality of literacy in realiz-
ing career plans than did the talk of students at Chavez or Roosevelt. "Why is
reading important?" I asked each group. They typically responded as though the
question were entirely self-evident. "I don't want to be a little clown," one student giggled. Others were more mocking in expressing the unthinkable. "I wanna
be a waitress," one girl snickered with an "uneducated" accent; "I wanna be a taxi
driver," one boy guffawed. I asked them what they would be doing in 10 years,
when they were 19, and why they thought education was important. While students at all three schools talked about needing an education "to get a good job,"
only the students at Crest Hills could name specific universities they planned to
attend; nearly every student named one of three major institutions in the state.
Moreover, only students at Crest Hills indicated a knowledge of the postgraduate
education required for the kinds of "good jobs"—in medicine, law, and higher education—that their parents held and had "talked to [them] about." Although they
couldn't name them, several students also told me about "these tests" their parents told them were in their future whose outcomes would largely determine ad-
mittance to professional programs; one student knew there were "books in the
library" that would help you study for them. A good deal of parental anxiety was
also communicated to me in these interviews. One group of students caught this
particularly well. Imitating his father's voice, one student mimicked, "You can
be whatever you want to be," to which a girl added, "Except, my mom says that
. . . a gas station isn't the best job you can get." I asked why not; the boy
replied, again mimicking his father, "It just isn't." And the girl clarified: "She
says that some people who haven't, um, all the way gone to college, uh, uh,

like, if they dropped out of school they would go to a gas station or something like that."

But while students were knowledgeable and accepting of certain realities, they seemed at times to be less than enthusiastic about facing them. Their whole future, as they saw it, rode on "getting smart," which was an outcome of passing The Test; then you could get a job to get money to buy a house. Luckily, the students told me, there were these books to help you pass The Test so you could get smart. But none of this was assured, these students also explained. In another interview, I asked the students, "What happens if you don't get to go to college?" They explained the consequences to me, and then the following exchange took place:

Steve: J. C.'s not going to college.

Tiff: He's gonna work in a supermarket, probably.

Mark: How do you know?

All: Because [unintelligible] he's not getting good grades.

Steve: He's not going to college.

Mark: You know that already? [Students nod] In the third grade you know that?

Steve: But he's gonna like, live on a ranch.

Jorge: Yeah.

Mark: Is that what he wants to do? Is that what he says? [Students nod]

Then one boy remarked wistfully, "I want to live on a ranch," to which another added, "Like his [J. C.'s] brother."

"Like his brother?" I asked. They both agreed, and I asked the second boy, "You don't want to live on a ranch [too]?" But he asserted, "*I want to*," and one girl added, "Yeah, me, too."

In the course of the study, I came to see the boy, J. C., whose future these students seemed to regard with equal parts fear and envy, as something of a folk figure to the class. For the boys especially, he was their own James Dean, a marginalized character destined to live a life as romantic as it was unthinkable for them. He was well liked, especially by the boys. During small-group interviews, students paid more attention to his remarks than they did to other students', and he was the only student in the class besides Emily (another marginalized person: They told me she was going to Harvard) whom they talked about in interviews in which they were not present.

He seemed like an unlikely future "hood" to me, however. J. C. was not among the boys who made trouble for the librarian during story times, and in my conversations with him, he was always polite, open, and cooperative. He was also relatively articulate, and although it took many drafts, his animal report seemed as well written and researched as any other student's in the class and more so than some. J. C.'s most singular trait was the amount of name-dropping he did. Over the course of five interviews, he told me his family was from Alberta, Canada, but owned a ranch in a mythically "western" region of the state, that Nolan Ryan was a family friend, that he was the godson of a former governor, and that in 10 years he would probably be the ex-governor's aide, because he was blind and "needs people to drive him around and fly."

For all his and others' talk, J. C. seemed terribly insecure more than anything else, like someone struggling to come to grips with, and put a public shine on, a future that his third-grade classmates ultimately found wanting. This was made painfully evident in the final interview session with J. C. and three classmates. The three boys in the group had been teasing each other throughout the interview, looking through some books I'd brought and making puerile comments like, "Here's Jorge, and here's his wife," but when I asked them where they would be in 10 years, when they were 19, the conversation turned rancorous:

J. C.:   Well, I'm going to be going to some other thing. I'll be, I'll be—

Mark: Will you be working on a ranch?

J. C.:   I'm gonna go to some other—

Jorge: He'll be hanging out with his friends at the alley, drinking beer.

J. C.:   Shut up, Jorge.

Mark: Let's hear [J. C.].

J. C.:   I'm gonna, I'm gonna go to something it's like college, it's called, my dad told me about it—

Mark: Like a technical school?

J. C.:   Yeah, a technical school.

Mark: Okay, okay . . .

There was a long, embarrassed silence. And then J. C. turned and looked Jorge in the eye. "You don't even know what a techn-technical school is, Jorge," he stammered.

Jorge looked back at him and coolly dared, "What is it, J. C.?"

"Something where you don't go to college, you just, instead of having to go like six years to get your degree, you only go like two years." The other three people at the table—Emily, the girl bound for Harvard, a boy, Steve, and myself—leaned back in relief. J. C. had proven that he *did* know about technical schools: His life had a plan—and a meaning—after all. Then Steve mumbled some approving words, and everybody could see how J. C.'s plan, a degree in two years instead of six, made a lot of sense.

Following this incident, I spoke with Elaine Dawson about J. C., and she confirmed that he was one of the two boys whom she felt were potentially "headed in the wrong direction" and that the problem was partially, but not essentially, academic. J. C.'s brother, the one who "lived on a ranch," was one of the two older brothers of her students who had gotten into trouble and been "boarded out." The family had been very prosperous and prominent in the community, but the "talk" around school (and also around Madison Heights) was that the father's investments had gone sour, and the family had declared bankruptcy but was now on the financial mend. She described the parents as demanding and difficult to deal with; they were very defensive about J. C. and had made accusations in conferences that she had never had made against her before. She also told me that the mothers of several other boys were concerned about the influence that J. C. had over their sons; there had been an incident in which J. C. and two other boys were spotted on their bikes far from home and in a place they had been forbidden to ride, and the mothers were certain it was J. C.'s doing; they did not want their boys over at his house anymore, because they "weren't sure of what was going on there."

I was left to marvel, at the end of our conversation, about the envelope of talk that surrounds each individual child at Crest Hills and how that envelope gets constructed from the voices of the students themselves, their parents, the school, and ultimately, public sentiment in Madison Heights. I wondered what the actual connections might be between the failure of the family's business, the judgment of the community, and the developing problems of J. C. and his older brother; but I had to wonder even more at the discursive processes that the evidence suggests conflated the problems of the father with the sons, at the talk that I have little doubt went on in homes throughout Madison Heights, at how that talk came to school, at the family's resulting anger and humiliation, at all the "face work" that J. C. did with me during interviews, and finally at J. C.'s very public—and, I suspect, very symbolic—repudiation of the college track.

In summary, the discourses of the library at Crest Hills were not discourses that attempted to compensate for any perceived deficiencies in students' educational/life experience but instead were discourses intended to enrich and add narrative layers of meaning to their experience in preparation for their eventual entry into the professional-managerial workplace and its class privileges. In pursuit of that future, students picked up and read the library's rationalized, formal system of text classification, as well as its literature, as though both were manuals. Story-time discourse not only provided opportunity and encouragement for students to cultivate conventional, objective positions in relation to text-based knowledge; it also taught students how to use information and conversational skills to gain attention and recognition for themselves. Book talk extended these lessons and provided narrative models of heroes whose detached subjectivity and managerial skills won the day. Finally, students' internalization of the rule-governed nature of all these discourses came to light in the ways that students made sense of texts they are asked to sort into groups.

These rituals of talk achieved their effect mainly because they serviced larger metadiscourses within the community of Madison Heights and the managerial-professional culture at large. Those discourses, as the children at Crest Hills heard them, were mainly about the future: They were Calvinistic in tone and stressed the relationship between the morality of hard work, the delay of gratification, and ultimate success in life, connections that Barbara Ehrenreich has argued become increasingly difficult for parents to convey to each succeeding generation in a society as affluent and driven by images of consumption as ours is.

I also have to marvel, then, at how ironically important people like J. C. and his family were to the affluent, professional middle class. J. C.'s classmates might have been fascinated by his persona and intrigued by the novelty of a non-professional life, but it is unlikely any of them would have traded places, because they all suspected, as Jorge ungraciously pointed out, that J. C. would someday end up "hanging out with his friends at the alley, drinking beer." The incident reported above suggests it was the object lesson of J. C. and his family's fall from grace and dignity that helped to keep everyone else's children from jumping off the social fast track, too.

CONCLUSION

Although they possessed an enviable level of basic skills and an impressive array of material advantages, students at Crest Hills were still a long way from being free—that is, from constructing social positions as readers that would routinely allow them not to be reproduced by but to negotiate with, and so produce, their own meanings and reality from the texts and discourses of the library and its community. I have argued here that it was because the congruence of discourses of home and school effectively suppressed, or concealed, the constructed nature of reality at Crest Hills that students were channeled into believing that there was a single, "normal" way of seeing the world and the future, which anyone with common sense would be eager to adopt.

To make my point, I may at times have overstated the case against discursive congruence as the instrument of hegemony in the library. Certainly some overlap between home and school and library in discursive practices, some linguistic "transparency," is essential if students are ever to learn how to construct any meaning at all from the library and its texts. Crest Hills seems to be an extreme example in one direction, one that pushes to their limits the unacknowledged assumptions of sociolinguistic perspectives and in doing so reveals their base in the dominant ideology of industrial capitalism; while on the other hand Chavez Elementary provides an extreme example of the consequences of repressing, as opposed to suppressing, the possibility of alternative worldviews and the incongruence between home and school cultures. Is there no middle ground in school and library discourse, then? One that balances reader-subjects between the dominant texts of the society in which they find themselves and their home discourses? One that embraces, rather than suppresses or represses, the contradictions between the two, and in doing so allows students to construct, or rather to reconstruct, their own subject positions as readers and produce their own meanings? In my research, the library at Roosevelt Elementary seemed to be a working example of how such a middle ground might be (re)constructed; and it is to a presentation and analysis of its particular practices that I turn as the final case in this book.

4

Liminality: Roosevelt Elementary

Raul:	It tells about this ninja turtle, Raphael.
Mark:	Oh. That's in the biography section?
Raul:	Um-hmmm.
Mark:	Ninja turtles . . . Raphael. Okay, is it about Raphael, or is it about the guy who wrote—
Raul:	It's just about—
Cristina:	—about his paintings and all that—
Rachel:	—what he draws—
Laurie:	—when he was a little boy and stuff like that.
Rachel:	I like Leonardo DaVinci . . . Michelangelo did funny drawings . . .
Raul:	Just crazy . . .
Rachel:	He liked to party.

READING THE SCHOOL

Roosevelt Elementary is located approximately two miles from the city's central business district. The school is in a working-class residential area that is bounded on the north by a major shopping strip and on the east by a busy transportation artery; the area is also divided by a major railroad line. There are many apartment complexes and small, tightly spaced single-family homes in this part of town but no public housing projects within Roosevelt's student attendance area. A higher percentage of private (and more expensive) rental property is the probable reason that Roosevelt has a slightly higher percentage of student transfers than Chavez (both schools lost population during the school year) and a rate double that of Crest Hills (which gains students). The high rate of transience, combined with a lack of geographic cohesiveness and a lack of "presence" in the area (the school is tucked away on a side street toward the bottom of a hill), makes Roosevelt's characterization as a neighborhood school less fitting than either Chavez's or Crest Hills's.

In 1992–1993, the 750-plus students at Roosevelt were more ethnically diverse than at either Crest Hills or Chavez. Two thirds of the students were Hispanic (mostly Mexican-American); 27 percent were European-American, and 8 percent were African-American. Eighteen percent of all students participated in either bilingual or English-as-a-second-language programs. Exactly three quarters of the students were designated "low income," a positive difference of 27 percentage points from the district average of 48 percent. But the percentage of students designated as "at risk," 40 percent, was 5 points lower than the district-wide percentage.

Quantitative measures consistently placed Roosevelt slightly below the mean in terms of student academic achievement across the district and the state. In the 1992–1993 school year, 56 percent of third graders "demonstrated mastery" on the state-mandated criterion-referenced skills test, 3 percentage points lower than the district-wide percentage and 1 point lower than the statewide percentage. The composite (math and reading) score for third graders on norm-referenced achievement tests (ITBS) was at the 48th percentile, 13 points lower than the district but only 2 points below the mean. When only measures of reading are considered, however, Roosevelt fell considerably farther below the mean. Grade three reading scores on criterion-referenced skills tests were 5 percentage points below the district and 9 points below the state percentages of mastery, while for norm-referenced measures, they were 16 points below the district and 9 points below the national average.

In interpreting these quantitative measures, and particularly in comparing them to other schools, it is important to take a larger view of the school's ethical and curricular stance toward testing, as well as the attitudes and economic circumstances of the student body. While testing was a concern at Roosevelt, and teachers felt some pressure prior to a testing period to "teach for the test," the administration did not make test performance the yearlong preoccupation for teachers that it did at Chavez, nor was I given the impression from conversations with the staff that the quality of a teacher's work was judged exclusively by his or her students' test scores. Information collected through participant observation of students in the school library and of third graders in their classroom and through focused interviews with students about their reading could be more indicative of students' competencies and attitudes toward reading at Roosevelt. I never encountered, as I did regularly at Chavez, a student who was unable to identify basic sight words or read orally with some degree of fluency, and I never heard anyone, adult or student, suggest that a text was "too hard" to read; on the contrary, I regularly observed second graders in the library attempt to use the card catalog without hesitation, and I watched students in the third-grade class that participated formally in the study intrepidly look through encyclopedias, magazines, and informational books for specific information or just to browse. In focused interviews with these students about the library books they had checked out, students were able to discuss these books' contents in detail and with enthusiasm; none of the students indicated that they had had any problem in reading them (although they also indicated that they had not read each book from cover to cover).

On balance, when Roosevelt's lower-than-average reading test scores are weighed against the school's comparatively less-than-obsessed attitude toward testing, the general inconsistency of test results across years, and students' positive attitudes toward reading and informally observed competence in using text, the school program actually appears to be moderately successful, particularly in light of high percentages of children from low-income households and relatively high rates of transience. Combined consideration of qualitative and quantitative demographic measures placed Roosevelt firmly within the median third of all elementary schools in the district during 1992–1993. In many but not all ways, Roosevelt was about as "average" an elementary school as could be found in an urban district whose neighborhood schools were highly segregated by property values and subsequently by ethnicity and socioeconomic status.

READING THE LIBRARY

Roosevelt was established in 1988 in a move to consolidate and replace two older, more cramped schools. The one-story building, which sits on 11 acres, covers 83,000 square feet in area and is shaped like a wide H with a third vertical bar through the center of the letter. The northeast wing of the building contains the gymnasium and cafeteria; the south-central wing contains administrative offices and the teachers' workroom, and the remaining north and south wings are classrooms. The library, which at 4,550 square feet is by far the largest single space in the school, is located in the central, horizontal portion of the building, just west of the central north-south wings. Doors to the north and south open onto main hallways leading to classrooms in all wings of the building. The library actually stands in the center of the school's instructional space and adjacent to the teachers' workroom and administrative offices.

"The World We Live In"

With 39 years' experience in elementary schools, the last 27 of which have been spent as a librarian in the same school district, 70-year-old Louise Currie was widely regarded as the dean of school librarians in the city, if not throughout surrounding counties and smaller school districts. She was appointed librarian at Roosevelt before the school opened, and although she did not select the original books for the school's collection (these were ordered by her supervisor from master lists of books chosen by "experts"), she did bring with her some 3,000 books that she had culled from an elementary school that was closing. At the time I was there the library had over 11,000 volumes, most of them recently published and in very good condition. Louise Currie boasted that her library had "the most comprehensive collection in the district"; by most standards, and from my knowledge of five other school libraries in the district, the collection did appear to be well above average.

While the library's architectural design was set before Louise Currie's appointment as librarian, she counted this library as "the most wonderful facility I have ever worked in" and said she "wouldn't change a thing" about its design.

Architecturally, the library at Roosevelt was something of a showplace for the school and the district and resembled more than anything else a modern, suburban church (see Figure 4.1). Its wood-paneled ceiling slanted upward from north and south walls to a central beam that ran the length of its "nave" from east to west at a point at least 30 feet from the floor and created a light, airy atmosphere within a single large, open space. An angled set of carpeted risers for storytelling stood in the front and center of the room and was named the "kiva" by the librarian, after circular rooms found in the ruins of prehistoric Anasazi Indian ruins that are popularly thought to have been used for sacred rituals.

Not only the naming of the story corner but the arrangement of the library's collection, a task that fell to Louise Currie when she arrived, can also be interpreted as iconographically sacred. In the opening line of the tour she conducted for students and adult visitors (and in a school with a largely Mexican-American, and Roman Catholic, student population), the librarian would sweep her arm in an arc along the central beam of the ceiling and note that "you can draw a line down the center of the library and all the fiction is on the left"—on the side reserved for Mary, the good working-class wife and mother in Roman Catholic churches and lore—"and all the fact books are on the right"—on the side of Joseph, the fatherly carpenter. But she herself was a lifelong Presbyterian and, as her business cards and conversation indicated, was a dyed-in-the-wool, highly professionalized, "librarian/learning resource specialist." A more likely interpretation, then, might see this division as iconically reproducing the division of life in the modern age into dichotomized realms of the subjective and objective, the "made up" and the "true," pleasure and work, or the feminine and the masculine—the same division that the dual ordering of texts in public and school libraries historically represents (see Chapter 1). To further underscore the division, the words FICTION and FACT in black capital letters 12 inches high were taped to the left and right walls, over the bookshelves that line them. Bookcases were also along the walls on either side of the kiva; SPANISH was written in large black letters above them on the left wall, and BIOGRAPHY was written on the right. Additional bookcases stood out along the north and south walls in angular rows. The card catalog was across from the checkout counter in the front, and between the library's two entrances.

If there was a religious significance to the library's design, however, it competed with the very obvious appointments of the middle-class living room, or parlor. A set of adult-sized comfortable chairs and a low "coffee table" toward the back and center were duplicated by a miniature set of child-size wicker furniture, including a sofa, two rocking chairs, and matching coffee table (complete with throw rug beneath it), in front of the kiva and the picture book shelves that lined the kiva's walls. There were also three freestanding racks for magazines and paperbacks in the library and a few seldom-used study carrels. Throughout the room, dried and artificial flower arrangements, numerous knickknacks, statuettes, and a collection of ceramic owls along the top shelf of the reference section occupied odd corners and empty top shelves; no books stood to display their covers here, as at Crest Hills and Chavez. The center of the room was filled with round tables that seated four or five and were easily rearranged for meetings and other public gatherings. In keeping with the library's stated theme, "The World We Live In," two large inflatable globes hung suspended from the ceiling of the li-

Figure   4.1
Roosevelt Elementary Library Floor Plan

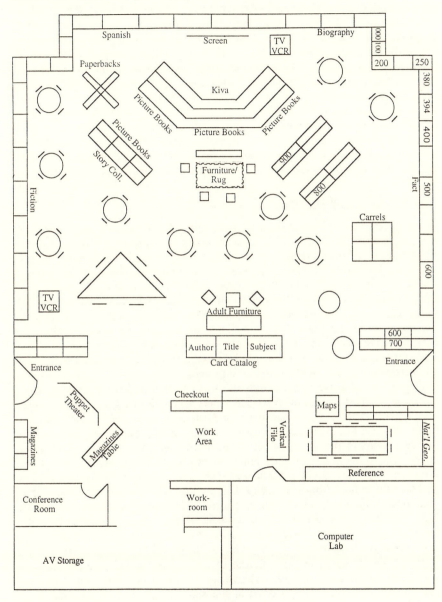

AV = Audiovisual
VCR = Videocassette Recorder

brary. On the back wall behind the counter and workspace, a large soft-sculpture map of the world hung 15 feet above the floor; on the north wall over the reference section, there was a printed world map with six clocks lined up beneath it to indicate different time zones; a map of the United States with its time zones also indicated by clocks was placed on the opposite wall facing the world map.

Finally, it is important to note how explicitly and carefully each portion of the library was labeled. For the primary divisions of the library—fact, fiction, Spanish, biography, and reference—the labels were in words; at the subcategorical level, however, sections were indicated by letters (A, B, and so on) for fiction and three-digit Dewey numbers (e.g., "340"; "798") for nonfiction on laminated signs that protruded from between books on the shelves; no other subject indicators were provided, save for small, freestanding signs on top of bookcases that marked the start of a new Dewey category numerically, by title (e.g., "400 Language"), and with a cartoon of a caveman performing some illustrative action.

Scheduling and the Rhythm of the Library

"It is a point of pride with both Robert Smith [Roosevelt's principal] and me that this is an 'open' library," Louise Currie explained, meaning that except for pre-k, kindergarten, and first-grade classes, no visits or story times were regularly scheduled for grades two through five. In her years of librarianship, Louise Currie ran a library with scheduled weekly visits for all classes only one year—the year before she came to Roosevelt—and that year, she said, "was the easiest of my career." The advantages of an open library, she said, were two. First, open scheduling made the library more available to teachers and students whenever they needed to use it; second, because she was not occupied for large parts of the day with scheduled classes, she could be more available to individuals who "really need professional help" in finding information.

The result, as Louise Currie admitted, was that "this library's circulation rates are not as high as at some other schools where all the teachers bring their classes once a week." Unscheduled checkout periods meant that student contact with the library in some teachers' classes was spotty; she reported that most teachers sent groups of kids to the library to check out books on a weekly basis, but many never came to the library or made much use of it in their teaching. In fact, except for when they were sent by a teacher or came to the library as a class, children's access to the school library seemed relatively limited; I seldom saw many children in the library at lunchtime, or before and after school, as I did at Crest Hills. Still, the librarian argued, for those teachers who chose to take advantage, the opportunities of an open library were richer than in a scheduled one.

Informal junctures and rituals, however, did provide a predictable rhythm to the workday. The librarian oversaw a cadre of volunteers, retired women and men who helped several days a week to shelve books and perform other time-consuming clerical activities. They arrived at the start of the school day and went straight to work, while she made hot water for coffee and tea and played light classical music from the local public radio station. Some mornings an early primary group would arrive around eight for story time or a few students might enter, sent by a teacher to return books or to look up some specific information. There was a break at midmorning for coffee or tea and graham crackers, and then work resumed. More classes arrived after the break to check out books or to do research; many days the librarian conducted classes in library instruction at this time. Toward noon, some volunteers left and others arrived. Traffic picked up after lunch; there were more story times, and there always seemed to be at least one class or group of students using the facilities. The school day ended with a general straightening up for the following morning or, many times, with preparations for a principal's or staff meeting later in the day.

Louise Currie's mission, she said, was to "teach children to be independent in the library." Her program of decontextualized instruction defined successful use of the library in bottom-line terms, as the retrieval of books or of discrete pieces of information from the library's collection of texts; it was the only significant deviation, as the librarian herself acknowledged, from what "the professional literature recommends." Pre-k, kindergarten, and first-grade students, who were "so new to any kind of a structured situation," were socialized to check out books with their teacher's assistance and to sit quietly in the kiva during story times. In one 22-minute period with a pre-k group that was behaving very meekly and cooperatively, the librarian read one book and played five "finger games," designed, she explained later, to focus the students' attention on her and get students to put their hands on their laps. The book for the day was *Sylvester and the Magic Pebble* (Steig 1969), which one child immediately recognized as a Caldecott winner ("It got the award!"). As the librarian explained, "We're making a real effort here" to teach students to recognize illustrators' trademark styles and to identify award-winners by their medallions, because "we want children to recognize quality."

From the second grade up, Louise Currie limited her formal contact with classes to four or five 45-minute sessions at each grade level ("I just don't think I have that much to teach about the library"), in keeping with her open library policy. Second graders were introduced to the card catalog ("Just the subject catalog—that's all they really want or need") and a "featured author" (of fiction). In the third grade, students were instructed in the "proper" use of the encyclopedia and other "ready reference" works; these lessons focused on the use of guide words, on identifying the important words in a topic, and on recognizing different types of maps, charts, and graphs. Lessons with the fourth grade focused on the Dewey Decimal System and included detailed practice using the card catalog. The fifth grade largely repeated lessons learned in the earlier grades.

It was in the fourth grade "that I really zero in," Louise Currie noted. It was at this grade that she explained the "meaning" of the Dewey Decimal System, using a master narrative that situated not only the system but the user in a grand scheme of human cultural evolution. The story, which was recorded in synoptic form in a pie chart that was hung at a child's eye level on the side of a bookcase, was repeated in fuller form on freestanding cards that sat atop the bookcases where the books of a particular category were kept; but in its original telling, the librarian used special laminated charts measuring 12" x 18" that contained the original illustrations, drawn by a parent at another library many years ago.

In the story, which the librarian said she got from a professional journal and which she believed was first told by Melvil Dewey himself, a caveman stumbles out into the light of day and asks himself the question that "naturally" comes to mind: "Who am I?" Because of this First Question, books dealing with identity, such as philosophy and ethics, come first in the system hierarchy as the "100s." Next that caveman asks himself, "Who made me?" and from this question springs the next category, that of religion, the "200s." The story progresses in this manner, from questions about his next-door neighbor (the social sciences, or "300s"), to how to talk to that neighbor (languages, the "400s"), to questions about the natural world (the sciences, or "500s"), to how to use his knowledge (the applied sciences, or "600s"), to how to use his leisure time (fine arts and recreation, the "700s"), until the caveman becomes a man of letters himself (the "800s," or literature) and in his final years leaves a record of his experiences for the benefit of future generations (the "900s": history, geography, biography).

THE MEANING OF THE LIBRARY

How are messages about the use of the library and its texts communicated at Roosevelt Elementary from the perspective of Peircean (Peirce 1931/1958) semiosis? Because of its caveman allegory, its churchlike architecture, and its kiva story corner, it might at first seem obvious that, as at Chavez, iconicity—the communication of meaning through properties of resemblance—would be the dominant mode of signification via the practices of the librarian at Roosevelt. But unlike Chavez, where students were presumed to lack an interest in the library or an understanding of the importance of literacy, and so Mary Strauss felt she must work to inculcate a sense of literacy and an interest in the library through rituals that equated reading with physical exercise and quantity with quality, Louise Currie saw the library and its texts as a resource to students who had grasped the significance of the library a priori but who were probably lacking the knowledge necessary to navigate its textual order. This concern with the order of things is also different from the focus of librarian practices at Crest Hills; there, Barbara Henry assumed not only that students knew a priori what a library and books were for but that students had already or soon would pick up its order on their own—assumptions that led her to focus instead on how to use text based information and the discourse conventions of literary discussion to negotiate power relations. At Roosevelt, the rituals of library lessons and story times were most often focused on learning the order of the library itself by coming to recognize the relation of one genre of text to another—for example, of the juxtaposition of fiction, along one wall, to nonfiction, along the opposite wall—and by drawing students' attention to the salience of surface-level signs posted above or in close relation to different types of texts. Thus, students were directed to the card catalog when they entered the library and asked for information; they were shown the Dewey Decimal numbers atop or along bookshelves when searching for a book; they "learned to recognize quality" by looking for a silver or gold medallion on the cover of a novel or picture book; and directional signs were large and conspicuously placed. Although iconicity was clear and present within the library at Roosevelt, Louise Currie did not emphasize its significance in her interactions with students, nor were her interactions with upper grades lessons in how to position oneself to read aesthetically and with abstract purpose or in the symbolic exercise of power through the exchange and control of information. Instead, the dominant mode of signification via librarian practices at Roosevelt was indexicality, in which signs function by virtue of their spatial or temporal contiguity with an object, essentially pointing to, or directing attention toward, that object.

Because the index takes the medial position in the chain of semiosis (and also in the act of communicating a message) between the icon (which, remember, connects the sign and its object by virtue of some *resemblance* between the two) and the symbol (which acts by virtue of a *conventional* or arbitrary and unmotivated connection between sign and object), we might suppose that the index as a sign performs a merely instrumental function in the process of communication. We then might also suppose that indices, as mere pointers, are less implicated ideologically in any process of cultural reproduction or hegemony. For unlike the practices at Chavez, whose iconicity addressed students there as aliterates whose conversion must be obtained through metaphoric associations, and unlike the practices at Crest Hills, whose symbolism addressed students as future managers of its discourses, the indexical practices at Roosevelt addressed students as potential accessors of text-based knowledge and users of library resources. In other words, while the signs of Chavez and Crest Hills attempted to cast library patrons in specific roles as social actors, the signs of Roosevelt's library were more open and more liminal in this regard.

But a case can also be made that the middle-class decor, the clarity of its arrangement, the use of award-winning picture books in grades k-1, the profusion of well-placed labels, and Louise Currie's direct instruction in library skills were designed to indicate explicitly to working-class students the same avenues of access to, and use of, text-based information that middle-class students at Crest Hills pick up on their own. Taken as a whole, the library's design might serve as an easily accessible map that "fostered" (positive word) rather than "prescribed" (negative word) ideologically appropriate ways to think about and use certain genres of text. Theoretically, because the successful acquisition of these indices as tools of thought would not presuppose adherence to any particular ideology, the tools of access in the library could be used to retrieve and use information in an infinite variety of ways and for an infinite variety of purposes—even against the ideological stance the library represented and supported, if the user so desired. Here, then, would be a library of which Lisa Delpit (1986, 1988) would approve—one that would strive to educate its student users directly in the competencies of what Delpit characterizes as the "culture of power," competencies that, according to her, are indispensable in getting ahead in the world but that would otherwise remain unfathomable to working-class ethnic minorities and other students who are not in the middle or upper class.

This line of reasoning raises two additional issues, however. The first is moral and ethical and questions the fatalism and cynicism of an argument that implies that there is only one system, it's bigger than you and me, and that to "get ahead" in it, the sooner you decide to "go along," the better off you'll be. As was detailed in Chapter 3, this is the same chamber of commerce mentality that pervaded Crest Hills; and while it did seem likely that the students there would eventually prosper materially, it seemed less than certain that in the process they were also acquiring perspectives that would guide them to think more creatively and critically about the world, much less suggest they had a mandate to change it for the better.

The second issue stems from the false supposition that as a class of sign the index is purely instrumental, that is, ideologically inert, in its own effect. As Richard Parmentier (1987) points out in his discussion of Peircean semiotics, "Every index, in order to convey information, must embody an icon" (22). The example he provides of this, "The falling grass is an index of the wind, but it is also an icon in that the direction of the grass's fall resembles the direction of the wind" (22), while illustrative of the point, refers to a primal level of perception that occurs without a social component of influence, in which the chain of semiosis, or the apprehension of meaning, moves from *sensibility* —that which is known but is not consciously apprehended—to *intelligibility*—that which can be named and whose relations to other signs are at least partially grasped. Although, as Peirce claimed, a cycle, or chain of semiosis, always moves in the same direction, from sensibility (iconic meaning) to intelligibility (symbolic meaning) regardless of whether signification is based in verbal or visual or other types of stimuli, on the level of semiosis at which language operates, iconicity—that is, resemblance—depends on social conventions that link words and expressions with objects.

In effect, the function of indices in this context is to point to a symbolically, socially determined "interpretant," or meaning, in which the conveyance of information by indices of human manufacture is contingent on the mutuality of conventionalized resemblances, or iconic symbols, between the sender and receiver of indexical signs. Where mutuality is lacking—and here I want to make it clear that "mutuality" as I conceive of it is not a binary, all-or-nothing phenomenon but rather is continuous and refers to partial congruence or incongruence in resemblance—the possibility exists that what a sender may intend an index to "point to" and what from the receiver's point of view an index points to may not be recognized as exactly the same object. In cases where a speaker is trying to make an abstract, conventional sign intelligible to others by presenting concrete examples and then drawing his or her audience's attention to indices of that sign in the examples, the result may be that sensibilities are confused. But although the audience has not perceived a resemblance in the same way it was intended, the chain of semiosis is not necessarily broken; instead, the audience may still work toward intelligibility, or conscious, symbolic understanding. But because that understanding is based in differently grasped resemblances and contiguities, it will be different from the speaker's understanding (although reasoned and intelligible nonetheless). The ironic consequence of such a situation may be one in which, often unbeknown to either side of an exchange, two relatively *parallel*, and so separate but contiguous, strands of thought or chains of semiosis play themselves out in a communication act. As will be discussed in the following section, these sorts of elisions, or gaps between meanings that were intended and meanings that were made, were a dominant feature of the instructional discourse between Louise Currie and the students during story times and in her presentation of lessons in library skills and occurred with a frequency unobserved at either Crest Hills or Chavez.

READING STUDENT RESPONSE

Dual(ing) Conversations

To translate the discussion above from Peircean terms, because the robust and yet contingent nature of human systems of communication is often ignored or overlooked by cultural economists who view knowledge as a commodity, such reasoning errs critically in the assumptions it makes about the nature of language and other sign systems as media of communication; and it is this error that helps to explain, as will be seen, the nature of students' responses to Louise Currie and the library. That error lies in the underlying assumption that language is a transparent medium by which a human sender can transmit a message to a human receiver in terms so explicit that what was intended will almost always be the same as what is understood.

A model of communication like this, however, also depends on certain commonsense assumptions about how language works—assumptions that, when applied to actual communications events, are quickly contradicted. The model assumes that the meanings of words and expressions and their referents are fixed and shared by all parties, that those words are combined (and understood in combination) using rules that are equally well defined and grasped by all parties with equal facility, and that the context within which they are used is one that all parties share the same understanding of. Further, there is an implied assumption that successful communication occurs only if the message received is understood in the same way as the message sent; any gap between the two is viewed as an error in transmission. In Louise Currie's story times and in her presentations of library skills, these sorts of gaps were legion; and yet they did not seem to lead to a breakdown of communications between the librarian and the students but instead seemed to force a change in the nature of the lessons from transmission to dialectical exchange.

To see how this happens, I present a small portion of one (of many similar) episodes I observed in the library at Roosevelt. This was the second of four lessons on the encyclopedia that Louise Currie conducted in the spring with teacher Mariellen Wilson's third-grade class. Twenty students sat on risers in the kiva (story corner); the librarian stood before them and began with a brief review of the first lesson. Her main discursive strategy throughout the lesson was a slightly modified form of the classic initiate > respond > evaluate (IRE) sequence of instruction identified by Mehan (1979). She did a little talking in which she tried to drop clues right and left, stopped to pose a leading question, gave a sprightly "You're exactly right," and moved on.

The central objective of this lesson was to get students to categorize topics they might find information about in an encyclopedia as either people, places, things, events, or ideas by providing examples (icons) and pointing out features in these examples (indexes) that placed them in certain categories (symbols). The librarian moved quickly through the first three categories but had more difficulty with the last two (I was unable to identify students by their voices from the tape):

Librarian: Okay, let's go on now. People, places, things. There are two other kinds of information that the encyclopedia always reports on, and you're not as likely to think about them. So I'm going to help you find the—search out the answer in your mind. Two Sundays ago, we all sat around our television, late in the afternoon or early in the evening, watching what?

Student: Commercials.

[Everyone laughs]

Librarian: We do watch commercials, don't we? We can't avoid them.

Student: Movies!

Librarian: No, two Sundays ago, or has it been three? I think it was just two Sundays—

Student: Superbowl.

Librarian: Superbowl! Yes, the Superbowl. Everybody was interested, and you can find information in the encyclopedia and other reference materials about the Superbowl games. [*Students ooh and ahh*] So those Superbowl games are representative of something else that happens in our lives—

Student: Sports.

Librarian: Sports are— [Writes "events" on board]

Student: Football.

Student: Baseball.

Students: [*Reading*] Events.

Librarian: This is a new word to you perhaps: *events*. What is an event?

Student: Like a contest?

Librarian: Like a contest.

Student: Like a race.

Librarian: It could be a race.

Student: Sports?

Librarian: Sports.

Student: Gymnastics?

Librarian: It could be gymnastics if it were a special gymnastics event. Uh, what about the . . . the Persian Gulf War? You might in another year, for sure, be able to find it in the encyclopedia. What would that be? It wouldn't be people, although people were involved, would it?

Student: Place.

Librarian: It wouldn't be a place, although places were involved in it.

Student: Things.

Librarian: It could be a thing, or the Persian Gulf War itself might be an—

Student: An event.

Librarian: An event. You're exactly right. Wars, uh, are events, just like Superbowl games are. But Superbowl games are fun; wars are not. But they all fall into this general category of an event. Another good word that you probably know better might be happening. If it's a happening, it's something that happened special, and it is an event. Can you, you be sure and tell us, Mrs. Wilson [*the teacher*], if you can think of another way that we can make this clear to the boys and girls.

Invariably and no matter, it seemed, how many clues she dropped or how carefully she worked to phrase a point or a question, students seldom gave the librarian the answer she was looking for on the first try. It is also important to note how eager the students were throughout the lesson to please her with the "right" answer; they grew restless toward the end of this 45-minute session but never showed signs of disinterest or frustration with her instruction. Once the five categories had been introduced and discussed, the librarian returned undaunted to the topic of the encyclopedia. She posed a series of "questions" students "might want to find the answers to" in the encyclopedia. The question that drew the most extended discussion was, "Did Indians take part in the Boston Tea Party?"

Librarian: Think carefully, kids, before you speak out to be sure you're right, will you? Let's look at this question. Did Indians take part in the Boston Tea Party? What are your two possible key words?

Student: Boston Tea Party.

Librarian: Boston Tea Party and—

Student: Indians.

Librarian: Indians, that's exactly right. Which one—I want to see hands on this— which one did you think would be the quickest, easiest place to find an answer to that question if you were researching it?

Student: Tea?

Librarian: Pardon?

Student: Shhh!

Student: Uh, tea.

Librarian: You said tea? There's more to it than that. What is it?

Student: B?

Librarian: B? For what?

Student: Boston.

Librarian: You'd have to go for the Boston Tea Party. Does anybody know what the Boston Tea Party is? Let me tell you, just to give you a brief description—

Student: People in Boston have tea parties?

Librarian: Hmm?

Student: People in Boston have tea parties?

Librarian: That's a good guess. People have tea parties in Boston, and I expect they do, but this, notice this one is capitalized. That means that it is pretty important, doesn't it? It was something that happened. Okay, the Boston Tea Party. In the early days of our country, we didn't, we were not the United States of America. I hope you already realize that. But, what country did we belong to? Anybody know?

Student: (*unintelligible*)

Librarian: Did somebody say Britain? Does anybody know what country we belonged to?

Student: The United States.

Librarian: I've already told you we were not the United States. What country—

Student: Egypt.

Student: Great Britain.

Librarian: Great Britain, that's exactly right. Or England. We belonged to England, I guess you'd say. Okay. They were . . . those people, those early people in our country . . . were taxed and taxed by the English people, by the people of England. . . . King George wouldn't listen to them; he just kept taxing them. He taxed the tea that they were buying, in order to make money for England, and the people were not getting any advantage of it. So, they decided—

Student: Shoot him.

Librarian: —what can we do to make him listen to us, so that he'll know, and they decided they would stage the Boston Tea Party. And what they did was dress up like Indians and go down when the big shipments came in of tea and dump it all in the water. And it has been called by historians since then the Boston Tea Party.

Student: Ohhhh!

Librarian: I was in Boston a few years ago, and I went aboard one of the old ships, the U.S.S. *Constitution*. Guess what they served us on that ship?

Students: Tea!

Librarian: You're exactly right! They surely did! Okay. So did Indians take part in the Boston Tea Party—

Student: Ye—

Librarian: —from what I've told you? Listen: The people dressed up like Indians to participate and throw the tea into the water. Did Indians take part in the Boston Tea Party.

Student: No.

Librarian: No. Who did?

Student: The people.

Librarian: The people. But they dressed up like Indians. So you see, *Indians* wouldn't be a good word. You'd never find it, because Indians didn't really take part in it, did they? They just looked like Indians. . . . Okay. Is the Boston Tea Party representative of people, places, things, events, or ideas?

Students: [*Loud and clear*] People.

Student: People.

Student: People.

A lengthy discussion ensued in which students identified the Boston Tea Party as representative of people (colonists dressed as Indians), places (Boston), things (tea), and ideas (civil rights). Finally, the librarian explained the "right" answer: it was an event.

Librarian: Remember: People were involved, but it's not certainly a person you're looking up. Places were involved, but we weren't interested in Boston as a place so much. It was an event, a thing that happened in our history. The Boston Tea Party, and that's the way you'll find it.

Student: I saw a cartoon about that. They were dumping these big barrels of tea in the water and shooting bombs everywhere.

Librarian: [*Laughs*] I'll bet they didn't have bombs then, but they probably were shooting some firearms, weren't they? Good, I'm glad you realized that's what this was.

The same sorts of exchanges also took place at other times and in other instructional contexts, like story times, where Louise Currie did not attempt to feed correct responses to students with leading questions. For one story time with a pre-k group, she read *Sylvester and the Magic Pebble* (Steig 1969). As an introduction, she discussed the title page and said that the book had been printed in New York City. Then she showed the students a pebble, which they promptly identified as a "rock." Several children asked if pebbles were found in New York City. "I don't know," the librarian said, giving an answer in the spirit of the question, "they have so much pavement there." A few moments later, the students wanted to know if the pebble "came with the book." She told them, "No, I got this one from the planter here in the library."

Louise Currie was not the only adult who had adventurous conversations with the students at Roosevelt. Although she seemed to understand the worldview of her students clearly, teacher Mariellen Wilson was often caught off guard by students' sense making, and I found during my interviews that communicative contexts that seemed completely transparent to me at the time could be understood by students in very different ways. In my first meeting with Mariellen Wilson's class, she asked me to explain the questions I would be asking the students and the sort of interaction I would have with them. At one point in my presentation a girl in the class asked, "Will you be like a counselor?" Without fully considering what a counselor at Roosevelt was likely to discuss with students, I said yes. "No, no," Mariellen Wilson interrupted. "He's not your counselor. You're not supposed to tell him things that are private. He's not a counselor. You're only going to talk to [him] about school and the books you read."

As a final instance, a week later in the encyclopedia lesson that followed the one described above, Louise Currie met with the students in the "ready reference" section of the library. The entire class sat around two large conference tables that had been pushed together, and each student had in front of her or him a volume of the *World Book Encyclopedia*. The librarian demonstrated how to use guide words, then set the students to work finding a political map, a terrain map, a chart, and a captioned picture. But the students paid little attention to the worksheet before them and instead used the occasion to browse in their volume of the encyclopedia, pausing to nudge the classmate next to her or him to share photographs and subject headings they recognized. One girl was excited to identify Leonardo DaVinci from a photograph (he had figured in a lesson Mariellen Wilson had presented to the class); a boy giggled at a "nasty picture" of Michelangelo's *David*; another girl noticed that her volume was "CI–CZ" and that her "country" (the class was doing reports) was in it. Librarian, teacher, and I circulated among the students, working with them individually to complete the worksheets; in my case, at least, I ended up doing most of the work locating the information while the student I was working with continued to browse.

As I observed and interacted with students at Roosevelt, what stood out most for me repeatedly was how very different the nature of students' meaning-making processes was compared to Crest Hills, where adults and students both seemed to share an interest in moving toward conventional meanings, or to Chavez, where students' most significant uses of texts occurred "under the table" and often against adult intentions. Students at Roosevelt did not resist or conform to the lessons of the librarian nor, as will be seen, to the library as an informational system. Instead, they seemed to take advantage of gaps in the "official" logic employed by adults in explaining how systems—in this case, the library and its texts—worked to deploy their own logic in attempting to make sense of the library as a system. Of course these students' ways with words and text could be construed as nothing out of the ordinary but simply as "kids being kids," whose limited knowledge and experience led them to make sense of their reality in ways that children everywhere do when left to their own resources. But that is precisely the point I am making here: Because while it was nothing out of the ordinary to watch "kids be kids" in their interactions with adults at Roosevelt, these kinds of exchanges at Chavez (where it was more common to watch kids act like disgruntled laborers) or at Crest Hills (where The Future was the motive educational force) were equally as rare.

A case can also be made that the entire decontextualized lesson was misguided from the start and that a more appropriate strategy might have been to present students with topics and let them generate categories. There probably also is enough evidence in the transcript to convict Louise Currie of Piagetian negligence, since it is likely that the students' inability to categorize the Boston Tea Party as an event was because they had not yet reached the stage of formal operations. But in her defense, the transcript shows that the librarian was aware that students would have problems with these two categories and took steps to scaffold their understanding of them. And it also seems clear that however useful Piagetian theory may be in explaining some of the students' responses, many more have little, if anything, to do with concrete-abstract distinctions. A Piagetian critique would also misread the wholly pragmatic purpose of the lesson, that is, to orient students to the logic of the encyclopedia and the library as established systems instead of imposing its own Progressive educational agenda on a situation without first taking into account the librarian's own reasoned and good intentions—to provide all students in the school with at least a minimal orientation to the formal structure of the library, an orientation that they might not otherwise ever receive—within a situation where, due to her position as librarian, no "authentic" instructional context presented itself.

In her further defense, Louise Currie used a good deal of narrative in her lessons; she constantly tried to engage students in interaction; her responses to students were respectful, open, and unpatronizing; she made a serious effort within the parameters of the lesson structure to be topical and relevant; and the tape shows that her tone of voice and demeanor were buoyant and friendly throughout the lesson, even when the conversation was the most derailing. As Lilia Bartolomé (1994) has noted in her critique of "methods fetishism," particular instructional strategies in themselves are not likely to make the critical difference in whether students are successful at school learning. Citing the work of Ray McDermott (1977), Bartolomé points out that "numerous teaching approaches and strategies can be effective, so long as trusting relations between teacher and students are established and power relations are mutually set and agreed upon" (186). Considered in this light, the librarian's lesson was a very effective one, albeit not in ways that she intended. Even though students may not have learned to use encyclopedias in ways that she advocated, they did successfully engage her in an extended dialectical exchange about how textual knowledge is ordered, requiring her, at times, to see things their way and never surrendering their own prerogatives. Using communicative practices that Doug Foley (1990) has described as "making-out games," these students also gained valuable practice in the development of communicative competencies that could have served them well in negotiating authoritative meanings later in their careers.

What stands out most in Louise Currie's interaction with the students, then, is the difference between the logic employed by the librarian in explaining the logic of bibliographic systems and the logic deployed by the students in attempting to make sense of the library and its texts. The logic of conversations, according to Paul Grice (1989), depends on what he terms the "co-operative principle," or the shared assumption of all parties involved in a conversation that they are making a good-faith effort to understand and be understood by each other. According to Grice, a "successful" (i.e., accurate) transaction of meanings is contingent on four loose rules, or "maxims," since (as a general rule) in any given conversation, one or more is violated. These maxims, in brief, are: (1) quantity, or the imperative to provide no more and no less information than is required to make a point; (2) quality, or the imperative to be accurate and truthful, and to say no more than what one has evidence to support; (3) relation, or "relevance," in which what is said supports and does not detract from what is meant; and (4) manner, which includes avoiding obscure and ambiguous turns of phrase and being succinct and orderly in one's delivery. Our own life experience tells us that in normal conversations one or more of these maxims is regularly violated, causing a gap or rupture in the smooth flow of information and meaning from one person to another. Belief in the cooperative principle and an intuitive grasp of conversational maxims, however, leads both parties in a conversation to strive toward the construction of rational meaning through a process Grice terms "implicature" (24–31).

If we go back to the context of Louise Currie's lessons and story times, a good case can be made that it was only through implicature and their faith in the co-operative principle of rational conversation that the students were able to make any sense of her instruction at all. As John Stephens (1992) explains, however,

"Since these maxims suggest a norm, and are in fact often violated, the ways in which they are utilized or breached become a key aspect of signification, and enable an audience to make interpretive or evaluative judgments about what is represented in the text" (36). It is in fact only through implicature—by breaching the gaps created by violations of the maxims of communication—that people create their own meanings, and their own understanding of the world. If this is the case, then it raises interesting philosophical questions about whether it is pragmatically correct to say that miscommunication occurred between Louise Currie and Mariellen Wilson's students. For if we go back and look at every student response to every question from the librarian, we will find that while the responses were frequently not what she had in mind, nonetheless they were all rational, given the information students had to work with. How, then, can we say the answers were "wrong" or, from the students' point of view, that the lesson was a failure?

For persons who are used to thinking of teaching in mechanical terms, as an act of "transmitting" knowledge from the informed to the ignorant, and of language as a neutral instrument, whose efficiency, much like a telephone system's, is to be judged in proportion to the lack of distortion in the signal from the sender to the receiver, the point I am making must seem intolerably perverse. We have only to consider the alternative, however, to see that this is not so. Suppose that the maxims of language were never violated and that communications were perfectly, clearly transmitted from one person to another. In this case, no other meaning than that conceived by the communicator would be possible; communicants and communicators would be virtual prisoners of their ideational system. We would be a very different species indeed, since, lacking any capacity for inferential reasoning, our cognitive abilities would be entirely limited to dealing with the face value of what we were told.

Of course, we might justifiably wonder what meaning the students did take from these lessons, if it wasn't the meaning intended by the librarian, and that, frankly, would be a difficult question to answer. In the case of these lessons, while the students probably didn't learn much about accessing information, they did successfully engage Louise Currie in a serious dialectic exchange about how textual knowledge is ordered, forcing her, at times, to see things their way; they didn't surrender their points of view and successfully avoided being told how to think about the library; and they gained valuable practice in the development of communicative competencies that could serve them well in negotiating authoritative meanings later in their school careers.

Knowing the Library/Knowing Its Text(s)

It would be some cause for concern, however, if this were all the students learned from their trips to the library; after all, a library ought to be more than a field for dialectic maneuvering. In my observations of subsequent skills lessons with this class and with others, in observations of students' skills in locating books, and in focused interviews and tasks requiring them to categorize texts on their own terms, the students at Roosevelt demonstrated a sophisticated, situated knowledge of the library and of texts as information sources that, while different from the formal, procedural knowledge promoted by the librarian, was still instrumentally powerful.

Second-grade students at Roosevelt were formally instructed in the use of the card catalog and the ordering of books on the shelves, and they did not seem at all intimidated by the process, even though from my observations their enthusiasm was not rewarded with much success in using it to find titles and locate books on topics of their choice. Typically, the descriptors students had in mind in their searches did not match the catalog's descriptors. They knew to use the first letter of a topic's principal word or phrase and to use the last name of a person but did not generalize beyond that immediate descriptor; two students looking for information on Muhammad Ali, for example, looked under "A" for Ali, but when they found nothing, they were stymied until I suggested they try "boxing." If they did find a listing, students made frequent errors in copying down the call number, or they became confused in locating that number, or many times the book was checked out. Students seemed to derive great pleasure, however, and a great sense of competence from looking up a subject, copying down the title, author, and call number of a book, and then trying to find it on the shelves. The following excerpt from one interview with students in Mariellen Wilson's class illustrates their grasp of their own access strategies (again, I was unable to identify speakers fully):

Mark: How would you find out about Bill Clinton?

Student 1:   Biography.

Mark: What would you do? You know who Bill Clinton is?

Student 1:   The new president.

Student 2:   I know where you'd go: in the card catalog, and look for Clinton, the K, and um, and then look for Clinton, Bill Clinton?

Student 3:   But you gotta look under C in Biography.

Mark: How [would you find a book about] Egypt?

Student 1:   "E."

Student 3:   Countries or fact.

Mark: Would you know where to go to find—

Student 3:   800s.

Mark: 800s . . .

Student 3:   900s.

Mark: 900s for Egypt? Okay.

Student 4:   I don't know the library.

Mark: You don't know? Could you just go in and go right to the place, or would you have to use the card catalog?

Student 2:   You have to use the card catalog and write down the place before you find it.

Student 3:   I don't have to.

Mark: Why don't you have to?

Student 3:   Because I know this; I know libraries.

Mark: You know this library? How long have you gone to school here?

Student 3:   I've just been here two years, but I learn fast.

Student 4:   I've been here four years and I still haven't figured out how to use the card catalog.

   These students' tentative and uneven knowledge of procedures might lead an adult observer to conclude that those who claimed to know what they were doing were merely reciting what they had been told about how to access information. However, because each group that I spoke with talked at length and in detail about using the card catalog, and because I did observe many students using the card catalog in the library (though without much practical success), I suspect that students did, in fact, fully believe that rummaging through its drawers before moving to the shelves or seeking help from others was a crucial part of their search process.

   But in spite of these difficulties, and in addition to a weak understanding of the Dewey classification numbers needed to make sense of the library's subcategorical signs, many students were successful in finding books on a given subject, either because through repeated visits to the library they had developed a working knowledge of where books on specific subjects were located or because they were with a peer who had that knowledge. Students in Mariellen Wilson's class seemed to be working from two separate bodies of knowledge, the official, card catalog–cum–Dewey numbers explanation of which they were explicitly aware and a more situated, implicit, working knowledge of topical associations in combination with a knowledge of spatial relations among books on the shelves. They could give a ballpark explanation of how to access information about many topics.

   The students I interviewed at Roosevelt seemed to have developed, then, through a combination of experience and instruction, a heuristic for finding books that was (roughly) as follows: (1) decide if the book is fact or fiction; (2) identify the first letter of the salient word in the author's last name, the title, or the subject; (3) look that up in the card catalog; (4) make a guess about where a book on that subject is located in relation to other subjects whose location is known; (5) look around for the title in that section. But this heuristic would be seriously compromised in its usefulness without a sense of categorical boundaries that grouped books by topic in a way that was roughly congruent to the categorical boundaries of the Dewey system. To observe the ways that students in Mariellen Wilson's class categorized texts, as at Chavez and Crest Hills groups of two or usually three students were asked to sort 35 books representative of the texts that might be found in a children's library or bookstore into groups that made sense to them, then give each group a name.

   Although each group used a mixture of subject and genre categorization criteria in its sorting, the tendency for five of the six groups was to sort texts by subject criteria much more than by genre. For the most part, consideration of whether a text was a periodical, fact or fiction, a reference work like an atlas, an encyclopedia, a dictionary, or even prose or poetry was a secondary consideration in the decisions students made. For example, one group categorized the books under the headings: Outside Livers; Science; Things about Animals; All about Writing; All about History; Most about America; Blacks; Statues; Smiling Children; Ps (the letter P was the main word of their titles); and You Can Look Things Up in Them. Another group sorted the books under the headings: History; People; Science; States; Zoology (Mariellen Wilson had organized a third of the class into a "College of Zoology"); and Books We Don't Know Where to Put. Tape recordings of their conversation during the sorting sessions show that students seemed to be most swayed by key words in the title (e.g., "Egypt" in *The Egypt Game*, or "Americans" in *A Book of Americans*, which is an anthology of poetry) or by an image on the cover; for example, books in the category "Zoology" all had pictures of wild animals on their covers. In another example, the distinction between what was classified as "Real Stuff" and what was classified as "Picture Books" in a third group depended largely on how representational as opposed to cartoonlike the cover illustrations were. Even after I urged students to look through the books before making their decisions, and on occasion challenged a decision by pointing out textual features that did not match the features of other books in the same category, students would argue that their way made more sense; and that way most often involved looking for visual clues—key words and images on the covers and inside the books—that *indexed*, or pointed to, a likely main topic.

Overall, then, students' criteria for categorization and titling at Roosevelt bore a closer resemblance to the *substance* of the Dewey Decimal System and was less attentive to textual genre than were the categories formed by students at Crest Hills; there, with one exception, students paid close attention to the formal genres of the library or grouped the same books by imposing a criteria on them that "managed" the texts as objects (e.g., by size or alphabetical order). The criterion of students at Roosevelt were also "truer" to the Dewey categories than the organizational criteria of students at Chavez, who focused largely on each text's utility or relevance to family members and themselves in making their groups.

To be sure, however, the correspondence between student categories and Dewey categories was not exact; and while there was a strong resemblance, students' categories did not seem to represent any conscious effort on their part to reproduce the Dewey system. For example, the Dewey 900s included history *and* geography *and* biography; but one group separated these three topics into two categories, "About the World," and "People," while another group separated them into "States and Countries," "History," and "People." In another case, only one group had a separate category for "Poems," which in the Dewey system and the library at Roosevelt are in the 800s, under "Literature." And books that would be considered "Folktales" and housed in the Dewey 300s at Roosevelt were most frequently placed with fiction, picture books, or even in the category of "History." In fact, many of the departures that students made in their categorization were at the same points that the system's logic seems to make the least practical sense in contemporary terms; and these were also the same points at which librarians in the three schools made the most significant modifications in shelving. In short, the ways that students at Roosevelt made sense of the 35 texts presented to them were more rational than *rationalized*, and in some critical ways, they made as much sense as the formal ways that the library and the Dewey Decimal System make sense of texts.

The remarkable thing about the library at Roosevelt, then, was that in spite of its rationalized, proceduralized, professionalized systematicity, or perhaps in some ironic ways because of it, many students still found the ways and means to make sense of its organization on their own terms and to use its texts to their own informational advantage. The reasons for this, I will argue, are multiple and complex.

First, with respect to Louise Currie's program of instruction and policies for library use, its "open library" policy was honored in some critical ways. When they entered the library, students for the most part were left to their own devices; they asked for help if they needed it, but many did enjoy the chance to follow their own interests. It also seemed that while close attention was paid to the proper way to do things, the penalties for breaking the rules were slight or nonexistent. While there was a nominal rule that students could only check out two books at a time, for instance, no one monitored the cards for a particular teacher's class to see how many books a student had out; many students, from my inspection of several third-grade classes' cards, had four or more books out in their names. Nor did the librarian make more than a very informal assessment of whether students had "gotten" her instruction the way she intended it; my analysis suggests, in fact, that the real benefit of these lessons might have been to provoke students to begin to make their own sense of the library and its texts as much as it was to provoke the internalization of its external logic.

But these factors alone cannot account for the enthusiasm, the earnestness, the unconventionality, or the lack of constraint that students at Roosevelt displayed toward the library and the meaning and uses of its texts. Students at Crest Hills, for example, had as much or more open access to the library, enjoyed regular story times and frequent, personal attention from a friendly and highly knowledgeable librarian, were monitored even less than at Roosevelt in their book checkouts, and were never evaluated or penalized for failing to "get" the librarian's point during story times. Yet they were very constrained and conventional in the ways they went about ordering and using text and were markedly less enthusiastic about learning for its own sake than were the students at Roosevelt. Accounting for the response of students at Roosevelt requires an examination of the ethos or set of values that was communicated by librarians and teachers through their practices rather than in those practices when examined out of context. In the library at Roosevelt, that ethos can be explained in three ways: through an analysis of librarian-student interaction as a ritual process; through a critical reading of the narratives of the library; and finally, in the reconstructed image promoted in the rituals and narratives of the library of the reader-subject as a socially reconstructed agent.

RECONSTRUCTIVE PRACTICES

Reconsidering Rituality

In characterizing students' responses to the library at Chavez in Chapter 2, I noted how librarian Mary Strauss's characterizations of the act of reading and the intended effects of her program were consistent with the ways that Geertz (1983) and Turner (1969, 1974, 1982, 1992; see also Ashley 1990) have theorized ritual processes. During rituals, individual initiates become anonymous; they are depicted by their initiators as undergoing "a 'leveling' process, in which signs of their preliminal status are destroyed and signs of their liminal non-status are applied" (Turner 1982, 26). They submit to ordeals and exercises with arcane meanings that are often narratively justified and whose purpose is to bind them to the values of the group in advance of their participation as full members and thus ensure its continuance. Consequently, ritual processes are fundamentally very conservative in nature; they are preoccupied with maintaining the stability and the historical continuity of a group's identity and its social structures by passing along symbols and meanings to initiates in settings where their reality and significance are compressed and heightened and so are made sacred and seemingly placed beyond alteration. And yet, as Victor Turner has also noted, it is through ritual that the problems confronting societies themselves are addressed and the identities and capacities of individual members are not merely suppressed or repressed within the process but are also expressed and developed; moreover, Turner has argued, it is within rituals that individuals in socially fragmented, industrialized societies find the means not merely to cope with their alienation but to turn that alienation to their culturally transformative advantage.

How can this be? Two factors, one having to do with the conditions of liminality and the other with the conditions of alienation within, in our case, an industrialized life world, can be identified. The first factor results from the condition of being temporarily displaced from society as an initiate, outside responsibility to its members and so outside its punishments for violating its strictures. Because, in their state of anonymity, anything they do "doesn't matter," initiates are given license to play with their given reality in ways that no vested member of a society would think of doing. "Dead to the social world," as Turner (1982, 27) puts it, they can, and do, raise hell. Thus,

[l]iminality may involve a complex sequence of episodes in sacred space-time, and may also include subversive and ludic (or playful) events. The factors of culture are isolated, in so far as it is possible to do this with multivocal symbols. . . . Then [the symbols] may be recombined in numerous, often grotesque ways, grotesque because they are arrayed in terms of possible or fantasied rather than experienced combinations. . . . In other words, in liminality people '"play" with the elements of the familiar and defamiliarize them. Novelty emerges from unprecedented combinations of familiar elements. (27)

Within culturally cohesive, intact social groups or societies, Turner continues, where social activity is all of the same piece, rituals are highly formalized and set apart from daily life; they are clearly marked rites of passage from one social condition to another. Within such congruent life worlds, temporal/spatial distinctions between work and play do not need to be observed so keenly, so that even though initiates play with elements of their culture during a liminal period, they are actually *working* at acquiring knowledge of "how things work" symbolically within their social order. The play itself is ritualized and bounded—initiates may raise hell, in other words, but they do so in expected ways—and play's effect is to socialize initiates to their new status within society. There is a high-stakes intensity to this sort of play; it is seldom "leisurely." Initiates do construct themselves within this liminal state, but they construct themselves into beings that ultimately fit within the form and function of their society.

As I also noted in Chapter 2, the efficacy of ritual processes of this sort is very dependent on the true belief of everyone involved. It requires tremendous implicit social coherence and shared understandings within a group, understandings that cannot be seriously challenged or interrupted by external forces. But industrialized life worlds are seldom characterized by such unitary belief and inclusiveness, as Turner, writing in the latter part of his career, also noted. Instead, industrial societies are more often marked by social upheaval and by the transience of their populations, as individuals, families, and fragmented social groups disburse from one region to another in search of ever-better "career opportunities" or, as often, just plain work. Industrialized societies are not nomadic or even migratory, for that matter, for these imply a coherent social group moving methodically within a specifiable geographic terrain; rather, they are *diasporic*, and their condition affects not only those who move but those who are left and those who are "moved in" on. The people with whom one works are likely not to have the same religion or to have come from the same region with the same cultural practices. Most significantly, they are usually not the same individuals one grew up with, so they often do not share a common history and they lack a common cultural memory. Where they do—in the inner parts of major cities or in southern and southwestern parts of the United States, for example, between whites and African Americans or whites and Chicanos—what is remembered and reproduced can be a relationship of institutional oppression and antagonism. The work ethic that prevails in these instances insists that both laborers and employers conform to a single code of cultural practice in the name of "getting the job done." Paradoxically, then, we must all agree to relate civilly to each other as strangers in the name of a common humanity (as defined by the dominant group); otherwise, we'd spend our time trying to relate culturally, labor itself could not be performed, and the work of industrialized societies would not get done.

The consequence of this ostensible division of work from culture in industrialized societies, according to Turner, is the redefinition of work as *labor*—that is, its (partial) extrication from social, performative activities that identify one's total being, who one is, in society and so the division of activities that are laborious (that are "work") from those that are leisurely (that are "play"). The lack of true belief within a fragmented society that separates the activities of work from play for Turner means that the conditions of social regeneration via liminality and communitas that take place within intact cultures with cohesive, shared rituals are shifted within fragmented societies. Whereas liminality in intact cultures is produced during sacred moments that are seasonal, that are collectively generated, and that are "centrally integrated into the total social process" (Turner 1992, 57), such moments within fragmented, industrialized societies tend to be secularized, to be produced by specific individuals or groups of individuals, and to "develop most characteristically outside the central economic and political processes, along their margins, on their interfaces, in their 'tacit dimensions' [though liminoid ideas and images may later seep from these peripheries and corners into the center]" (57). Such conditions are more "liminoid" than liminal;

they represent "in a sense, the dismembering, the *sparagmos*, of the liminal; for various things that 'hang together' in liminal situations split off to pursue separate destinies as specialized arts and sports and so on, as liminoid genres" (56). This difference is more than academic, for as Turner (1982) explains:

I see the "liminoid" as an independent and critical source—like the liminoid "works" of Marx, written in the secluded space of the British Museum Library—and here we observe how "liminoid" actions of industrial leisure genres can repossess the character of "work" through originating in a "free time" arbitrarily separated by managerial fiat from the time of "labor"—how the liminoid can be an independent domain of creative activity, not simply a distorted mirror-image, mask, or cloak for structural activity in the . . . "mainstreams" of "productive social labor." . . . "Antistructure," in fact, can generate and store a plurality of alternative models for living, from utopias to programs, which are capable of influencing the behavior of those in mainstream social and political roles . . . in the direction of radical change, just as they can serve as instruments of political control. (33)

I've gone on here at some length about the difference between work/play in cohesive and more fragmented societies and between liminal and liminoid situations because making the distinction helps to explain the differences in the rituality of librarian-student interactions at Chavez, Crest Hills, and Roosevelt Elementaries and consequently of the ways students were able to make sense of and use its resources. Those differences principally have to do with how each librarian and the students at each school implicitly conceptualized the relationship between work and play and how that relationship was dialectically worked out between elder and initiates during the ritual of story time and other formalized library visits. For example, the motivational reading program and the activities of Reading Rally Day at Chavez Elementary can be seen as its librarian's well-intentioned attempt to turn the work of reading into a playful activity for the children there. From the students' point of view, however, I suspect that the program's underlying assumption of deficiency—the assumption that students were not just "blank slates" but *resistant* slates whose reading must be regulated and monitored at every turn lest the program's message not get written—coupled with their community's working-poor experience of the relationship between work, play, and leisure, led them to characterize the activities of the program not integratively as work/play but as *labor disguised as play* and to seek every opportunity to turn what the librarian regarded as a (highly controlled) liminal situation leading to social integration into a more fragmented, liminoid one. But this was one bent not on temporarily reversing the social order of the library in order to learn it but on subverting that order by finding every gap and contradiction in the library program they could and using those spaces to read on their own terms.

Still, such liminoid, as opposed to liminal, conditions possess enormous potential within a society. They enable individuals and groups of individuals not to be merely integrated within a stable social order but to construct social identities on terms more amenable to them and to (partially) reconstruct social practices in the process. But at Chavez this didn't happen. As I discussed in greater detail in the conclusion to Chapter 2, conditions there were too penal, and the gap between the structural knowledge the librarian presented to students and the structural information students needed and were interested in was too great for students ever to reconstruct the meaning of the library in a fully functional way. Students at Chavez knew that the library had a system, for instance, and they knew the card catalog was its key; but lacking opportunities either to pick up its rules or to learn them outright, they were effectively prevented from conforming to or breaking its code. One consequence, as reflected in the results of the book-sorting task I gave them, was to organize texts in ways that reflected their per-sonal/functional interests in reading but that did not connect them to the way the library or society organizes knowledge. While their actions in this situation stood as a tribute to the power of human agency and a critique of the library's programs, it also seemed clear that because they had to do so sub rosa and with-out benefit of any explicit knowledge of how the library actually works as a sys-tem, their actions often had the ironic effect, as Paul Willis pointed out in his study of resistance, *Learning to Labor* (1981), of also helping to socialize them to assume subordinate roles in the workplace and in society.

The difference in the potential of liminal versus liminoid conditions is made even clearer by the example of Crest Hills. Although the community there was part of an industrialized society, the stability of its student population and their ethnic and socioeconomic homogeneity, combined with the longevity of its li-brarian's tenure and the congruence of its literacy practices and future-oriented ethic within the community's homes, school, and library, produced microcondi-tions similar to societies that prevail in nonindustrialized and in culturally intact communities. As I argued in the conclusion to Chapter 3, a true belief in The Future kept students both in line and on track and fostered liminal, not liminoid, situations that allowed both the narratives and the discursive practices of the li-brarian to tutor students in their future managerial roles. Even the rebellion of the boys during story times against Barbara Henry's attempts to persuade them that "in the years to come" their leisure reading practices would be the same as their practices in the workplace can be read as part of a liminal, rather than limi-noid, process; for although the boys were making distinctions between leisure-re-lated and work-related practices through their rebellion, they did so in a very gen-dered way and in fact were encouraged to do gender by the librarian, whom, it seems, *expected them to rebel* and to do so in very predictable ways that repro-duced *gendered* distinctions between how work and play are related, which, as I noted in Chapter 1, have been primary, functional characteristics of the literacy and life world practices of the middle class since the eighteenth century. Ironi-cally, then, the practices of the library at Crest Hills both combined (during story times) and distinguished between work and play (in the Dewey Decimal System and students' browsing patterns) in the service of preparing students to assume gendered, social class practices in the future.

Finally, the practices of the library and the interactions of its librarian with students at Roosevelt can be characterized in ritual terms as producing conditions that were more liminoid (more playfully subversive) than liminal (ritually repro-ductive) in the responses that were evoked from students; and yet, unlike the lim-inoid situation at Chavez, students at Roosevelt were able, it seemed, not only to critique but to reconstruct the meaning of the library in ways that enabled them to use its resources on their own terms. Students at Roosevelt were re-ceived into the library as initiates, and librarian Louise Currie also saw her job as one of inculcating middle-class values of literacy and text use in student initiates through a series of rituals designed to impart proper ways to access the knowledge (or "information") of the culture. In anonymity, students there were taught to approach the card catalog and access texts through a prescribed series of steps that my observations suggest they only partially understood or mastered initially; there were similar exercises taught for using the encyclopedia and for book checkout and return. There was also an air of formality and of seriousness to these processes on the part of both students and librarian; as will be seen in the next section, Louise Currie herself was a true believer who had come to her profession through visits to her hometown's public library as a child. Like the librarians at both Chavez and Crest Hills, she, too felt the transformative power of the library deeply and constantly conveyed that sense of power to students in her demeanor and in her library's procedures, programs, and decor.

Yet there is a significant difference in the way interactions in the three libraries proceeded: At Chavez, labor was disguised as play, producing liminoid moments of resistance in unexpected spaces that proved ultimately reproductive, while at Crest Hills the play of story time was turned to the future purposes of managerial work, producing liminal moments of rebellion that were ritual in themselves and equally reproductive. But at Roosevelt, it was the work of using the library itself that was turned to play by the students, and not in ways that any elder could predict or encourage, because the play that students engaged in mostly was verbal and derived from the students' own earnest attempts to comprehend the meaning of the librarian and the library as a system. So when a ludic inversion of meanings occurred, it could not justifiably be censored, as at Crest Hills, or managed through increased surveillance and muffled through the rhetoric of reading programs, as at Chavez. At Roosevelt, the agenda of story times and other library visits was shared with students in ways that were not true at the other libraries, ways that produced liminoid moments of dialectical exchange between structure and antistructure and between societas and communitas that were as reconstructive as they were reproductive.

The significance of this sharing of the agenda and the true dialectical exchange between the social forces of societas and the liminoid forces of communitas should not be underestimated here, for the renewal of the social order itself and, within fragmented societies, of individuals' sense of belonging and identity within a fluid social order is predicated on it. As Turner puts it, "Communitas exists in a kind of 'figure-ground' relationship with social structure. The boundaries of each of these . . . are defined by contact or comparison with the other" (1982, 50). Each needs the other, one to provide continuity and stability, the other to promote adaptation and critique, if a society is to thrive and if individuals are to give meaning to their lives. As was noted in Chapter 2, "What is certain is that no society can function without this dialectic" (Turner 1969, 129).

Interestingly, the same understanding of the dialectical, social nature of classroom interaction appears in mainstream *educational* research as well, although it is seldom explained in terms as cosmic as Turner's. For example, Courtney Cazden (1988) makes a similar ironic point in the final chapters of *Classroom Discourse*. While Cazden's central project is to summarize almost two decades of sociolinguistic research and to demonstrate very convincingly that didactic participation structures like IRE are inherently alienating and incongruent with many students' home cultures' language and literacy practices, she also notes that "any classroom contains two interpenetrating worlds: the official world of the teacher's agenda, and the unofficial world of peer culture" (150). Cazden notes that in much productive classroom talk "there is an interpenetration of the official and unofficial, illegal parts of the total classroom-speech community" in which "the dilemma for the teacher (or in this case, the librarian) is not what her academic objectives should be . . . but what rules about talking should be enforced to advance those objectives most effectively" (152).

In summary, in the library at Roosevelt Elementary the dialectic by which societies and individuals construct and in turn reconstruct each other was enabled by the tension created when student initiates in a state of liminoid anonymity encountered the web of signs that formed not only the library's textual structure but its ideological code. Under this condition students were able not only to construct a working knowledge of the library and its contents but also to find, in the inconsistencies of each text's webbed construction as well as in the webbed construction of the collection of texts available to them as a whole, the means to reconstruct a reality more in line with their own social position and subjective view of the world. To see how critical and perhaps how delicate this dialectic tension is we need only have compared its presence at Roosevelt to more asymmetrical relations at Chavez and at Crest Hills.

Victor Turner's theory of ritual processes, then, provides us with a very useful frame for comparing and contrasting ideological processes within the three libraries of this study and for demonstrating how these processes draw from and contribute to cultural structures embedded deep within human behavior. But rituality does not in itself explain why conditions at Roosevelt should be so different from Chavez or Crest Hills or, more important, how students there knew how to play with the work of the library or why its librarian should be so tolerant of their play. At Roosevelt, as at Crest Hills and to a lesser extent at Chavez, procedural knowledge of this sort appeared to be conveyed narratively, in the story that Louise Currie told of her own career, in the stories that she recommended and shared with students, and in the apparent meanings that students took from them. It is to a critical examination of these narrative spaces within the practices of the library at Roosevelt Elementary that I now turn.

Narrative Spaces

The most pervasive and "official" narrative of the library at Roosevelt was the one encoded in the caveman cartoons that graced the signs marking the main subject headings of the 10 Dewey categories, in the posters that Louise Currie used to teach the Dewey Decimal System formally in the fourth grade, and in the pie-chart synopsis of the story that hung on the side of a bookcase on the "Facts" side of the library. In that story, let's recall, a caveman progressed from total ignorance of himself and the world in the 100s, through a growing awareness and sense of empowerment within the metaphysical, physical, and social worlds (in the 200s to 600s), to a point where, having freed himself from the burdens of production and survival, he was free to express himself as all self-made bourgeois should, that is, aesthetically, through the fine arts (the 700s), through literature (the 800s), and finally, through historical texts that celebrated the accomplishments and geopolitical legacy of his own kind (the 900s). In the cartoon il- lustrations for this story, the caveman at the lower end of the hierarchy bore a strong resemblance to that protobumpkin, L'il Abner: His muscles bulged, his fingers twiddled, his eyes stared blankly, and question marks popped out of his head. But by the 700s he had become someone of means and refinement: He held a pencil or a book and he maintained an air of pensiveness—he was more self- possessed.

There exists in this story the strong potential to portray the caveman as the prototypically smug bourgeois subject—as, historically, Melvil Dewey himself was (Garrison 1979)—who secures the world for himself through a philosophical idealism that is actually "a form of rage which wants to subsume the object in the categories of thought, eager to capture and assimilate all that is different from itself" (Best and Kellner 1991, 225). But as Louise Currie told the story, the caveman was a more modest individual than most self-made men. As a subject he was less estranged from his fellows and the world of objects than the typical bourgeois hero: It was he who made friends with the caveman next door, who learned the languages of others to talk with them, and who studied nature, not to gain control of these social and physical worlds but to "commune"-icate within them. He was portrayed as a humble soul who came from nowhere with nothing and with pluck and earnestness and study educated himself and earned his own way in the world, eventually coming to enjoy the fruits of his labors and retiring to pass them along to his progeny. He was portrayed as the First Library User from the librarian's point of view, but he also could have been the First Autodi- dact. His story enacted for the benefit of its audience Bourdieu's (1984) account of the petit-bourgeois attitude toward legitimate culture, self-improvement, and upward social mobility but with none of Bourdieu's attendant cynicism: that if one takes advantage of educational opportunity to "get some culture," then one will almost surely be entitled to the status and rewards that come with its acqui- sition.

The same leitmotif presented itself in the story Louise Currie told of her own childhood and education. Her father and mother were both orphans. Her mother left school in the eighth or ninth grade, but her father finished high school. "The foster family that was raising him . . . wanted to send him to college, but he felt he should get out and go to work." He met Louise Currie's mother after the ser- vice and got a job at the Magnolia Petroleum Company. "He worked out there for forty years, you know, good, steady, dependable shift work . . . and really, he left an estate that was kind of unbelievable, because he didn't make a bunch of money.

"Here were these two people who grew up as orphans . . . and they were just kind of out-on-the-town, somebody had to raise them, and they never let me for- get I had to go to college. They never let me forget it." In her own education, Louise Currie recalled that she was "very impatient" to go to school: "I recall circling the letters in the newspaper and trying to figure what it all was." She started school when she was five. At the end of the school year the class was tested in the cafeteria "by the ugliest woman I ever saw." The woman told the students that they did not have to take the test if they did not want to, and Louise Currie "started not to do it, then I thought, oh, it's so easy, I'll just go ahead and mark the pictures and stuff. . . . I got in the 1-A class."

About her childhood reading, Louise Currie recalled that she was lucky in that "anything I was big enough to read I could read. They [her parents] didn't censor or really pay any attention to what I was reading. I guess they were too busy making a living and stuff, but I read anything I wanted to read, and read widely." The local public librarian (whom Louise Currie, who was herself 70 years old, still visited) "had gathered together a group of us little girls . . . and she was guiding our reading. Most of them were from the other side of town, which was where the rich folks lived—we lived over where the poor folks lived—and she introduced us to first editions and served hot chocolate with whipped cream."

Louise Currie borrowed $100 from an aunt to pay her tuition to the local junior college and then talked her way into a job and some financial assistance. "You know," she told me, "people say bad things about Franklin Roosevelt, but his programs really helped me." She finished two years of college, then she married and planned to become a housewife. But World War II intervened; her husband went overseas and she managed to take another year of college courses through a university's extension service. After the war, her husband entered college at a state university, and she worked to support them but was able to take a few more courses. She also had two children during this time but finally finished her undergraduate degree in "social science."

In her own life, Louise Currie achieved—and not through marriage, as she told the story, but through her own efforts—entry to the middle class; at the end of her career, this library was a final expression of that struggle. Its text, as written by its librarian, communicated in its procedures and in its interior design a preoccupation with the ideology she acquired in her graduate studies (she eventually acquired a master's degree in library science) and, over years of association with the ALA and many nationally known experts, of "how a library should be." That ideology embraced strict adherence to codes of professionalism and rationalized practice as dictated by the research and the experts, combined with a late Victorian, bourgeois focus on form and the aesthetics of good taste, which in theory ought to have made the library a culturally alienating experience for many working-class children. But in the telling of her own story, it became clear that Louise Currie still identified herself as a child who was much like the children of Roosevelt: that is, from a working-class (she said "poor") family who lived on the wrong side of town and whose efforts to acquire the social graces and advantages of the middle class were consciously (l)earned. "You see kids," she told me, "who are really poor kids who achieve a whole lot because they have a lot of inner motivation; I was one of those."

Louise Currie's own story helps to explain many seeming contradictions about the library at Roosevelt, especially its middlebrow character and rule-driven systematicity, conditions that were paradoxically undermined by many other policies and by her own tolerance and good humor toward the students. These factors effectively loosened the controlling influences of the system and opened the library up to its patrons' own uses. This reading also helps to explain how this librarian could paradoxically invoke the classist assumptions of the deficit hypothesis in one clause and the desires of the working-class child in the next. For example, in one interview she stated:

For some of the children in this school, their lives are so barren and so full of problems that this is *the most beautiful place they're ever going to be* [her emphasis]. . . .
I want them to be able to go away from this school with the feeling "that was the
place where it was warm, and they loved me, and *I was free to do some things on my
own* [my emphasis]."

In short, the library at Roosevelt remained an open space at least partially because while its librarian had clearly appropriated the *images* and the rhetoric of
the bourgeoisie, her own reflexivity had effectively mitigated against its coinci-
dent contempt for the ways of the working class in the *substance* of her practice.
Finally, this reading of Louise Currie's life story helps to explain why, although
her layout of the library clearly reproduced the historic differentiation of fictional
and nonfictional texts, and the responses she gave to formal interview questions
about the importance of reading repeated the standard librarian talk about loving
fiction, in her practice with children she emphasized the informational and reference texts of the library. It is, I suspect, because she understood through lived
experience that her own social mobility was built on the acquisition of more
than a "taste" for things "literary."

In other narratives of the library, similar themes—of self-reliance, of the
steady accumulation of capital through persistent investment, of modesty, and of
a generous and sincere extroversion—also reveal themselves. This can be seen
most clearly in the one children's novel that Louise Currie recommended to the
second grade, *Eddie's Valuable Property* (Haywood 1975). In a series of episodic
chapters, when 10-year-old Eddie prepares to move to a new town, his father de-
clares that Eddie will have to get rid of "all that junk" he's been collecting and
storing in the basement by having a garage sale. When the boxes are opened,
Eddie's father recognizes the contents as valuable antique toys. Throughout the
story, it is not only luck that brings Eddie fortune; it is his talent for finding
value in objects (and in people) that others do not see or have little regard for.

Like his spiritual brother the caveman, Eddie's materialism does not extend to
his acquisition or treatment of people as commodity objects, nor is it associated
with any physical or social isolation from others. Quite to the contrary, it is Eddie the newcomer who befriends an isolated boy at school and brings him into
his expanding circle of friends. When the girls at school want to make Eddie a
member of their "Eye Glass Club" but won't also ask Roland and another boy,
Jimmie, to join, Eddie responds by forming his own club; he digs around in one
of his boxes of valuable property, finds an ear trumpet, makes paper trumpets for
his friends, and teaches his friends their running joke: "When we get to school,
I'll give you your horn and you must hold it to your ear. When the kids say,
'What's that?' you say, 'How's that?' " (148).

The same sort of conversations that characterized adults' exchanges with students at Roosevelt also characterize many of the exchanges of Eddie with his
friends. One of them, a boy named Boodles, claims to "read the dictionary a lot.
That's how I know so much about words" (60). The following dialogue suggests
something of the ways that these students might deconstruct formal academic
ways of knowing:

"Eddie's getting an old dog with a pedigree," said Boodles. "It must have something
the matter with its feet."

"It is not an old dog, and it does not have anything the matter with its feet. It's a young old English sheepdog with a pedigree," said Eddie.

"That's it!" said Boodles. "Any word that begins with *ped* has something to do with feet. You know, like pedals on a bike. You put your feet on 'em, don't you?"

"You're right!" said Anna Patricia. "My mother always gets a pedicure."

. . . "Oh!" said Boodles. "Well, if he's young, he must have been born with this pedicure thing." (39–41)

Another book that the librarian recommended to students was *Snot Stew* (Wallace 1989). This book was by far the most popular story in Mariellen Wilson's class, one that students in interviews repeatedly and enthusiastically discussed and continued to check out over the four-month period that I was with them. The story begins with the abandonment of a litter of kittens by their mother. Eventually, two kittens are taken as pets, but their socialization into the life of a middle-class human family is far from smooth. Their human hosts, the kittens learn, have a tendency to be over-attentive and sentimental one moment, and violent in their enforcement of certain unwritten rules (don't sharpen your claws on the furniture; stay off the table) the next. They observe and discuss the culture of their food suppliers carefully in the interests of self-preservation and soon figure out the names of rooms and furniture; they also learn to read the moods and personal ticks of each family member and how to negotiate the rules of the "games" humans play with them and each other, especially the fights between the human brother and sister. In one of these games, which the kittens call "Snot Stew," a little boy in the human family grabs a toy belonging to his sister. She demands its return, but he claims it is his; soon they argue back and forth, slurring the words "Is not!" and "Is too!" until the exchange sounds like: "Snot!". . . "Stoo!" (56–58). The joke of course is that the kittens hear the word *stew* and run for their food bowls in the kitchen, only to feel tricked. The students in Mariellen Wilson's class found this joke to be hilarious and explained it to me with relish. Given their own semiotic proclivities, this is hardly surprising. For them, the story seemed to act as a map of social relations that they could both relate to and study. It also provided an interesting twist to the motif of most children's novels, for, as with those novels, it tells of abandoned protagonists who must learn to depend on their own resources in the body of the novel and who learn to do so successfully; but its protagonists' eventual stance is considerably different. Instead of achieving union with middle-class domesticity, the narrator remains ambivalent about her association with humans and to the end continues to study them with a detachment that assures her psychological, if not physical, independence.

The guiding narratives of the library, then, including the story Louise Currie told about her own life and education, share three critical elements that help to reconstruct the mid-Victorian, modernist problematic of the abandoned, isolated, and eventually domesticated subject who "finds her/himself" at the conclusion of so much contemporary children's literature. First, no characters above are estranged from their family, friends, or community in a way that causes them to treat or be treated as objects, and yet each manages to maintain a reflexivity in social relations that frees him or her as an individual from many of the constraints of the conventional ideology. Second, this reflexivity most commonly reveals and constructs itself in verbal semiotic play, indicating that the characters view the world itself as an open text whose meanings are up for negotiation. Finally, and perhaps as a consequence of the first two elements, the characters in each of the narratives view their circumstances without cynicism or self-pity; even though many live in penury, each believes that the person who reads the world as an open text and looks in places when or where others choose not to look can build his or her own estate and negotiate a share of the world.

The sort of transformation of textual reality into worldviews and ultimately life practices that I am suggesting was enabled by library practices at Roosevelt was contingent on a stance toward the value and authority of texts as well as a way of reading that was very different from the practices both at Chavez and at Crest Hills. Such a "stance" or spatial positioning, in turn, is contingent on ways of conceptualizing relations among space, time, and social being (and practice). This is a *geographic*, as opposed to a primarily *historical*, way of considering how human subjectivities are the reciprocal product and producer of not only a historical, but a spatial dialectic; and in this dialectic, the pursuit of one's desire and the desire of others is dependent on a condition of ambivalence between metaphorical and material realities. The description, or mapping, of such spaces by will be the primary undertaking of the final chapter of this book. As a way of introducing that undertaking, I conclude with a consideration of important differences that the ethnographic study of Roosevelt Elementary makes apparent between the curriculum of the school library and its primary other, the school classroom.

CONCLUSION

For teachers and researchers accustomed to thinking about students' acquisition of literacy within the context of school classrooms, the idea that it is conditions of anonymity and explicit, didactic instruction that are key to creating a learning environment that was, in the words of Louise Currie, "warm" and "where [students] can do some things on their own" must seem counterintuitive if not completely counterproductive and contrary to all the evidence. After all, innumerable studies within the last two decades have repeatedly shown that effective teaching and learning in classrooms depend on mutual understanding and caring within intimate settings, where students feel they are "known." On the same note, many literacy experts have also argued that students learn more thoroughly and are better able to use their knowledge in functional ways when literacy tasks are presented in authentic situations—that is, in contexts where procedures and structures can be scaffolded for them naturally.

In response, because teachers and students spend extended periods of time together within relatively close quarters and focus on the acquisition of specified curriculum content, the necessity of personalized learning within authentic contexts does seem crucial to creating a *classroom* zone where students are known and comfortable with its organized learning agenda. Moreover, there is little doubt that teachers like Mariellen Wilson who included the use of the library in their teaching created rich contexts in which students' literacy could develop. But taken on its own, the school library was potentially a very different kind of educational space from classrooms and one that could provide an important alternate learning agenda to the domesticity of classrooms because it operated within different parameters. This is the case for two reasons. First, because school libraries open themselves to all the students in a school, they are of necessity far more public places than classrooms, places where students may not always be well known. A lack of intimacy in this setting does not necessarily create the condition of alienation, however; except for scheduled lessons and other visits arranged by teachers for specific purposes, students at Roosevelt were left to their own devices in the library, but their emotional and psychological comfort was never threatened or impinged. Under these conditions, anonymity may permit students a rare chance within the school day to elude the domesticating gaze of more capable others (Vygotsky 1978) who may inadvertently constrain interpretive possibilities in their rush to capitalize on "teachable moments" (Routman 1991). Under these conditions a school library may present itself to students as a safe but public space—a liminal/liminoid space—in which individuals can find the freedom to pursue agendas that the immediacy of the classroom precludes.

The second reason has to do with the lengths of time that students spend in libraries compared to classrooms. Even in classrooms where library texts are an integral part of the curriculum, students usually spend relatively short periods of time in the library and may only visit it two or three times a week. Unless they come from homes where parents and older siblings help students to learn about the organization of public libraries during their visits, students' opportunities to pick up these skills on their own will be haphazard. Louise Currie knew this, and that is why she felt her didactic instruction, decontextualized as it was, was needed. Her four or five scheduled "skills lessons" a year effectively provided students with a sense of familiarity with the library as a system, even as their openness allowed great freedom of interpretation—providing, in effect, students with a "road map" to the library but no directions. Again, literacy experts may argue that a more authentic way to impart the same knowledge would be for teachers and librarians to work more closely together during student projects that required accessing information in the library, as Mariellen Wilson and Louise Currie did occasionally. But I would also note that without the tolerance of a librarian like Louise Currie or the restraint of a teacher like Mariellen Wilson who could see the sense making within her students' "fooling around," and not step in to prevent "mistakes," this sort of learning context would not necessarily also open the system itself up to critique by students and so might become another vehicle for the uncritical transmission, rather than the reconstruction, of knowledge. In the end, when the total contexts in which students are able to interact with texts are governed by domestic principles of careful supervision, the totalizing influence of that order may not only nurture the development of literacy skills; at times it may also inadvertently stifle alternative readings and uses of texts, as at Crest Hills, or actively work to smother oppositional voices and agendas, as at Chavez.

While domestic values were also strongly represented in the decor and interior design of the library at Roosevelt and upheld in the arguments that Louise Currie used to justify her program, their totalizing influence was effectively mitigated by the stories that she recommended to her students and that she used to explain the library's system, as well as by her own good humor and tolerance of students' alternative readings of her program. I have tried to show this is because rather than working to resolve all the inherent contradictions of school librarianship,

Louise Currie's perception of the social agenda of the library was the negotiated product of at least two different ways of seeing the world, simultaneously from the perspective of the working-class child and from the perspective of an adult who is thoroughly ensconced in the discourses of her profession. While she invoked the deficit hypothesis in her characterization of the students she served, and showed enormous enthusiasm for the professional discourses of school librarianship as the proper and official response to social and educational deficiency, she could quickly turn and in her interactions with students almost assume the position of a child herself, a child who was reconstructed from the living memory of her own childhood and interaction with libraries and librarians. Rather than try to iron out the contradictions between the subject positions of the missionary adult and the apostate child, Louise Currie's main achievement was to construct practices that honored one as they accommodated the other; and these practices effectively permitted the children in her care some space in which to read and make sense of the library in terms that negotiated, but did not submit to, its order.

The case of Roosevelt Elementary and of Louise Currie would probably be regarded by standard sociologies of education as an anomaly—as the fluke case of an individual within a school setting who, through a combination of serendipitous circumstances, managed not to be "reproduced" by the educational system and so, in her practices, found ways not to reproduce in students either resistance or conformity to the dominant middle-class ideology of reading. But, in fact, if we took a more generational view of Louise Currie's experience, she could be seen not as an isolated individual at all but as the current link in a long line of oppositional practitioners reaching back to her own childhood librarian, and perhaps that librarian's librarian, and extending through dialogical links with her own students into the future. Louise Currie might then be seen not as an isolated subject but as part of the historical undercurrent of alternative practice in education that has always, although at times with greater or lesser openness, interrupted the currents of mainstream educational practice (Teitelbaum 1991).

If this is the case, then as the educators of educators and the theorizers of change, we ought to take a lesson from their example and, not by opposing or trying to redirect mainstream currents but by joining and widening historical undercurrents already there, help to make more and new spaces where educators and students can do their humanizing best to reconstruct our world. A theorization of that space, and of the heterogeneous—as opposed to unified—subjective positions that the data of three school libraries and my reading of them suggest, is the project of the final chapter of this book.

5

Toward a Geopolitics of School Libraries

A whole history remains to be written of spaces—which would at the same time be the history of powers (both these terms in the plural)—from the great strategies of geo-politics to the little tactics of the habitat, institutional architecture from the classroom to the design of hospitals, passing via economic and political installations. It is surprising how long the problem of space took to emerge as a historico-political problem. Space used to be either dismissed as belonging to "nature"—that is, the given, the basic conditions, "physical geography," in other words a sort of "prehistoric" stratum; or else it was conceived as the residential site or field of expansion of peoples, of a culture, a language or a State. . . . The development must be extended, by no longer just saying that space predetermines a history which in turn reworks and sediments itself in it. Anchorage in space is an economico-political form which needs to be studied in detail.

—Michel Foucault, "The Eye of Power," in *Power/Knowledge*

CONCEPTUALIZING SPACE

Here at the end of this comparative study of three school libraries, I think it must be imperatively clear that Michel Foucault was right and that coming to terms with the ways that school libraries are ordered by, and are meant to order, the desires of adults and children requires that we read further than what is usually considered appropriate or possible in the educational and library science literature. It requires that we not stop at the decoding of practices, discursive and organizational, as they occur within a space whose dimensions and positioning are dismissed as largely accidental and beyond their control, and that we instead look at how space is used to enact relationships, both ideological and tactical, between power and knowledge within school settings.

The opening chapter of this book did, in part, achieve such a task in that it dealt with the ideological and tactical internal ordering of school libraries as gendered political spaces and showed how the early practices of school librarianship, practices that are little changed in their ethos from practices today, were not merely shaped by but actively shaped and actually created both the school library and its primary organizing principle: the division of "fictional" texts of leisure from "nonfictional" texts of work. There is also a way, however, in which the three chapters that followed the first could be read as undoing this proposition; for when each of the three libraries studied is placed in comparison with the others, what seem most salient are not the similarities but the startling differences among the ways librarians in each setting interpreted their mandate and exercised their authority within similarly ordered spaces. When considered as an independent variable, the ordering of texts in school libraries would not seem to influence the actual behavior of librarians and children; so one could argue that the practices of librarians and also the responses of children to them had little to do with space and much to do with variation in the social backgrounds of the librarians and the children they served—that is, in historical, rather than geographic, conditions.

On the other hand, it is very possible that the similarity in the ordering of all three libraries renders its effects invisible, and that to conceptualize the library positively as a physical ordering of texts and then look for the Newtonian effect of that order on the practices of librarians and library users is to misconceive the significance of the library as librarians and users themselves conceptualize—and use—it: as a "space." If adults and children conceived of the school library as a space in exclusively positive terms, that is, if they only thought of it as a collection of texts ordered in a particular way, one against the other, then the only significance the library would have for them would be the ordering of its texts, and the only measure of its significance on their behavior would be the comparative observation of practices across libraries. In Peircean terms, its level of signification to the people associated with it would not extend beyond the level of the icon, as a diagram, and the index, as a set of proximal associations. Other factors besides the order of the library, and most of them determined by the personal history of librarians and users, would appear salient in determining differences in practices, and the order of the library itself would appear to be little more than a historically determined vestige. But if adults and children conceptualized the school library as a space in terms that were more than physical, and defined that space as different from other spaces where different agendas were also exercised, then we would be justified in conceiving of the library not exclusively in terms of its physical, internal ordering but in terms of its social significance within its larger setting, the school, and ultimately of the school within the lives of students, within their cultures, and within society at large. The library could be conceived of and would need to be analyzed as a social space, a space that was both "real," that is, physically present and concretely ordered in a particular way, and yet existing also as a cultural sign whose meaning as a sign depended on its juxtaposition to other spaces-as-signs as they, too, existed in the imaginations of the social beings whose lives they touched.

In this conception (again in Peircean terms), the library would be a fully symbolic entity, one containing and dependent on a real physical space rendered comprehensible in itself in iconic and indexical terms but also understood and rendered socially and culturally significant to the adults and children associated with it as a concept, a concept whose meaning was constructed by its relations to other, differently ordered spaces in the school and in the lives of those adults and children. We would not be able to dismiss the order of the library as vestigial, then, because the ways in which that order differed from, extended, or imitated the order of other spaces in the life worlds of adults and children would be crucial to its meaning—and its use—by them. The library could be metaphorized as a text, and its order would be the structure of that text; the influence of its order on the practices of adults and children, and the differences in practices from library to library, would be accounted for in the same way that we account for differences in meaning that any two or more readers take from a text, not as the failure of that text and its structure to influence meaning but as meaning constructed through dialectical exchange between the text and different readers' differing subjectivities. So in the social imaginations of adults and children, there would be three dialectically constituted and highly interdependent constructions that would need to be accounted for in the analysis of their practices in the library: the subjectivities of adults and children; the geography of the library, which would be composed of its internal set of relations and its positioning vis-à-vis other school spaces; and history, or rather the robust set of systemic relations that Michel Foucault alluded to in the quote above among economy and politics but just as much among culture, language, and gender (to name a few areas of the whole)—relations originating in the past that act as the template for systemic relations in the present. Historical relations and their legacies have been the subject of Chapters 1 through 4 in this book, and subjectivities as they relate to history and geography will be the closing topic of this chapter. For now I will consider the ways that the geography figures into the practices of the school library.

There is abundant evidence from this study that in the imaginations of adults and children in schools the library is geographically conceived of not in Newtonian terms but in sociocultural, and ultimately political, ones, as a space whose meaning derives from what it permits when contrasted to what other spaces in the school, most notably the classroom, often do not permit. Historically, the establishment of children's reading rooms in public libraries and later in public schools produced a physical space within the setting of the school that was contrary to the didactic, rote traditions of the elementary schools of the period—an actual space in the midst of a larger institution designed as a protofactory (Callahan 1962; Spring 1972; see also Willis 1981), a space in which children's desires were recognized as potent and legitimate forces in their education. From the beginning also, children's librarians acquired their practices not in normal schools or teacher education programs but in schools of library science and from the practices of charity workers. These practices derived not only from their lived experience of literature as a potent form of pleasure and information but probably also from their pragmatic, local acknowledgment that the order of the space over which they presided—a space dominated not by individual desks but by tables, chairs, and bookcases—and the amount of time and contact they had with individual children effectively precluded them from exercising the same kind of overt control over the bodies and so, in a Foucauldian sense, over the minds of their constituency that teachers were able to exercise. Instead, the tropes-in-trade of librarians necessarily had to be "guidance" and "influence"—gentler, deeper forces that, if applied not over a single year but across the career of an individual child in a school, might have as profound an effect as any teacher's will to power in a given year.

In formal interviews and other more informal interactions, the three librarians in this study consistently identified themselves and their practices as part of the tradition of school librarianship, a tradition that they implicitly defined in contrast to the practices of the teachers in their school. As I noted in Chapter 1, although each librarian had originally been a classroom teacher (as all school librarians in the state were required to have been), none of the three saw herself as a teacher who now worked in a library but, in pointed contrast, defined her identity as that of a librarian who used to be a teacher. All three named the American Library Association and its state affiliate as the group with which they associated and attended its state and national conferences, rather than the conferences attended by teachers, for example, the state education association or the state and International Reading Association (IRA) conferences. Finally, in her conversations with me, each consistently spoke of her systemic role within the school, a role that implicitly separated her from the faculty and that named the teachers as "other" to the librarian, just as a school administrator or counselor might speak in global terms that placed him or her in a "higher" position than teachers.

That these librarians placed the agenda of the library in contrast to the agenda of the classroom was underscored in at least two of the three libraries in individual ways; the exception here was, predictably, Crest Hills, where Barbara Henry sometimes made overt attempts to link classroom projects with students' library visits during story times. Louise Currie, on the other hand, stated more than once that she wanted her library to be a place where "it was warm" and where children could do some things on their own, implying that their classrooms might not be such places, and that the regular school curriculum did not provide such opportunities. Mary Strauss was less indirect; she acknowledged that her motivational reading programs and her control of children's browsing and book checkout violated many of the principles of school librarianship; but she justified her practices with the argument that since many of the teachers at Chavez were not readers themselves and did not value reading fiction for its own sake, she was duty bound to compensate for their failure to motivate and overtly direct the reading of their students. Mary Strauss's acknowledgment that the role she was playing—a role she stated belonged to teachers—was in many ways contrary to the role that the ethos of librarianship said she should be playing, and the deep conflict that she projected in her conversation testify to the importance of library-classroom divisions in defining the cultural place and practices of the library.

There is, finally, evidence that children believed the library to be a space with an agenda that was very different from their classrooms' and that this belief influenced what they were and were not willing to do in the library. The most obvious illustration of this was the reaction of the boys at Crest Hills to Barbara Henry's attempts to suggest that, from now on, the sort of reading stance they took routinely in their classroom work would be the stance they would learn to take when they read for pleasure. Although boys and girls in Elaine Dawson's class routinely used the library to research class assignments, the space of the story corner had always been reserved for their ludic participation in the reading of texts that met their, and not their teacher's or the librarian's, desires. Students at Chavez also made it clear in interviews and in the steps they took to circumvent the restrictions of Author Fan Club and other reading programs that they knew, in principle, that the resources of the library were intended to meet their interests and not the interests of the librarian. The refusal of a normally cooperative and very bright student like Miguel to read fiction and instead to insist on his right to read the biographies of minority sports heroes like Jackie Robinson, and the frustration of his teacher and librarian with the assertion of that right, was also grounded in the tacit understanding of all concerned that the library was, in the final analysis, a place where readers' desires held first priority. Evidence of the assertion of this principle on the part of students was less apparent at Roosevelt, perhaps because as a space the agenda of that library was so open to students in the first place. The dialectic between students and the librarian that occurred during didactic library skills sessions with the students, however, hints at the need, within the library, for students to be allowed to make sense of the library and its texts on their own terms.

I want to be very clear about the argument I am making here. I am not arguing, for instance, that classrooms and libraries are antagonistic in their relations or that they can be contrasted in simplistic terms as totalitarian versus libertarian regimes. In actual practice, the agenda of either space often spills over into the other; teachers send children to the library to do research for curricular projects that are often very specific and controlled, librarians work with teachers' plans in the library, and children behave under these circumstances as diligent students who must meet production requirements; likewise, teachers bring library books into the classroom and allow, in group projects and other "creative" activities, work to accommodate the desires and interests of children as best they can. I am arguing, however, that when these crossovers occur, they are reckoned as accommodations to the needs of each other, as "exceptions that prove the rule." The cultural rule remains, despite the philosophy or creativity of an individual teacher or the rigidity or fussiness of an individual librarian, that classrooms are fundamentally spaces devoted to literacy as work, and libraries are fundamentally spaces devoted to literacy as the pursuit of personal desire. Moreover, these differing devotions are read by adults and children in the differing history and geographic arrangement of the two spaces, the differences are deeply felt, and the two spaces, along with all the other differing spaces of a school and of the school as a space that differs from the home, the church, the playground, the mall, or the streetcorner, depend on their differences to identify the function and nature of activities within a given space.

THE SCHOOL LIBRARY AS HETEROTOPIC SITE

This geography, or cultural conceptualization of space, is radically different from the geographies that prevailed in other periods of history, according to Michel Foucault (1986). It produces different social arrangements, different distributions in power and knowledge, and different opportunities for individuals and groups to produce and assert their identity with, against, or apart from the dominant ethos and practices of mainstream society. Ironically for someone whose career seemed mainly given over to the explication of spaces, during his lifetime Foucault only discussed space in geographical terms in four brief articles. Three of these occasions were published interviews in which Foucault responded extemporaneously to interviewers' questions about his apparent, but largely unarticulated, metaphorical and material interests in space. The fourth occasion was a lecture given to a group of architects in 1967 and published posthumously in English in 1986 as "Of Other Spaces" in the journal *Diacritics*.

In these lecture notes, Foucault advances two related propositions. The first is that, contrary to the nineteenth century, which was consumed with representing the world in temporal, historical terms whose dominant themes were "of development and of suspension, of crisis and cycle, themes of the ever-accumulating past," the dominant preoccupation of a period characterized by exponential increases in population and new technologies in transportation and communication will be the reordering of the world not in terms of distance and sequence, spatial and temporal, but in terms of propinquity and interconnection:

The present epoch will be above all the epoch of space. We are in the epoch of simultaneity: we are in the epoch of juxtaposition, the epoch of the near and far, of the side-by-side, of the dispersed. We are at a moment, I believe, when our experience of the world is less that of a long life developing through time than that of a network that connects points and intersects its own skein. (22)

Foucault's second proposition is that a history of space—of the ways that cultural conceptions of space have changed over time—can and ought to be written for the understanding it would provide of present relations between space and cultural practices with regard to the distribution of power and knowledge in a given period. For example, Foucault notes that the hierarchical cosmology of the universe that supported hierarchical, vertical arrangements of power and knowledge during the Middle Ages also constituted the ordering of spaces during that time, so that medieval space could be described as "the space of emplacement" (22), in which a static, enclosed cosmology ordered by an immediate deity diagrammed a static, enclosed society in which everyone was born into, and knew, their place. With Galileo came the displacement of the earth from the center of the universe and by implication, the displacement of divine ordinance to a prime, but very distant, position; but in Foucault's analysis, "the real scandal of Galileo's work lay . . . in his constitution of an infinite, and infinitely open space . . . a thing's space was no longer anything but a point in its movement, just as the stability of a thing was only its movement indefinitely slowed down" (23). Space, and tracing one's own path and order within an undelineated, virtually endless space, became a matter of plotting one's path in time in relation to other objects' paths in time; history became determinant, while geography was viewed as its circumstance or as its physical product.

Although changes in the ways that space is conceptualized in different time frames are not accounted for by Foucault, I am supposing that they are due to changes in the material circumstances in which societies are constituted. I am also supposing that the shift Foucault saw in the present epoch from the definition of place by its coordination in time to a definition of the site as a location "defined by relations of proximity between points or elements"—that is, in geographic rather than in historical terms—has much to do with two conditions. The first is the closure of the notion of the geographic "frontier," or of spaces largely uninhabited (or written as uninhabited; see Pratt 1992) and therefore open to the imagination of society. And the second is the collapse of spatial and temporal distance as a defining condition of possibilities by technologies of transportation and communication, that is, by the elimination of material, physical constraints that produce the need for other practices of separation and containment.

At any rate, the defining principle for Foucault by which space is ordered in our time is not cosmologically or mechanically/temporally driven but is, instead, largely semiotic in its processes. Our sense of where we are and of what location means, and the significance that places have for people in their social imaginations are constituted negatively from their sense of what they are *not* and, therefore, of what other practices they enact. The meaning of a space, like the meaning of a word, is defined in its negativity by its differences from other spaces. And those differences are perceived as both material and metaphorical; that is, they are sensed in both physical and intuitive ways. For although we have displaced the influence of God in this scheme, according to Foucault, a sense of the sanctity of space itself remains with us; our presence in a particular space, and our awareness of what that space is in juxtaposition to other spaces, retains the power to legitimate practices that would be almost inconceivable and certainly inappropriate within other spaces; and it is this sense of sanctity that stabilizes and orders our practices as social beings. Thus, there are spaces designated for work and for leisure; and their spatial designation separates the activities of work from leisure and ensures that the two won't be confused. There are also, as Foucault notes, spaces designated as private and as public; as cultural and as useful; for families and for other social groups—in short, a life world of spaces constituted in opposition to each other.

What characterizes all these spaces is their quality of heterogeneity, of their difference from one another and of their delineation as sites by their relations to all the others; and it is within this condition of heterogeneity, of multiplicity in not only the relations that order sites but in the relations that order the identities and possibilities of the people who frequent them, that Foucault suggests possibilities for creative response to a system bent on individualizing, normalizing, and bringing desire under control can be made or found. Foucault describes certain sites, defined by particular sets of relations, that interest him most. These sites "have the curious property of being in relation with all the other sites, but in such a way as to suspect, neutralize, or invert the set of relations that they happen to designate, mirror or reflect" (1986, 24). They are of two types: the utopia, a place with no real place where society is presented in some perfect form meant as a corrective model for its very real problems and tensions; and heterotopias,

places that do exist and that are formed in the very founding of society—which are something like countersites, a kind of effectively enacted utopia in which the real sites, all the other real sites that can be found within the culture, are simultaneously represented, contested, and inverted. Places of this kind are outside of all places, even though it may be possible to indicate their location in reality. (24)

What makes the relationship between sites and their heterotopic counters unique and, perhaps, hard to grasp in abstraction, is the extent to which heterotopias concentrate the meanings and contradictions within the principal sites of a life world in images that open that world to examination and contestation. They are not so much scale models of those sites as they are their ordering forms and functions combined and sometimes inverted, that is, twisted to perform some other function that exposes what would otherwise be concealed within a society.

Heterotopias are places removed from the normal sphere of activities in daily life. As examples, Foucault names the boarding school, the honeymoon trip, the prison, the cemetery, the garden, the library, the vacation resort, the brothel, and the colony, among others. Each of these examples, in turn, is an example of one of five descriptive principles that characterize heterotopias as sites. The first principle is that all societies, not only our late industrialized one, have hetero-topias, which are of two main types: the heterotopia of crisis, where people go when they are in some transitional stage—during puberty, during marriage, dur-ing birth, so that what happens to them can happen in a space that is apart from every day life; or the heterotopia of deviation, a recent innovation to the notion of crisis, where people whose prognosis is not so much transitional as frequently terminal are placed; these are the prison, the psychiatric hospital, and the rest home. The second principle of hetertopias is their ability over time to change their cultural function; Foucault's example is the movement of the cemetery, which in medieval times formed a sort of "city of the dead" located within a vil-lage or city, to the suburbs, where it has become an individuated site of decay. As its third principle, the heterotopia juxtaposes "in a single real place several spaces, several sites that are in themselves incompatible." Within a formal gar-den, for example, nature itself is bent to the designs of human imagination, and plants, stones, and other human-made structures that would never be found to-gether otherwise are combined to form a representation of the world that is at once apparently, delightfully "natural" and yet utterly contrived; a zoological gar-den makes this point with even more force. The garden is a "sort of happy, uni-versalizing heterotopia" (26)—a site that makes the relations between humanity and nature seem far more congenial than they are.

The fourth principle of heterotopias is their connection to time, or rather to slices of time, and to the ways that they attempt to represent, arrest, or preserve time within space. Clear examples are museums and, of course, libraries, spaces dedicated to the organization and representation of society in ways that render it immemorial; but the vacation resort where people go to "get away from it all" also achieves its function by abolishing the demands of "real" time, as do fair-grounds, where mundane reality is interrupted by the temporality of the carniva-lesque for fleeting periods of the year. This fourth principle of temporality is closely linked to Foucault's fifth principle, that heterotopias always presuppose a system of opening and closing that both isolates them and makes them penetra-ble, places that are "not freely accessible like a public place . . . [and where] to get in one must have a certain permission and make certain gestures" (26). One's reasons for entering them must be clear, and one is obliged to observe certain practices, to behave in a prescribed sort of way, while in them. Prime examples of these spaces are the barracks, the bath, or even the motel room—a space where, at least in Foucault's imagination, "a man goes with his car and his mis-tress and where illicit sex is both absolutely sheltered and absolutely hidden, kept isolated without however being allowed out in the open" (27).

Parameters

As a site that is socially defined as other to the classroom, the school library makes a perfect example of a heterotopia. It is, in accordance with Foucault's fifth principle, an enclosed space that is ostensibly open to the use of everyone in a school, and yet is also curiously private in its practices, and is organized by a code of classification and numeration that must be acquired, either through private tutorial or group ritual, and that must be adhered to if a user is to find anything on the library's shelves; this code is also a prime cue to users of the library's sanctity as a space.

In accordance with Foucault's fourth principle, the school library is linked to slices of time in both ways that Foucault describes. Like the public and university libraries it imitates, the school library contains the "best" books of the culture that are suitable for children, many of which are "classics," books whose quality is so great they are "timeless" in their knowledge and their appeal; and in the nonfiction section, they are arranged by a system that, at least according to Louise Currie, recapitulates the phylogenetic progress of the human species from caveman to bourgeois savant. But the school library is also a place that requires "visiting": It is a place to which individual students or small groups or an entire class escape from the normal routine of the classroom, a space that interrupts the normal process of a school day, and so, for all its quiet rituals, it is also a place of festivity (which, again, accounts for the Dawson boys' resentment of the librarian's suggestions about their reading during story time). This juxtaposition within the same space of spaces devoted to festival and to memorial, and within the book collection, the juxtaposition of the texts of work and production to the texts of leisure and desire, is in accordance with Foucault's third principle. As a whole, the school library is arranged much like a garden, a diagrammatic representation of the literary cosmos; and like a garden, its effect is meant to delight and to make this representation of the world and the juxtaposition of texts and spaces devoted to opposing sets of practices seem more congenial than they actually may be.

Foucault's second principle may not seem to pertain so directly to school libraries since, as I have argued throughout this study, the mandate and practices of the school library and of librarianship seem little changed from their inception in the late nineteenth century. But when the formation of school and children's libraries is considered as part of the history of libraries as institutions, then a radical change, from an institution that until the late nineteenth century was an idiosyncratically ordered signifier of social status and power to a publicly funded institution charged with the "uplifting" (and intellectual ordering) of the masses via their desire, is made apparent. A sense of crisis provoked this change in the library's cultural function, and it was a sense of crisis, and of a strongly felt need on the part of librarians to motivate a transition in the literacy of their clientele, that motivated the practices of at least two of the three librarians in the study.

For Mary Strauss, the crisis she attempted to address was a crisis of desire. Children in her school were not learning to "love books," and particularly fiction, as she believed they should, with consequences that were almost beyond contemplation for her; for if children would not love fiction, how would they learn to read, how would they come to know a wider world than their own, and how would they get ahead in life? The response to this crisis was the organization of the library as a preemptive heterotopia of deviation, governed by principles of surveillance and individuation, where reading habits could be more efficiently corrected. That these procedures eliminated much of the difference between the ethos of the school and classroom and that of the library and violated the sanctity of the library as a space was not lost, on an unarticulated, intuitive level, on the students at Chavez, many of whom continued to find ways to have their desires as readers met.

Barbara Henry's sense of crisis was both more and less pressing, for her concern was that the literate stance that children took in the early years of their lives should be transformed to the literate stance that would allow their participation in the activities of the professional-managerial class; her concern was one of the acquisition of the proper standards of taste, without which she knew the children at Crest Hills would always seem, and feel, out of place. She was concerned not with correcting but rather with shaping the desire of students within the library. Yet her concerns were no less serious, in a way, than Mary Strauss's concerns, as the developing ostracization of two children whose tastes and interests deviated from the professional-managerial norm—J. C., the third grader who didn't want to go to college, and Emily, the animal behaviorist banished in her peers' discourse to Harvard—seems to illustrate.

Crisis operated in a different form at Roosevelt Elementary, but in a way that was similar to the way I have portrayed it as operating in the early years of school librarianship, when librarians thought of their libraries as promoting an alternative view of education and of literacy. Unlike Chavez and Crest Hills Elementaries, where it was children who were presumed to be in a state of crisis due to the social and human environment outside the school, at Roosevelt it was not only children's home environments but the curricular environment within the school that was implicitly recognized as the source of crisis. Louise Currie's expressed desire not to shape tastes or to bring children to "the love of fiction" but to create a place "where it was warm, and people loved me, and I was free to do some things on my own" speaks as much to the cultural poverty that she ascribed to children's home lives as to the curricular poverty of the classrooms in which many children in the school were educated. The third-grade teacher with whom I worked, Mariellen Wilson, and her students were a notable exception to this rule, Louise Currie told me; and indeed, Mariellen Wilson's classroom was an extraordinary place that covered the standard curriculum—spelling tests, workbooks, textbook mathematics, and preparation for the next standardized test—in the morning. However, in the afternoon, or between tests, or whenever there was "wasted time" in the regular schedule, the same classroom became an "other" space, a heterotopia called "Mrs. Wilson's University." Then and there the structure of the university Mrs. Wilson had attended was parodied: the three clusters of student desks in the room became three colleges, of math, science, and zoology; Mrs. Wilson's college diploma hung from the top center of the blackboard as its sign of accreditation; and students did "research" on earthworms brought from home, on dolls and doll making, on sharks, or on whatever seized their, and Mrs. Wilson's, imagination—all of which led to forays into the heterotopia of the library for books on these subjects. The library at Roosevelt was open and prepared to accommodate these forays, provoked by crises in the desires of children and teacher to use texts in ways that the libraries at Chavez and Crest Hills seldom anticipated.

BEATING HEGEMONY

Metaphor and Ambivalence

There are two other characteristics of heterotopias that Foucault's analysis implies and that their application to the three libraries in this study makes explicit. First, it seems from all of Foucault's examples and from the example of school libraries as well that a heterotopia is always a place that is visited, a place where one goes but plans not to stay; and second, a heterotopia must be a place where people's desire is never neglected, or ignored, or denied, but is attended to in one way or another. How attention is paid to desire, however, is another matter, and it is this second characteristic of the ambivalence of heterotopic spaces to the liberty of the people who visit them that makes it difficult to claim that the heterotopia is necessarily a space of effective resistance or reconstruction within our social order.

The problem I am discussing here is not an original one in the theorization of space as the geographic bypass to the social cul de sac of modern history. As both Doreen Massey (1993) and Neil Smith and Cindi Katz (1993) have noted, a great number of feminists, postcolonialists, and poststructuralist/postmodern theorists and aficionados, people who are looking for ways to "beat" hegemony and have largely given up on historical dialecticalism as itself ironically reproductive, now put their hopes in spatializing narratives in which "marginalized" groups create spaces in the contradictions of modernity in which they can, as I myself once explained elsewhere, "finally, just be themselves" (Dressman 1995, 243). Victor Turner's (1969, 1982, 1992) application of ritual theory to the negotiation of power relations in industrialized societies, for example, which played a prominent role in the theorization of resistance, reproduction, and reconstruction in Chapters 2, 3, and 4 of this book, is clearly predicated on the existence of liminal/liminoid "sites" where alternative identities are assumed and new relations are played with, spaces within a society where historically constituted relations of power and knowledge can be (momentarily) inverted and parodied. The use of space in the work of Turner and others (Keith and Pile 1993; in education, see Chávez and O'Donnell 1997; Giroux 1992; McLaren 1993) is often metaphorical and frequently very poetic, and its power consists in not only inverting notions of absolute, modernist space in ways that invite its critical observation and analysis but in projecting an environmental response to hegemony that relies on a concept of human agency whose source is not historical (and is even characterized sometimes as antihistorical) and so may not be historically oppressive or ironically reproductive, either.

But there are inescapable consequences when metaphors give means to action in a material world, especially when spatial metaphors and space itself are used to evade history and to deny the reality of historically and materially constituted force. Using concepts of space in an antihistorical way may solve some theoretical dilemmas, but the possibilities it produces are themselves contradictory, since ignoring the practical distinction between metaphorical and material space can provide opportunities for those who privilege not historical analysis but an overdetermined "historicism," or mystification of hindsight (see Foucault 1984, 250; Soja 1989, 21), to reassert themselves in ways that can effectively isolate and contain—and sometimes eradicate—any sites that do not conform to social and institutional norms.

As an example that is outside but related to this study, consider the recent experiences of teachers in elementary schools who embraced the Whole Language Movement in the late 1980s. By referencing their practices to examples of literacy instruction and research conducted by school-based, rather than university-based, researchers, and largely not in the United States, Whole Language was able, for a time, to displace discourses about school literacy and so produce a metaphorical, discursive space that made it possible for many elementary school teachers in the United States to effectively counter the hegemonic influence of the educational-industrial complex of school district politics, university research, and basal textbook companies and begin to act in ways that were more consonant with their own beliefs about children's acquisition and use of literacy (Edelsky 1990; Goodman 1992). The movement's disregard for history, for "the tried and true," and in many individual cases teachers' whole-scale abandonment of basals, spelling tests, and "phonics," as well as their refusal to pay any tribute within the school day, their curriculum, or the material space of their classrooms to what in the eyes of many parents, teachers, and district personnel were the indices of "a well-run classroom," became the negative space, at least in California, in which school administrators could place the blame for falling test scores on Whole Language's "New Age methods" and "chaotic classrooms." In reality, however, the blame more rationally could be placed on the state's inattendance to issues of bilingualism, its outrageously high teacher-student ratio, and its per-pupil spending (second lowest in the nation; see Colvin 1995; Dressman, Mc-Carty, and Benson in press).

In the case of school libraries, we need to imagine, before we criticize the ambivalent legacy of school library culture and the apparent contradictions in the practices of the librarians studied, what might happen were librarians to "get radical" in their practices and their spaces and begin to meet the desires of children in more consistent, seemingly less constraining ways—that is, were they to fully operationalize the metaphorical principle of the school library's agenda as it contrasts with the agenda of the school and the classroom. What would happen, for instance, were Louise Currie to completely eliminate her "skills lessons," if Mary Strauss had a change of heart and began to act in ways that were antagonistic to her school's test-driven curriculum and culture, or if Barbara Henry decided that the doing of gender must be eliminated in her practices and in the arrangement of texts in her library? In each case, the textuality of the library would be changed dramatically, and the constraints on children's literacy within that space probably would be loosened; but the likely political consequences, as each librarian was seen to disregard the beliefs of teachers, administrators, and parents about how a library should operate, would be disastrous.

Under circumstances such as those described and imagined above, a sense of ambivalence about one's loyalty to a metaphorical, idealized spatiality versus a historically justified and materially constituted life world is the condition that enables us to understand—and in the space between the two to negotiate—a compromise between reinvention and reproduction, between one's desires and the exigencies of one's moment. And so ambivalence of the sort practiced by Michel Foucault throughout his career toward the relationship between history and geography, and more important, between concrete and abstract conceptualizations of space and their relation to human agency, lies at the center of this ethnography and of the political geography of school libraries. Yet in the case of Foucault, such ambivalence has been easily confused with indecision and imprecision about the uses of space and spatial metaphors. As Neil Smith and Cindi Katz (1993) read him, for instance, Foucault has "radically denied" the distinction "between material and metaphorical space . . . and the collapse of this distinction is marked by a deeply ambivalent dismissal cum retention of geographical space" (73). Such a rhetorical move, they claim, results in Foucault's failure to "recognize how social agents produce space and socio-spatial relations within and against the economic, political, and juridical imposition of produced space and spaces" (73–74). In other words, if we conceive of "the world" as mutually constituted by a triad of interdependent agents, that is, historical, geographic, and human (named here as descriptors rather than as things-in-themselves), then Smith and Katz seem to be charging Foucault the Structuralist not only with privileging the historical-geographical axis of the triad but with virtually eliminating the difference between history and geography and space and time and, in the process, ignoring the possibility of human agency as a force of resistance and social change.

This reading of Foucault's work, however, overlooks both its own prejudices and the complexity of Foucault's "rhetorical" uses of ambivalence, for in striving to maintain clear-cut distinctions between metaphorical and material uses of space, Smith and Katz seem to privilege the geographical-human axis of the triad and, in so doing, to radically deny/evade the reproductive agency of historical forces. In my view, a more "complete" and perhaps more sympathetic reading of Foucault finds him not purely "structuralist" in his uses of space and time at all but deeply preoccupied with issues of human agency and with the conceptualization of practices that might interrupt hegemonic discourses of power/knowledge between and within history and geography and space and time. As evidence in support of this reading, in "Space, Knowledge, and Power" (Foucault 1984), the interviewer, Paul Rabinow, repeatedly quizzes Foucault about the relationship between architectural design and technologies of social control; for one way to read Foucault's analysis of, say, the panopticon is to conclude that the historical growth of cities, in combination with shifts in the ways that architects and engineers perceived the relationship between space and human behavior, produced determining institutional and physical structures whose effects, in time, were beyond anyone's control—structures that are themselves the primary sources of liberatory or oppressive practices. In response to Rabinow, Foucault adamantly resists this reading of his work, insisting instead that "I do not think that it is possible to say that one thing is of the order of 'liberation' and another is of the order of 'oppression.' " Then he elaborates:

There are a certain number of things that one can say with some certainty about a concentration camp to the effect that it is not an instrument of liberation, but one should still take into account—and this is not generally acknowledged—that, aside from torture and execution, which preclude any resistance, no matter how terrifying a given system may be, there always remain the possibilities of resistance, disobedience, and oppositional groupings. (245).

Conversely, Foucault also insists that no institution or physical structure can ensure liberty, although architecture "can and does produce positive effects when the liberating intentions of the architect coincide with the real practice of people in the exercise of their freedom" (246). Foucault repeatedly asserts throughout the interview that "Liberty [and so also oppression] is a practice" (245)—and he makes it clear that a "practice" is not to be construed in behaviorist terms as environmentally reactive but rather as an act or set of acts undertaken by socially constituted human agents. Ultimately what Foucault is resisting in this interview is the application of his work within a concept of space as an adamantly positive entity rather than as a dialectically materialized one; it is Foucault who is being consistent here with his own concept of space as historically constituted by relations between people and places, against the suggestion of his interviewer that one or the other must prevail.

When read in this way, the power of Foucault's insights, and indeed the strength of his position as a historian/philosopher/social critic, is not undermined by, but is largely dependent upon, his ambivalence about the determinancy of historical/geographical/human interrelations. Edward Soja (1989) echoes this position in his call for "a triple dialectic of space, time, and social being; a transformative re-theorization of the relations between history, geography, and modernity" (12). A similar point is made by Doreen Massey (1993), who consistently asserts that "the spatial is integral to the production of history, and thus to the possibility of politics, just as the temporal is to geography" (159)—in other words, that space, time, and an agency located in individuals constituted as social beings not be thought of as either discrete or fully determining each other—a way of thinking that requires our vigilance against privileging one or two of the three over the other(s) in analyzing both metaphorical and material, socially and historically produced, structures. It is just such a position of Foucauldian ambivalence that I believe ought to be taken when we think about school libraries as sites of history, geography, and social being. The stance that such ambivalence permits is key to recognizing the ways that school libraries, both ideally and in actual practice, figure into either the resistance, the reproduction, or the reconstruction of the social order via the literate practices of students, teachers, and librarians.

Adventure, Not Espionage

In the conclusion of his lecture notes on heterotopias, Foucault himself takes some recognition of the ambivalence of heterotopic spaces to human liberty, noting that heterotopias possess one "last trait," which is "that they have a function in relation to all the space that remains." This function, characteristically, is bipolar: Either a heterotopia acts as a space of illusion, whose quality brings the problematic social conditions of "real" space into sharp focus (Foucault's example is the "brothel," a space he romanticizes as disordered in contradiction to Puritan reality), or it acts as a space of compensation, a space "that is other, another real space, as perfect, as meticulous, as well arranged as ours is messy, ill constructed, and jumbled" (1986, 27). Foucault speculates, and I will quote him here at length for full effect:

Brothels and colonies are two extreme types of heterotopia, and if we think, after all, that the boat is a floating piece of space . . . and that, from port to port, from tack to tack, from brothel to brothel, it goes as far as the colonies in search of the most precious treasures they conceal in their gardens, you will understand why the boat has not only been for our civilization, from the sixteenth century until the present, the great instrument of economic development . . . but has been simultaneously the greatest reserve of the imagination. The ship is the heterotopia *par excellence.* (27)

Foucault concludes, "In civilizations without boats, dreams dry up, espionage takes the place of adventure, and the police take the place of pirates" (27). While it may be hazardous to extend such poetry too directly or too far, if reading can be a kind of sailing, of moving from novel to novel, from illusion to illusion and as far as subject categories that are the distant, perfected forms of a messier, more immediate reality, then in these closing images Foucault may be offering us a reconstructive way "out," a way of tacking across history and the reproductive dilemmas of mass literacy that were introduced in Chapter 1, and developed in the narratives of Chapters 2, 3, and 4. Ambivalence would be the medium, the condition for adventure as opposed to espionage. And as its vehicle, a reader would require, or would require to be captained by, a subjectivity that was also heterotopic in principle, formed from its relations with others and in relation to others, and juxtaposing in a single human site several subject positions that would otherwise be incompatible. The constitution of reader subjectivity as such an agent, or vehicle of adventure, will be the last topic of this chapter and of this study of three school libraries.

RECONSTRUCTING READER SUBJECTIVITY

Environmental Issues

To begin this explication of reconstructed subjectivity, it will be useful to briefly review the general atmosphere or conditions within which students operated as readers in each library—conditions that were formed not only by the ethos of the school and community but, as I have argued in each chapter, by librarian practices that were closely associated with the reader subjectivity of each librarian. If students' readings of the library at Chavez can generally be characterized as acts of resistance, and at Crest Hills as acts of conformity, then students' readings of the library at Roosevelt as a text might best be described as playful acts of disassembly and reassembly—or reconstruction—of text-based knowledge in terms that made pragmatic sense to them. As was detailed in Chapter 4, these reconstruction projects were ubiquitous within the setting of the library program; they were apparent in the library in students' off-center readings of Louise Currie's skills lessons and in the sense they made of 35 texts in ways that paralleled, but did not reproduce, the classification system of the library; and they were promoted by her through the petit bourgeois narrative of the caveman allegory and in her recommendation of children's fiction like *Eddie's Valuable Property* (Haywood 1975).

How is it that so much reconstruction of school and text-based knowledge was in evidence at Roosevelt, in comparison with the curriculums of two other schools and libraries within the same system, Chavez and Crest Hills? The answer can be traced in part to significant differences in the general academic climate and mission of the school. Although by any standard Mariellen Wilson was an exemplary teacher, and her classroom should not be construed as typical of other classrooms in the school, I did see many teachers in the library interact with their students in ways that were more relaxed and more oriented toward using textual materials than at the other two schools. Unlike at Crest Hills, where The Future loomed ominously on the horizon in the minds of students and teachers and the "fear of falling"—that is, of not making the grade and obtaining entry into the professional-managerial class—was a prime motivating factor in the actions of staff and students, at Roosevelt the future was presented as one pregnant with the possibility of upward social mobility. Nor did I hear, in my conversations with teachers at Roosevelt, of undue administrative pressure that was placed on teachers to raise achievement test scores by almost any means. To be sure, testing was not taken lightly there; in a state where schools are closed and principals can be fired for low scores, Mariellen Wilson felt she had to spend a good portion of the week before any battery of tests in preparing students. But it was also clear that neither Mariellen nor the school administration ever regarded the results of those tests as the certification of real academic achievement, as was the case at Chavez.

In short, the evidence suggests that the overall environment of Roosevelt as an elementary school was the product of a compromise between external political demands (testing), the faculty's own understandings of what was important for children to know, and finally the students' own basic interest in making sense of school materials on their own terms. But while a looser, roomier ideological environment at Roosevelt explains how reconstructive acts could occur there, that condition alone does not explain how or why they did happen. To understand that, we must first examine the origins of Louise Currie's tolerance of students' alternate readings of her program in order to understand the multiple factors in her own background that impelled her to behave, in contradiction to the standard practices she claimed to follow, in seemingly counterhegemonic ways. In order to do this, we need to examine how subjectivity was conceptualized at Chavez and Crest Hills Elementaries, as well as to explicate a theory of subjectivity, one that differs from the commonsense modernist notion of subjectivity first projected by Rene Descartes, because it "implies a range of positions from which the subject grasps itself and its relations with the real [from positions that] may be incompatible or contradictory" (Belsey 1980, 65).

Subjectivity and Social Agency Reconstructed

As many authors (e.g., Belsey 1980; Faigley 1992; Fiske 1987) have noted, modernist concepts of subjectivity are hardly distinguishable from the concepts of individuality and the self. In each case, the subject/individual/self is an entity whose distinction from other subject entities is ultimately biological in origin and, while influenced by factors in its environment, possesses a central consciousness or inner "voice" that transcends social influence and speaks for the self. Thus, the modernist, or Cartesian, subject is one whose position in relation to the world is expected to be fundamental, unchanging, unalterable, and unified: we are putatively "named" at conception, and it is exclusively to this name, and to its unfolding developmental plan, that we are expected to respond throughout our lives.

A startlingly clear example of this concept of the subject and of its serious consequences for persons who internalize its implications appeared in the March 7, 1994, edition of *Newsweek*. In the weekly feature, "My Turn," Margaret Brown, a 19-year-old woman confesses, "This is my nightmare—I'm a person created by donor insemination, someone who will never know half of her identity" (12). She goes on to state that " 'Who am I?' is a hard question to answer when I don't even know where I came from." In her unusual situation, the contradictions of the idealized, unified subject are laid wide open for inspection. For she, a child of Tennessee and Texas and student at a conservative Catholic university, is a true believer in a transcendent reality and in the biological determination of her subject position, so that she guesses she acts "just like [her] donor." She continues to speculate:

And, as my thoughts, opinions, and behavior are almost 180 degrees from most of my family members, I've never felt like a "piece of the puzzle" at family gatherings— especially around my father's side of the family. This isn't something I sensed strongly—I thought I acted differently because I was from Tennessee and they were from Texas—but the feeling was always there. (12)

The nightmare that Margaret Brown lives is one constructed by the narrative poetics of the concept of subjectivity by which she lives her life, in which every doubt-creating discrepancy between her values and her family's values that she observes in her late adolescence must be accounted for (or suppressed) by a genetic explanation rather than by the social condition of contemporary adolescence or differences in lived experience between herself and her family. If "getting yourself together" is the sine qua non of "getting a life," then Margaret, it seems, is doomed; by refusing herself the possibility of seeing her subjectivity as socially constructed, she can only "feel anger and confusion" and be "filled with questions" about her subject position in relation to the world in which she lives.

Similar, although not so clearly or dramatically expressed, concepts of subjectivity are central to understanding issues at Chavez and at Crest Hills Elementaries. The illusionary "naturalness" of the way students pick up the discourses and order of the library at Crest Hills was a function of congruence among the practices of home, classroom, and library. The condition of unaltering univocality that was created also created a sense that there was only one, and therefore transparent, way of seeing the world, that is, one relevant subjectivity. People who didn't see things from this position—or worse, people whose positions departed from the norm, like J. C. or Emily—"must have something wrong with them." To the extent that this unified sense of a transparent reality remained in force, true believers at Crest Hills could also continue to believe in the natural quality of their environment and in their own normality: They thought, therefore

they were, and that's all there was to it. But in the course of living, in the experience of the real contradictions and friction among differing people that present
themselves to students and teachers and librarians in their daily interaction, true
believers can find themselves at odds with their own beliefs, so that what is
normal or natural in a situation is not always that clear to them; then they may
begin to worry that maybe they aren't normal after all. Thrown off center in adolescence or by changing family situations, they become, like Margaret Brown,
lost or, as Barbara Henry described students she observed at Crest Hills who had
experienced some decentering in their lives, "brittle" and unable to cope if things
didn't go quite the way they were supposed to go.

The problem at Chavez was just the opposite. There, by way of Mary
Strauss's middle-class feminine subjectivity and Calvinist ideology, "Kids are
not readers by nature," and so every child was off center; no one was a reader—
her code word for the unified subject—until he or she was brought into the center
of bourgeois cultural experience through rituals of subjugation to the texts of
expressive realism. Were Mary Strauss, along with the rest of the staff at
Chavez, able to give up idealist views that forced her constantly to measure the
students and the school against "norms" that always left her "angry and confused"
and begin to build on, rather than ignore or try to eradicate, students' subjectivities there, the underground ways of reading for meaning that her students practiced might have had a chance of developing more fully. But that event would
have been contingent on a reconstruction of the librarian's and the staff's subjectivity to allow for multiple and conflicting points of view in the development of
their own practices and interactions with students.

What might that reconstructed concept of subjectivity look like, and how
might it "work" theoretically? John Fiske (1987) offers some help here. He ex-
amines three ways the way the word *subject* is used in English: the political (a
subject of the queen); the subject of idealist philosophy (as in Margaret Brown's
case); and the grammatical (as in the subject of a sentence). He notes that the
idea of a political subject—of someone subjected to the law—carries with it the
implication of "an identity that originates from outside, rather than inside, the
individual": "This last is important for it points to the major difference between
subjectivity and individuality: subjectivity is the product of social relations,
whereas individuality is seen as the product of nature, or biology" (49). This use
of the term stands in contrast to the way it is used in idealist (e.g., Cartesian)
philosophy, that is, of the subject who "thinks therefore he is" quite apart from
any condition of social interaction. Although, as was discussed above, it is this
concept of the subject that lies at the root of the modernist problematic, the term
still remains an important part of the reconstruction of subjectivity to the extent
that it helps to explicate the development of cognitive, psychological relations
between individuals and their social environments. The final use of *subject*,
which designates the producer of the action in a sentence, complements the political use of the word, which designates the subject as subjected to political discourse. Fiske concludes:

Our subjectivity, then, is the product of social relations that work upon us in three
main ways, through society, through language and discourse, and through the psychic
processes through which the infant enters into society, language, and consciousness.
Our subjectivity is not inherent in our individuality, our difference from other people,

rather it is the product of various social agencies to which we are subject, and thus is what we share with others. (49)

This last statement is crucial, because "social agencies," for example, family, school, library, church, social class, nation, religion, gender, and age group, to name a few, do not work smoothly in relation to one another in modern society. Consequently, "as there are contradictions between the agencies of society, so there will be contradictions in the subject" (50). Middleclass African-Americans, for example, may feel "split" about the plight of the inner cities, identifying with their inhabitants along the lines of race but sympathizing with predominantly European-American middle-class attitudes about welfare reform and urban renewal. In another case, liberal Catholics who identify in many ways with progressive social agendas may also feel split on the issue of abortion. Or closer to the present study (and closer to the core of many curricular issues today), teachers from working-class backgrounds who now live middle-class lives may feel split about how best to teach their poor and working-class students. Should they adopt the subjectivity of mainstream, middle-class educational practice and risk alienating their students but celebrating their own sense of arrival, or should they risk the loss of their newly gained social status and relinquish the security of socially approved practices to develop curricular approaches more in line with their students' subjectivities, a process with uncertain outcomes that would necessarily require them to reconnect on a daily basis with a past they thought they'd left behind?

In most cases, as at Chavez or Crest Hills, when conflicts among subjectivities arose in schools, there were usually enough ideologically congenial explanations about students' home lives, the "student centeredness" of the staff, or references to the power of the state legislature quickly brought to bear on the situation to iron out the contradictions and muffle any dissenting subjective voices, or burgeoning awareness of contradiction. In these cases, those ideologically sound narratives interpellated the teacher and the librarian as "professionals"—as the manager/guardians of the social order—and pulled them back to a unified (inter)subjective position, one in line with the dominant ideological function of the school.

But that, largely, did not happen at Roosevelt. Paradoxically, the librarian there (and Mariellen Wilson also, although as a teacher she was not a focus of the study) seemed to act from at least two subjectivities—those of the working-class child and of the middle-class professional—at once and without much attempt to resolve the tensions between the two. For example, although Louise Currie frequently invoked the deficit hypothesis in describing the students' home lives as "just empty," took great pride in her knowledge and enactment of the professional ethos of school librarianship, and was extremely didactic in her instruction, in almost the same moment, she could laugh at the ways that students undermined her didacticism and speak of wanting to create a place where it was "warm" and where children could come "to do some things on [their] own." Instead of acting to muffle the contradictions between subjective positions through alignment with the ethos of professionalism, or fully aligning herself with the students and risking her eventual marginalization within the school for being unprofessional and incompatible with the official curriculum, Louise Currie constructed, as Stuart Hall (1980) suggests, practices that negotiated the contradictions between subjectivities; and in the process, she abetted her patrons' playful de- and reconstruction of the library and its texts and opened spaces for them "to do some things on their own."

In the cases of Louise Currie and teacher Mariellen Wilson, a reconstructed and living memory of themselves as "poor" children was the factor, I believe, that interrupted their interpellation as middle-class subjects of the educational system. Both of Louise Currie's parents were orphans who struggled all their lives to make ends meet; in her telling, it was a combination of their preoccupation with making a living and her continuing dialogue with a children's public librarian in her hometown that gave her the opportunity—and the idea—to read "widely" and "whatever [she] wanted." Similarly, Mariellen Wilson's mother died when she was nine and her father was an alcoholic who was unable to care for her very well. In the third and fourth grade, she said "school was a good place to be"; she had some good teachers who not only liked her but liked to do some pretty interesting things. She decided then that when she grew up, she'd like to find a way to stay in the classroom—she'd become a teacher.

CONCLUSION

In summary, I have tried to demonstrate in this chapter, through the published comments of Michel Foucault, from evidence provided by the recent history of librarianship and of reading, and from the ethnographic study of three school libraries, that the geography of our epoch is a geography of difference; that the embrace of difference, and the ambivalence that embrace produces, provides the conditions in which individuals within a society ordered by exigencies of mass production and mass consumption can make or find the liberty to meet their desires; and that the school library can be read as the paradigmatic heterotopia where such a proposition can be tested within the context of literacy education. As has also been discussed in this chapter, however, the theorization of space alone as a counterhegemonic agent is no more likely to succeed than previous theorizations of history as our liberator, as the differential consequences of the three library programs detailed in this study should make very clear. The ambivalences produced by geography and history need also to be joined by a kind of ambivalence in the position of the dominant with regard to those "in their care," an ambivalence predicated on a concept of the mind as a space and of an imagination that is heterotopic in its principles of organization, an imagination directed from multiple points of life experience and identity. Where such ambivalence is ignored, denied, or otherwise patched over, the desire of the cared for is likely to be denied; where ambivalence about one's own social being is embraced, tolerance can thrive, liberty is produced, desire may be realized, and social agencies themselves can take more reconstructive forms.

As educators and as the educators of educators, then, our project could be the encouragement of just such ambivalence in the subject positions that readers in *our* care might take in their ways with text and in the ways they imagine their agency and interaction with others in their care. Such a project is less utopian than it seems at first consideration. For if we truly do live in an age whose sense of social space and social agency is heterogeneous, then the mind might be thought of as a space, too, one constructed as a heterotopia along the lines of Foucault's third principle, of the juxtaposition of seemingly incompatible spaces and positions within a single space. As educators, we might be able to act from the presumption that social being and social identity are truly heterogeneous as well and fully capable, once their geography is even tacitly acknowledged by social actors, of providing them with a heterotopic field of subject positions from which they can read and interact with others. As educators, we would not be responsible for the *production* of these positions but for promoting their recognition by the social agents in our care.

Our task, then, would be to prompt that recognition through a variety of pedagogical rituals and discourses that would ask participants, elder and initiate alike, to explore the differences and contradictions located within the site of their own social being; to promote, as readers, acts not of espionage but of adventure on themselves; and not to police subjects' positions for their lack of unity but to pirate the treasures hidden within the territory of their, and our own, multiple life experiences and identities. Such rituals and such adventuring are likely to produce a condition, at least initially, of disease with our, and our students', sense of place in the world, even as they open new possibilities for pleasure and for work. Yet paradoxically, in an age marked by the fragmentation of social life, a geopolitics of dis-ease within dominant discourses of identity and literacy education may also be education's best hope of reordering the world in ways that promote the realization, if not the guarantee, of liberty and that make schooling into a concern for, if not the fulfillment of, our desires.

Bibliography

WORKS CITED

Adamson, J. 1960. *Born free: A lioness of two worlds*. New York: Pantheon.

Adler, S. 1986. *Meet Samantha, an American girl*. Middleton, WI: Pleasant Company.

Althusser, L. 1971. Ideology and ideological state apparatuses. In *Lenin and philosophy and other essays*. New York: Monthly Review Press.

Altick, R. D. 1957. *The English common reader*. Chicago: University of Chicago Press.

Anderson, B., and J. P. Zinsser. 1988. *A history of their own: Women in Europe from prehistory to the present*. Vol. 2. New York: Harper and Row.

Anyon, J. 1981. Social class and school knowledge. *Curriculum Inquiry*, 11: 3–42.

Armstrong, N. 1987. *Desire and domestic fiction: A political history of the novel*. Oxford: Oxford University Press.

Ashley, K. M., ed. 1990. *Victor Turner and the construction of cultural criticism*. Bloomington: Indiana University Press.

Atwell, N. 1987. *In the middle: Writing, reading, and learning with adolescents*. Upper Montclair, NJ: Heinemann.

Avery, G. 1975. *Childhood's pattern*. London: Hodden and Stoughton.

Barthes, R. 1973. *Elements of semiology*. New York: Hill and Wang.

Barthes, R. 1974. *S/Z*. New York: Hill and Wang.

Bartolomé, L. 1994. Beyond the methods fetish: Toward a humanizing pedagogy. *Harvard Educational Review*, 64: 173–194.

Baum, F. 1900/1956. *The wizard of Oz*. Chicago: Reilly and Lee.

Baym, N. 1978.*Woman's fiction*. Ithaca, NY: Cornell University Press.

Belsey, C. 1980. *Critical practice*. London: Routledge.

Bernstein, B. 1972. Elaborated and restricted codes: Their social origins and some consequences. In *Directions in sociolinguistics: The ethnography of communication*, ed. J. J. Gumperz and D. Hymes, 55–69. New York: Holt, Rinehart and Winston.

Best, S., and D. Kellner. 1991. *Postmodern theory: Critical interrogations*. New York: Guilford.

Bobinski, G. S. 1969. *Carnegie libraries*. Chicago: American Library Association.

Boggs, S. 1985. *Speaking, relating, and learning: A study of Hawaiian children at home and at school*. Norwood, NJ: Ablex.

Bostwick, A. E. 1910. *The American public library*. New York: D. Appleton.

Bourdieu, P. 1984. *Distinction*. Cambridge, MA: Harvard University Press.

Bourdieu, P. 1990. *The logic of practice*. Stanford: Stanford University Press.

Bourdieu, P., and J. P. Passeron. 1977. *Reproduction in education, society, and culture*. Beverly Hills, CA: Sage.

Bowie, M. M. 1986. *Historic documents of school libraries*. Fayetteville, AR: Hi Willow.

Bowles, S., and H. Gintis. 1976. *Schooling in capitalist America*. New York: Basic Books.

Bradford, R. 1968/1986. *Red sky at morning*. New York: Harper and Row.

Bratton, J. S. 1981. *The impact of Victorian children's fiction*. Totowa, NJ: Barnes and Noble Books.

Brodkey, L. 1987. *Acdemic writing as social practice*. Philadelphia: Temple University Press.

Brown, M. R. 1994. My turn: Whose eyes are these, whose nose? *Newsweek*, March 7, 12.

Calkins, L. M. 1990. *Living between the lines*. Portsmouth, NH: Heinemann.

Callahan, R. 1962. *Education and the cult of efficiency*. Chicago: University of Chicago Press.

Caywood, C. 1994. Risk reduction. *School Library Journal*, 40 (10): 54.

Caywood, C. 1995a. The quest for character. *School Library Journal*, 41 (3): 152.

Caywood, C. 1995b. Risky business. *School Library Journal*, 41 (5): 44.

Caywood, C. 1995c. Tales of the dark side. *School Library Journal*, 40 (7): 31.

Cazden, C. 1988. *Classroom discourse*. Portsmouth, NH: Heinemann.

Cazden, C., V. P. John, and D. Hymes, eds. 1972. *Functions of language in the classroom*. Prospect Heights, IL: Waveland Press.

Chávez, R. C., and J. O'Donnell, eds. 1997. *Speaking the unpleasant: The politics of non-engagement in the multicultural education terrain*. Albany, NY: SUNY Press.

Christian-Smith, L. K. 1991. Readers, texts, and contexts: Adolescent romance fiction in schools. In *The politics of the textbook*, ed. M. W. Apple and L. K. Christian-Smith, 191–212. New York: Routledge.

Cleary, B. 1950. *Henry Huggins*. New York: Dell.

Cleary, B. 1983. *Dear Mr. Henshaw*. New York: Morrow.

Cockett, L. 1995. Entering the mainstream: Fiction about gay and lesbian teens. *School Library Journal*, 41 (1): 32–33.

Collins, J. 1993. Determination and contradiction: An appreciation and critique of the work of Pierre Bourdieu on language and education. In *Bourdieu: Critical perspectives*, ed. C. Calhoun, E. LiPuma, and M. Postone, 116–138. Chicago: University of Chicago Press.

Colvin, R. L. 1995. State report urges return to basics in teaching reading. *Los Angeles Times*, September 13, A1, A24.

Conford, E. 1992. *Dear Mom, get me out of here*. Boston: Little, Brown.

Connell, R. W. 1977. *Ruling class, ruling culture: Studies of conflict, power, and hegemony in Australian life*. New York: Cambridge University Press.

Cullinan, B., and L. Galda. 1994. *Literature and the child*. 3rd ed. Fort Worth, TX: Harcourt Brace.

Darton, F. J. H. 1932. *Children's books in England*. Cambridge: Cambridge University Press.

Davidson, C. N. 1986. *Revolution and the word: The rise of the novel in America*. New York: Oxford University Press.

Davis, L. J. 1987. *Resisting novels: Ideology and fiction*. New York: Methuen.

Defoe, D. 1719/1961. *Robinson Crusoe*. New York: Signet.

Deleuze, G., and F. Guattari. 1987. *A thousand plateaus: Capitalism and schizophrenia*. Minneapolis: University of Minnesota Press.

Delpit, L. 1986. Skills and other dilemmas of a progressive black educator. *Harvard Educational Review*, 56: 379–385.

Delpit, L. 1988. The silenced dialogue: Power and pedagogy in educating other people's children. *Harvard Educational Review*, 58: 280–298.

dePaola, T. 1981. *Fin M'Coul*. New York: Holiday House.

De Regniers, B. S. 1989. *The snow party*. New York: Lothrop, Lee, & Shepard.

Douglas, A. 1977. *The feminization of American culture*. New York: Alfred A. Knopf.

Dressman, M. 1995. Under the umbrella: Resisting the reign of rationalized educational reform. *Journal of Curriculum Studies*, 27: 231–244.

Dressman, M. 1996. Catholic boy: An account of parochial school literacy. In *Writing permitted in designated areas only*, ed. L. Brodkey. Minneapolis: University of Minnesota Press.

Dressman, M., L. McCarty, and J. Benson. In Press. <whole language> as signifier: Considering the semantic field of school literacy. *Journal of Literacy Research*.

Eagleton, T. 1983. *Literary theory: An introduction*. Minneapolis: University of Minnesota Press.

Edelsky, C. 1990. Whose agenda is this anyway? A response to McKenna, Robinson, and Miller. *Educational Researcher*, 19: 7–11.

Ehrenreich, B. 1989. *Fear of falling*. New York: HarperCollins.

Everhart, R. B. 1983. *Reading, writing, and resistance: Adolescence and labor in a junior high school*. Boston: Routledge and Kegan Paul.

Faigley, L. 1992. *Fragments of rationality: Postmodernity and the subject of composition*. Pittsburgh: University of Pittsburgh Press.

Fiske, J. 1987. *Television culture*. New York: Routledge.

Fiske, J. 1989a. *Reading the popular*. Cambridge, MA: Unwin Hyman.

Fiske, J. 1989b. *Understanding popular culture*. Winchester, MA: Unwin Hyman.

Flanigan, C. C. 1990. Liminality, carnival, and social structure: The case of late medieval biblical drama. In *Victor Turner and the construction of cultural criticism: Between literature and anthropology*, ed. K. M. Ashley, 42–63. Bloomington: Indiana University Press.

Foley, D. 1990. *Learning capitalist culture: Deep in the heart of Tejas*. Philadelphia: University of Pennsylvania Press.

Foucault, M. 1979. *Discipline and punish*. New York: Random House.

Foucault, M. 1980. *Power/knowledge: Selected interviews and other writings, 1972–1977*. Ed. C. Gordon. New York: Pantheon.

Foucault, M. 1984. *The Foucault reader*. Ed. P. Rabinow. New York: Pantheon.

Foucault, M. 1986. Of other spaces. Trans. J. Miskowiec. *Diacritics* 16: 22–27.

Fox, P. 1973. *The slave dancer*. Scarsdale, NY: Bradbury Press.

Franklin, H. R. 1976. Service to the urban rank and file. In *A century of service: Librarianship in the United States and Canada*, ed. S. L. Jackson, E. B. Herling, and E. J. Josey, 1–19. Chicago: American Library Association.

Garrison, D. 1979. *Apostles of culture: The public librarian and American society, 1876–1920*. New York: Free Press.

Geertz, C. 1973. *The interpretation of cultures*. New York: HarperCollins.

Geertz, C. 1983. *Local knowledge*. New York: HarperCollins.

George, J. C. 1972. *Julie of the Wolves*. New York: Harper and Row.

Giroux, H. A. 1983. *Theory and resistance in education*. Westport, CT: Bergin and Garvey.

Giroux, H.A. 1992. *Border crossings: Cultural workers and the politics of education*. New York: Routledge, Chapman and Hall.

Goffman, E. 1959. *The presentation of self in everyday life*. New York: Doubleday.

Goodman, K. 1992. Why whole language is today's agenda in education. *Language Arts*, 69: 354–363.

Goody, J., and I. Watt. 1963. The consequences of literacy. *Comparative Studies in Society and History*, 5: 304–326; 332–345.

Graesser, A., J. M. Golding, and D. L. Long. 1991. Narrative representation and comprehension. In *Handbook of reading research*. ed. R. Barr, M. L. Kamil, P. Mosenthal, and P. D. Pearson, 2: 171–205. New York: Longman.

Graff, H. 1987. *The legacies of literacy: Continuities and contradictions in Western culture and society*. Bloomington: Indiana University Press.

Grice, P. 1989. *Studies in the way of words*. Cambridge, MA: Harvard University Press.

Grimes, R. L. 1990. Victor Turner's definition, theory, and sense of ritual. In *Victor Turner and the construction of cultural criticism: Between literature and anthropology,* ed. K. M. Ashley, 141–146. Bloomington: Indiana University Press.

Guthrie, J., and V. Greaney. 1991. Literacy acts. In *Handbook of reading research*. ed. R. Barr, M. L. Kamil, P. Mosenthal, and P. D. Pearson, 2: 68–96. New York: Longman.

Hall, S. 1980. Encoding/decoding. In *Culture, media, and language,* ed. S. Hall, D. Hobson, A. Low, and P. Willis, 128–139. London: Hutchinson.

Hamlyn, H. M. 1946. Eighteenth-century circulating libraries in England. *The Library*, ser. 5, vols. 1–2, 197–222.

Harste, J. C., V. A. Woodward, and C. L. Burke. 1984. Examining our assumptions: A transactional view of literacy and learning. *Research in the Teaching of English*, 18: 84–108.

Hart, J. D. 1950. *The popular book: A history of America's literary taste*. New York: Oxford University Press.

Haywood, C. 1975. *Eddie's valuable property*. New York: Morrow.

Heath, S. B. 1983. *Ways with words*. Cambridge: Cambridge University Press.

Heath, S. B. 1991. The sense of being literate: Historical and cross-cultural features. In *Handbook of reading research*, ed. R. Barr, M. L. Kamil, P. Mosenthal, and P. D. Pearson, 2: 3–25. New York: Longman.

Heim, A. 1994. Beyond the stereotypes. *School Library Journal*, 40 (9): 139–142.

Hewins, C. M. 1901. Book reviews, book lists, and articles on children's reading: Are they of practical value to the children's librarian? In the proceedings of the Waukesha Conference, *Library Journal*, 26: 57–62.

Hodges, M. 1994. In service to youth. *School Library Journal*, 40 (7): 28.

Horkheimer, M., and T. Adorno. 1944/1993. *Dialectic of enlightenment*. New York: Continuum.

Huck, C. S., S. Hepler, and J. Hickman. 1993. *Children's literature in the elementary school*. 5th ed. New York: Harcourt Brace Jovanovich.

Humphreys, K. W. 1985. The book and the library in society. *Library History*, 7: 105–118.

Iser, W. 1980. Interaction between text and reader. In *The reader in the text*, ed. S. R. Suleiman and I. Crosman, 106–119. Princeton, NJ: Princeton University Press.

Jackson, S. L. 1976. Service to urban children. In *A century of service: Librarianship in the United States and Canada*, ed. S. L. Jackson, E. B. Herling, and E. J. Josey, 20–41. Chicago: American Library Association.

Jenkins, R. 1992. *Pierre Bourdieu*. London: Routledge.

Jones, D. 1990. The genealogy of the urban schoolteacher. In *Foucault and education: Disciplines and knowledge*, ed. S. Ball, 57–77.

Jordan, C. 1985. Translating culture: From ethnographic information to educational program. *Anthropology and Education Quarterly*, 16: 105–123.

Joynes, S. E. 1971. The Sheffield library, 1771–1907. *Library History*, 2: 91–116.

Kaufman, P. 1967. The community library. *Transactions of the American Philosophical Society*, 57 (7): 11–25.

Keith, M., and S. Pile, eds. 1993. *Place and the politics of identity*. New York: Routledge.

Kelley, M. 1984. *Private woman, public stage: Literary domesticity in nineteenth-century America*. New York: Oxford University Press.

Knott, D. H. 1976. Thomas Wilson and the use of circulating libraries. *Library History*, 4 (1): 2–10.

Knott, J. 1972. Circulating libraries in Newcastle in the 18th and 19th centuries. *Library History*, 2 (6): 227–249.

Kristeva, J. 1989. *Language the unknown: An initiation into linguistics*. Trans. Anne M. Menke. New York: Columbia University Press.

Labov, W. 1972. *Language in the inner city: Studies in the Black English vernacular*. Philadelphia: University of Pennsylvania Press.

Lofting, H. 1922. *The voyages of Dr. Dolittle*. New York: Fred A. Stokes.

Long, E. 1992. Textual interpretation as collective action. In *The ethnography of reading*, ed. J. Boyarim, 180–211. Berkeley: University of California Press.

Long, H. G. 1969. *Public library service to children: Foundation and development*. Metuchen, NJ: Scarecrow Press.

Lowry, L. 1989. *Number the stars*. Boston: Houghton Mifflin.

Lukács, G. 1920/1971. *The theory of the novel*. Cambridge, MA: MIT Press.

Lukens, R. 1982. *Critical handbook of children's literature*. 2nd ed. Glenview, IL: Scott, Foresman.

Lyotard, J. 1984. *The postmodern condition*. Minneapolis: University of Minnesota Press.

MacLachlan, P. 1991. *Three names*. New York: HarperCollins.

MacLeod, J. 1987. *Ain't no makin' it: Leveled aspirations in a low-income neighborhood*. Boulder, CO: Westview Press.

Mahy, M. 1990. *The seven Chinese brothers*. New York: Scholastic.

Mandler, J. M., and M. deForest. 1979. Is there more than one way to recall a story? *Child Development*, 50: 886–889.

Massey, D. 1993. Politics and space/time. In *Place and the politics of identity*, ed. M. Keith and S. Pile, 141–161. New York: Routledge.

McDermott, R. P. 1977. The ethnography of speaking and reading. In *Linguistic theory: What can it say about reading?* ed. R. W. Shuy, 153–185. Newark, DE: International Reading Association.

McLaren, P. 1993. *Schooling as a ritual performance: Towards a political economy of educational symbols and gestures*. 2nd ed. New York: Routledge.

Mediavilla, C. 1994. Books in the hood. *School Library Journal*, 40 (5): 40.

Mehan, H. 1979. *Learning lessons*. Cambridge, MA: Harvard University Press.

Milne, A. A. 1926/1961. *Winnie the pooh*. New York: Dutton.

Moll, L. 1992. Literacy research in community and classrooms: A sociocultural approach. In *Multidisciplinary perspectives on literacy research,* ed. R. Beach, J. L. Green, M. L. Kamil, and T. Shanahan, 211–244. Urbana, IL: National Conference on Research in English.

Monson, D. L., and S. Sebesta. 1991. Reading preferences. In *Handbook of research on teaching the English language arts*, ed. J. Flood, J. M. Jensen, D. Lapp, and J. R. Squire, 664–673. New York: Macmillan.

Moore, H. 1986. *Space, text, and gender*. Cambridge: Cambridge University Press.

Mowat, I. R. M. 1979. Literacy, libraries, and literature in 18th and 19th century Easter Ross. *Library History*, 5 (1): 1–10.

North, S. 1963. *Rascal: A memoir of a better era*. New York: Dutton.

Oakes, J. 1985. *Keeping track: How schools structure inequality*. New Haven, CT: Yale University Press.

Ochs, P. 1993. Charles Sanders Peirce. In *Founders of constructive postmodern philosophy: Peirce, James, Bergson, Whitehead, and Hartshorne*, ed. D. R. Griffin, J. B. Cobb, Jr., M. P. Ford, P. A. Y. Gunter, and P. Ochs, 43–88. Albany: SUNY Press.

Odell, L., and D. Goswami, eds. 1985. *Writing in nonacademic settings*. New York: Guilford.

O'Dell, S. 1960. *Island of the blue dolphins*. New York: Dell.

Ogbu, J. 1987. Variability in minority responses to schooling: Nonimmigrants vs. immigrants. In *Interpretive ethnography of education*, ed. G. Spindler and L. Spindler. Hillsdale, NJ: Lawrence Erlbaum Associates.

Orwell, G. 1936/1961. Excerpt from *Keep the aspidistra flying*. In *The Orwell reader: Fiction, essays, and reportage*, 118–148. New York: Harcourt, Brace and World.

Parmentier, R. J. 1985. Signs' place *in media res*: Peirce's concept of semiotic mediation. In *Semiotic mediation: Sociocultural and psychological perspectives*, ed. E. Mertz and R. J. Parmentier, 23–48. Orlando, FL: Academic Press.

Parmentier, R. J. 1987. Peirce divested for non-intimates. *RSSI: Recherches Semiotique/Semiotic Inquiry*, 7: 19–39.

Peirce, C. S. 1931/1958. *Collected papers of Charles Sanders Peirce*. Vol. 2: *Elements of logic*, 134–178. Cambridge, MA: Harvard University Press.

Philips, S. U. 1983. *The invisible culture: Communication in the classroom and community on the Warm Springs Indian Reservation*. White Plains, NY: Longman.

Plummer, W. W. 1901. The books themselves. In the proceedings of the Waukesha Conference, *Library Journal*, 26: 166–167.

Potter, B. 1902/1987. *The tale of Peter Rabbit*. New York: Penguin.

Power, E. L. 1943. *Work with children in public libraries*. Chicago: American Library Association.

Pratt, M. L. 1992. *Imperial eyes: Travel writing and transculturation*. New York: Routledge.

Purves, A., and R. Beach. 1972. *Literature and the reader: Research on response to literature*. Urbana, IL: National Council of Teachers of English.

Rosenblatt, L. 1978. *The reader, the text, the poem: The transactional theory of the literary work*. Carbondale, IL: Southern Illinois University Press.

Routman, R. 1991. *Invitations*. Portsmouth, NH: Heinemann.

Rylant, C. 1992. *Missing May*. New York: Orchard Books.

Scott, A. F. 1984. On seeing and not seeing: A case of historical invisibility. *Journal of American History*, 71 (1): 7–21.

Scott, A. F. 1986. Women and libraries. *Journal of Library History*, 21 (2): 400–405.

Scribner, S. 1988. Literacy in three metaphors. In *Perspectives on literacy*, ed. E. R. Kintgen, B. M. Kroll, and M. Rose, 71–81. Carbondale, IL: Southern Illinois University Press.

Scribner, S., and M. Cole. 1981. *The psychology of literacy*. Cambridge, MA: Harvard University Press.

Sendak, M. 1963. *Where the wild things are*. New York: Harper and Row.

Shor, I. 1993. Education is politics: Paulo Freire's critical pedagogy. In *Paulo Freire: A critical encounter*, ed. P. McLaren and P. Leonard. New York: Routledge.

Smith, N., and C. Katz. 1993. Grounding metaphor: Towards a spatialized politics. In *Place and the politics of identity*, ed. M. Keith and S. Pile, 67–83. New York: Routledge.

Soja, E. W. 1989. *Postmodern geographies: The reassertion of space in critical social theory*. New York: Verso.

Spain, D. 1992. *Gendered spaces*. Chapel Hill: University of North Carolina Press.

Speare, E. G. 1958. *Witch of Blackbird Pond*. Boston: Houghton Mifflin.

Sperry, A. 1940. *Call it courage*. New York: Macmillan.

Spring, J. H. 1972. *Education and the rise of the corporate state*. Boston: Beacon Press.

Steele, W. O. 1959. *Andy Jackson's water well*. New York: Harcourt, Brace, & World.

Steig, W. 1969. *Sylvester and the magic pebble*. New York: Windmill.

Steinbeck, J. 1936. *The grapes of wrath*. New York: Viking Press.

Stephens, J. 1992. *Language and ideology in children's fiction*. London: Longman.

Stone, I. 1961. *The agony and the ecstasy: A novel of Michelangelo*. Garden City, NY: Doubleday.

Stratton, J. 1987. *The virgin text*. Brighton, UK: Harvester Press.

Taylor, J. T. 1943. *Early opposition to the English novel*. New York: King's Crown Press.

Taylor, W.L. 1901. Books for children. In the proceedings of the Waukesha Conference, *Library Journal*, 26: 63–65.

Teitelbaum, K. 1991. Critical lessons from our past: Curricula of socialist Sunday schools in the United States. In *The politics of the textbook*, ed. M. W. Apple and L. K. Christian-Smith, 135–165. New York: Routledge.

Tompkins, J. M. S. 1932. *The popular novel in England 1770–1800*. London: Constable.

Turner, V. 1969. *The ritual process: Structure and anti-structure*. Ithaca, NY: Cornell University Press.

Turner, V. 1974. *Dramas, fields, and metaphors: Symbolic action in human society*. Ithaca, NY: Cornell University Press.

Turner, V. 1982. *From ritual to theatre: The human seriousness of play*. New York: PAJ Publications.

Turner, V. 1992. *Blazing the trail: Way marks in the exploration of symbols*. Tucson: University of Arizona Press.

Van Allsburg, C. 1991. *The wretched stone*. Boston: Houghton Mifflin.

Voight, C. 1983. *Dicey's song*. New York: Atheneum.

Vygotsky, L. S. 1978. *Mind in society: The development of higher psychological processes*, ed. M. Cole, V. John-Steiner, S. Scribner, and E. Souberman. Cambridge, MA: Harvard University Press.

Wallace, B. 1989. *Snot stew*. New York: Pocket Books.

Watt, I. 1957. *The rise of the novel*. Berkeley: University of California Press.

West, C., and D. Zimmerman. 1987. Doing gender. *Gender and Society*, 1: 125–151.

Wheeler, M. A. 1984. Fourth grade boys' literacy from a mother's point of view. *Language Arts*, 61: 607–614.

Wilder, L. 1935/1971. *Little house on the praire*. New York: HarperCollins.

Williams, R. 1977. *Marxism and literature*. Oxford: Oxford University Press.

Willis, P. 1981. *Learning to labor: How working class kids get working class jobs*. New York: Teachers College Press.

Wittrock, M. C. 1984. Writing and the teaching of reading. In *Composing and comprehending*, ed. J. M. Jensen, 77–83. Urbana, IL: National Council of Teachers of English.

Woolf, V. 1975. *A room of one's own*. New York: Harcourt, Brace, and World.

Wyss, J. 1954. *The Swiss family Robinson*. Garden City, NJ: Nelson Doubleday.

BOOK-SORT TEXTS

Aardema, V. 1975. *Why mosquitoes buzz in people's ears.* Illus. L. Dillon and D. Dillon. New York: Dial.

Anno, M. 1983. *Anno's U.S.A.* New York: Philomel.

Benet, R., and S. V. Benet. 1933/1986. *A book of Americans.* Illus. C. Child. New York: Henry Holt.

Berger, P., and J. Rolfe. 1990. *Michael Jordan.* New York: Warner Juvenile.

Bird talk. 1991. Mission Viejo, CA: Fancy Publications, March.

Bowyer, C. 1978. *Houses and homes.* Illus. B. Hersey, R. McCaig, and J. McEwan. London: Usborne.

Burne, D. 1988. *Bird.* New York: Alfred A. Knopf.

Cleary, B. 1990. *Ramona and her father.* Illus. A. Tiegreen. New York: Avon Camelot.

Cole, J. 1987. *Evolution: The story of how life developed on earth.* Illus. Aliki. New York: Harper and Row.

Corrigan, D. 1992. *The American firehouse cookbook.* New York: Crescent.

cummings, e. e. 1989. *hist whist.* Illus. D. K. Ray. New York: Crown.

Dinosaurs sticker book. 1990. New York: Chatham River Press.

Felder, D. G. 1989. *The kids' world almanac of animals and pets.* Illus. J. Lane. New York: World Almanac.

Garlake, P. 1990. *The kingdoms of Africa.* New York: Peter Bedrick.

Hall, K. 1991. *Skeletons! Skeletons! All about bones.* Illus. P. Billin-Frye. New York: Platt & Munk.

Hallinan, P. K. 1977. *That's what a friend is.* Chicago: Children's Press.

Hunt, J. 1993. *Illuminations.* Illus. J. Hunt. New York: Macmillan.

McDonnell, J. 1990. *Space travel: Blast-off day.* Illus. R. Collette. Chicago: Children's Press.

McGovern, A. 1974. *If you lived with the Sioux Indians.* Illus. J. S. Drew. New York: Scholastic.

Merriam, E. 1986. *A sky full of poems.* Illustrated by W. Gaffney-Kessell. New York: Dell.

Milton, J. 1990. *The story of Thomas Jefferson, prophet of liberty.* Illus. L. Padula. New York: Dell.

Montavon, J. 1991. *A history mystery: The curse of King Tut's tomb.* New York: Avon.

Myers, J. 1990. *Jumbo amazing question & answer book.* Illus. M. Mann. New York: Playmore.

National geographic. 1973. Washington, D.C.: National Geographic Society, October.

Page, M., and R. Ingpen. 1987. *Encyclopedia of things that never were.* New York: Viking.

Rand McNally children's atlas of the world. 1992. Chicago: Rand McNally.

Sharmat, M., and A. Sharmat. 1990. *Kids on the bus: School bus cat.* Illus. M. Johnson. New York: HarperCollins.

Snyder, Z. K. 1986. *The Egypt game.* New York: Dell.

Spier, P. 1980. *People.* Illus. P. Spier. New York: Doubleday.

Texas state travel guide (1991). Travel and Information Division. Austin, TX: State Department of Highways and Public Transportation.

Thaler, M. 1989. *The teacher from the black lagoon.* Illus. M. Thaler. New York: Scholastic.

Tofts, H. 1989. *The paper book.* New York: Simon and Schuster.

University of Chicago Spanish-English/English-Spanish dictionary. 1987. New York: Pocket Books.

Weiss, E. H., ed. 1993. *Free stuff for kids.* Deephaven, MN: Meadowbrook Press.

Wright, S. 1990. *A. Philip Randolph: Integration in the workplace.* Englewood Cliffs, NJ: Silver Burdett.

Index

About the Author

MARK DRESSMAN is Assistant Professor of Curriculum and Instruction at the University of Houston. He was a teacher in Morocco with the Peace Corps, on the Navajo Indian Reservation, and in Cincinnati for over ten years. He is the author of several recent journal articles.

ISBN 0-89789-495-2

HARDCOVER BAR CODE